basketball--
multiple offense and defense

Basketball

prentice-hall, inc., englewood cliffs, new jersey 07632

multiple offense and defense
by Dean Smith

with a special section on
the Shuffle Offense by

Bob Spear

foreword by
Bob Knight

coordinated and
edited by
Bob Savod

Library of Congress Cataloging in Publication Data

Smith, Dean E.
  Basketball, multiple offense and defense.
  Includes index.
    1. Basketball—Offense.   2. Basketball—
Defense.   3. Basketball coaching.   I. Spear,
Bob.   II. Title.
GV889.S56   796.32'32   81-8510
ISBN 0-13-072090-9   AACR2

basketball—multiple offense and defense
  by Dean Smith

with a special section on the shuffle offense
  by Bob Spear

©1981 by Prentice-Hall, Inc., Englewood Cliffs, N.J. 07632

editorial production/supervision
  and interior design: *Barbara Kelly*
cover design: *Diane Saxe*
cover photo: *Sally Sather*
manufacturing buyer: *Harry P. Baisley*

Printed in the United States of America

10 9 8 7 6 5 4

ISBN 0-13-072090-9

Prentice-Hall International, Inc., *London*
Prentice-Hall of Australia Pty. Limited, *Sydney*
Prentice-Hall of Canada, Ltd., *Toronto*
Prentice-Hall of India Private Limited, *New Delhi*
Prentice-Hall of Japan, Inc., *Tokyo*
Prentice-Hall of Southeast Asia Pte. Ltd., *Singapore*
Whitehall Books Limited, *Wellington, New Zealand*

To the athletes I have coached and to my wife Linnea and children Sharon, Sandy, Scott, Kristen, and Kelly.

Dean E. Smith

I would like to dedicate my portion of this book to the many cadets whose patience, dedication, and abilities made our system so productive; and, to my wife Dottie, who endured so many years of exhilarating highs and frustrating lows to remain the ideal coach's wife.

Robert B. Spear

contents

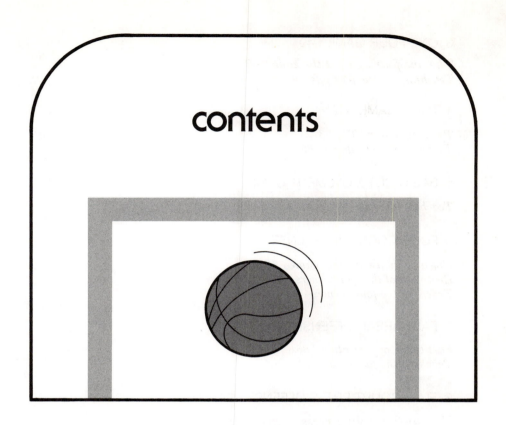

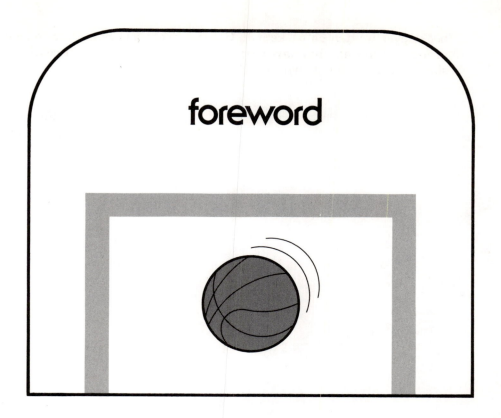

foreword

Basketball has been an integral part of the lives of Bob Spear and Dean Smith since each was a high-school player. In the years that have passed since their playing days, these two men have made a continual in-depth study of the game that so fascinated them in their youth.

Dean Smith's tremendous accomplishments at the University of North Carolina have placed him in a position where he has the unqualified respect of all in the coaching profession. This is a result not just of the championship teams he has produced but of the innovative and analytical way he approaches the game. Dean has a rare ability to look at the game in total perspective and no team in the country plays the complete game better or does as many things as well as his team does.

Among basketball people, no one is more highly respected for an open mind and studious approach to the game than Bob Spear. He is a fundamental and conceptual teacher on a par with the best the game has ever seen. Anyone who ever watched his Air Force Academy teams play saw the absolute maximum being obtained from the talent available. The greatest compliment a coach can be given is that "he gets everything there is out of his material." Bob epitomizes this phrase.

The combined efforts of Bob and Dean have produced a comprehensive study of the game of basketball that will become a constant source of reference for you. You are about to enjoy one of the most intelligent and best organized books ever written on basketball. Coaches Spear and Smith are to be congratulated on what they have written and thanked by all of us in coaching for sharing their thoughts with us.

Bob Knight
Indiana University
September 21,1980

preface

In the early 1960s, Coach Bob Spear, who was then head basketball coach at the Air Force Academy, and whom I had assisted in the late 1950s, asked if I would co-author a book with him on basketball. Since I had received many inquiries about our basketball program at North Carolina, I felt that the book might be a good idea.

We decided at the outset not to cover individual fundamental techniques such as the chest pass, etc., since many fine books were already written on the subject. Instead, we wanted to concentrate exclusively on team offense and team defense.

Sometime later, when Coach Spear resigned from the Air Force with a glittering record, he further suggested that we place our emphasis on North Carolina's basketball system. This book, therefore, consists of a description of the multiple offense and defense used at North Carolina, plus a section on the Shuffle Offense as coached and taught by Coach Spear during his years at the Air Force Academy.

Coach Spear is an excellent writer and quickly completed his contribution to the book. Our overall progress, however, was very slow simply because I found it difficult to sit down and put my thoughts on paper in book form.

I was also inclined to revise the material often, as the passing seasons at North Carolina brought about variations in our system (however, some of this material was written in the late 1960s and has gone to publication without revision). The net result was that the book was not getting done.

Then, some years later, Bob Savod, a supporter of Carolina Athletics, contacted me and volunteered to write recruiting letters and work at any other tasks that would assist our basketball program. Bob had some time available and wanted to help the program. It was at that point that we began to make some real progress as Bob pushed me to rough draft the chapters on the Dictaphone.

Over the years, I dictated the material in my own words and Bob managed to organize it in a clearer, more concise manner. Of course, everyone has his or her own writing style and Bob tends to use larger and often more appropriate words than I would use. This sometimes makes the text sound more like him than it does me, although I have changed some of his words.

We realize that much material is presented in the book and we are not suggesting that a coach use *ALL* these offenses and defenses in a single season. Although each of the offenses and defenses described have been used at North Carolina, they have not *ALL* been used at the same time.

We also hope that we never convey the impression at any of our clinics, or in our writings, that we think ours is necessarily the best system. Our ideas have worked well for us and hopefully they may do the same for you if you decide to adopt some of the principles.

The more years I spend in coaching, however, the more I realize that there is far more to the game than the Xs and Os described in this book. Mental attitude is so very important. Regardless of the offense or defense used, the players must have confidence in the system and be self-confident. In my opinion, the ability on the part of a coach to exude confidence to individual players and the team is more important than the particular offense or defense used.

This book is intended for coaches and aspiring coaches at all levels. These ideas have worked for us at the college level. They have also been used at the high school level. Since the middle sixties, the great coach at DeMatha High School, Morgan Wootten, has incorporated many of our concepts into his program. DeMatha probably would have been just as successful without the Run-and-Jump defense, the Four Corners, use of the tired signal, defensive huddles at the foul line, and multiple defense theory. Nonetheless, Coach Wootten's successful implementation of those concepts indicates that they can be used effectively at the high school level, especially if one teaches as well as Coach Wootten.

I would take this opportunity to apologize to the growing number of female coaches who may be reading this book. I have had difficulty updating my language to accommodate the women. For example, the term "person-to-person defense" is probably more appropriate than "man-to-man defense". In most cases, the male gender has been used but this should in no way indicate a lack of respect for our outstanding women coaches and women players. I believe the game of women's basketball will continue its rapid growth and will bring much enjoyment to many fine young girls taking part in it.

I also want to take this opportunity to express my gratitude to the players at North Carolina. In a sense, a coach learns most from his players. In this respect, I have been privileged to work with outstanding young men who have varied in their basketball talent, but have been all exceptional people. They have contributed extensively, if indirectly, to this book. Although it is impossible to mention all of them throughout the book, each letterman whom I have had the pleasure to coach is listed in a special section at the conclusion of this book. I believe we are fortunate to be coaches and have the opportunity to work with young men and women. Some have called it a privileged opportunity. Beyond most other considerations it is my hope that each of us will succeed in being a positive influence on the men and women who play for us.

Many coaches have helped shape my coaching philosophy and attitude through the years. In thanking them here however, I do not wish to imply that they should share the blame if some of the material in this book does not work out well for you. First, Dr. Forest C. "Phog" Allen, my college coach at the University of Kansas, and Dick Harp, who was assistant coach at Kansas during my playing days, contributed a solid foundation regarding coaching and the technical aspects of the game. Dr. Allen was a charismatic leader and extremely strong on fundamentals. Dick Harp is one of the brightest minds I have ever known in the game of basketball. I was fortunate to have served on the Kansas staff the year after my graduation under these outstanding basketball men.

Obviously, my co-author Bob Spear was a great influence on my thinking, particularly during the three years I assisted him at the Air Force Academy. Bob was a tremendous and patient teacher who gave confidence to the young men who played for him.

My coaching philosophy is also derived from Coach Frank McGuire, a basketball Hall of Fame member who brought me to North Carolina in 1958. Three of the happiest years of my life were spent as Coach McGuire's assistant. Coach McGuire exuded confidence to his players and certainly was a great game coach. During that period, I also had the opportunity to talk basketball with one of the great men who ever coached the game, Mr. Clair Bee, who has been an inspiration to many young coaches.

In addition, one who is familiar with the basketball philosophy of Coach Henry Iba will recognize many of his ideas in this book. Mr. Iba was kind enough to spend time talking basketball with me when I was assistant coach at the Air Force Academy. Our Kansas squads had played against Coach Iba's teams and we all held him in high regard.

I also learned from Chuck Noe, the former great head coach at Virginia, VPI, and South Carolina, who shared some of his ideas with me.

When Coach Ralph Miller was at the University of Iowa, he helped me by sending his written material on defensive basketball in addition to allowing me to study his Iowa team on film.

I would also like to publicly thank my former assistant coaches: Ken Rosemond; Larry Brown, who recently left UCLA to become head coach of the New Jersey Nets; and John Lotz, former head coach at the University of Florida, for their immense contributions.

I am most indebted to my present staff members, Bill Guthridge, who has turned down a number of head positions to remain at North Carolina during the past 14 years; as has Eddie Fogler. Coach Fogler co-captained our 1970 team and has helped me immensely while on our staff for 10 years. No coach could ever ask for more competent, bright, and loyal assistants than Bill and Eddie. They never receive the credit they deserve for Carolina's success.

Another coach I would like to thank is my father, Mr. Alfred Smith, who enjoyed coaching young men in high school at Chanute and Emporia, Kansas, for approximately 30 years. His dedication to helping young men inspired my decision to become a coach. Both he and my mother, Mrs. Vesta Smith, have played an active role in supporting me in coaching throughout the years. Dad still prefers that we not throw cross-court passes against a zone, nor allow a dribbler to go baseline. Dad's teams did win numerous championships and so I do continue to listen to him. However, I'm grateful to my sister, Joan Smith Ewing for supporting me in basketball arguments with Dad, but more importantly, being one on whom I could always depend for advice and counsel in all life's matters.

Finally I do wish to express gratitude to my secretary Betsy Terrell for her 20 years of loyal and dedicated service, and to our other secretaries Kay Thomas and Linda Lankford, as well as to Judy Savod for her typing assistance in preparing this manuscript. Thanks also to Sally Sather for her photographic contribution to the jacket cover of the book.

Dean E. Smith
Chapel Hill, North Carolina
May 17, 1981

introduction: the statistical basis for the system

Throughout this book we will make several references to the term *possession evaluation*. Our possession-evaluation statistics play an extremely important role in determining our goals as well as helping us evaluate the effectiveness of our offense and defense. Because it is an important criterion for us and relates to both offense and defense, we have chosen to cover possession evaluation at this early point in the text.

I have never felt that it was possible to illustrate how well we were doing offensively based on the number of points we scored. The tempo of the game could limit us to fifty points and yet we could be playing great offense. In some games we might score eighty-five points and yet be playing poorly from an offensive viewpoint. This would occur, for example, in a "run-and-gun" game.

From a defensive point of view, one of my pet peeves is to hear a team referred to as the "defensive champion" strictly on the basis of giving up the fewest points per game over a season. Generally, a low-scoring game is attributable to a ball-control offense rather than a sound, successful defense.

To more adequately judge the effectiveness of our offense and defense, we devised a statistical evaluation system while I was an assistant to Bob Spear at the Air Force Academy in 1955. We called it possession evaluation and it was first written for Coach Frank McGuire's book *Defensive Basketball*.[1]

Possession evaluation is determined by the average number of points scored for *each* possession of the ball by a team during the game. A perfect game from an offensive viewpoint would be an average of 2.00 points for each possession. The perfect defensive game would result in holding the opponent to 0.00 (scoreless). How well we do offensively is determined by how closely we approach 2.00 points per possession. How close we come to holding the opponent to 0.00 points per possession (as opposed to holding down the opponent's total score) determines the effectiveness of our defense. Our goals are to exceed .85 points per possession on offense and keep our opponents below .75 points per possession through our defensive efforts.

What constitutes a possession? Our assumption is that a team must have uninterrupted control of the basketball. The possession ends when the team no longer has complete control. If we attempt a field-goal, we no longer have complete possession even though we may recover the offensive rebound. We then begin another possession although the opponent has yet to gain control of the ball.

The jump-ball situation illustrates this continuous possession again. If we are in control of the ball and the opponent forces a jump ball, we no longer are in complete control. Therefore, we have lost possession. Should we recover the ball from the jump-ball situation, we will then have another possession.

---

[1] Frank McGuire, *Defensive Basketball*, Englewood Cliffs, N.J.: Prentice Hall, 1959.

In evaluating a basketball team, I like to use three phases of the game: offense, defense, and rebounding. Although I realize offensive rebounding is part of the offense, and defensive rebounding is part of the defense, I prefer to judge performance of the three phases separately. Our possession evaluation does this for us effectively and quickly.

The average points for each of our possessions gives us our offense. The average points for each opponent possession helps us determine the effectiveness of our defense. The total number of possessions helps us evaluate our rebounding effectiveness, although this can be altered by jump-ball situations.

I often have heard coaches comment after a game that their teams outrebounded the opponent by "X" number of rebounds. These coaches read the statistics and merely counted the number of rebounds per team. From our point of view, the total number of rebounds is not an accurate basis of determining a team's rebounding prowess in a game and I pay no attention to it. Let's use the following example to illustrate the point.

Team A shoots thirty-five percent from the floor and sixty percent from the foul line. Team B shoots fifty-six percent from the floor and eighty percent from the foul line. It is safe to assume Team B will be the leading rebounding team from a total rebound standpoint. The fact that Team A shoots poorly means there will be many more rebounds at Team A's offensive end of the court. Since Team B will have the inside position they *should* have many total rebounds. Team B shot so well that there were relatively few defensive rebounds available for Team A.

A more effective method of rating rebounding performance for us is the difference between total possessions on our chart. I realize that there is an average of four to five jump-ball situations in a college game. The recoveries will influence a team's total possessions. However, its influence is neglible compared to rebounding.

The easiest method to use to arrive at total possessions for each team is to count the lost possessions. Most teams keep statistics on shots attempted and made, foul shots attempted and made, and number of fouls. These figures, coupled with loss of ball *without* a shot, are the primary figures we need to determine our possession evaluation. With the rule of taking one-shot fouls out of bounds, the only statistic that needs to be taken is the *number* of times to the foul line.

The ways to lose the ball without a shot would be a bad pass, fumble, violation, offensive foul (without a shot attempt), or by being tied up for a jump ball. Before the rule change which brought about taking the one-shot foul out of bounds, it was easy to arrive at total possessions by adding the number of shot attempts, defensive fouls by an opponent, and loss of ball. The total possessions would then be divided into the number of points scored to give us the figures needed.

However, the rule change necessitated our changing the second figure on our chart (the number of defensive fouls by an opponent). For the new figure, we now need to calculate the number of times a team goes to the foul line. For example, if Team A is fouled early and takes the ball out of bounds without shooting the foul shot, they have continued to control the basketball and we consider that the same possession. When Team A finally shoots the ball, that shot is considered the end of that possession.

If Team A is fouled while shooting and goes to the foul line, they are considered to have lost control of the basketball after shooting the foul shots, and consequently, that completes the possession. Therefore, it is necessary to count the number of times each team goes to the foul line.

One particular play that gives our statistician difficulty is the offensive foul. If a player on Team A is dribbling the basketball and charges an opponent before a shot is attempted, it is clearly a loss of ball for Team A. That ends that possession. However, if a player from Team A is driving to the basket, shoots the ball, and then charges the defensive player, we must consider if the shot is counted as an attempt. It really becomes a defensive foul by the player on Team A. We can make that assumption simply because if the shot is attempted and counted whether it goes in or not, the possession is ended. The other team then goes to the foul line, which means it should be counted as a defensive foul.

In summary, we count the number of possessions by how *true* possession is lost. We make the following chart for each game.

UNC		OPPONENT	
_____ shots for	_____ points	_____ shots for	_____ points
_____ times to foul line for	_____ points	_____ time to foul line for	_____ points
_____ loss of ball	__X__	_____ loss of ball	__X__
_____ total possessions for	_____ points	_____ total possessions for	_____ points
total points ÷ total possessions =		total points ÷ total possessions =	
average points for each possession = UNC Offense and Opponent Defense		average points for each possession = Opponent Offense and UNC Defense	
Total Loss of Ball ÷ Total Possessions = Percent Loss of Ball		Total Loss of Ball ÷ Total Possessions = Percent Loss of Ball	

The important figures to us are (1) UNC points per possession (our offense), (2) difference of total possessions (our rebounding), and (3) our opponent's points per possession (our defense).

We also look carefully at the percent loss of ball rather than the number of times we lose the ball. Percent loss of ball is an accurate gauge of our ball handling and it also tells us if our defense has forced the opponent into frequent loss of ball. In addition, we would like to go to the foul line more times than our opponents.

I've heard coaches say "You can't throw the ball away more than ten times and expect to win." This again is misleading since it depends on the tempo of the game. If Team A loses the ball without a shot twenty times with one

hundred twenty possessions, it is doing better than a team who loses the ball
fifteen times in eighty-five possessions.

We run the fast break and make several passes, so consequently we expect
our percent loss of ball to be between fifteen and twenty percent. However, in
this style of play, our field-goal percentage is higher. Let's take a look at the
possession evaluation statistics of two specific games and draw some conclu-
sions from them.

Example A

UNC		OPPONENT	
68 shots for	68 points	87 shots for	62 points
24 times to foul line for	28 points*	18 times to foul line for	16 points*
27 loss of ball	X	25 loss of ball	X
119 total possessions for	96 points	130 total possessions for	78 points
96 ÷ 119 = .81 points per possession		78 ÷ 130 = .60 points per possession	
27 ÷ 119 = 23% loss of ball		25 ÷ 130 = 19% loss of ball	

*This game was played before the rule was changed pertaining to the first six fouls. Since all fouls were penalized
by foul shots, we simply counted the number of times fouled.*

In Example A, we selected a game in which I thought we were badly
outrebounded. The official statistic sheet shows UNC with fifty-nine total
rebounds and the opponent with forty-five rebounds. Yet our opponent has
eleven more possessions than we do. This would support my belief that we
were outrebounded. You would never convince the public that we were outrebounded since we had fifty-nine rebounds to their forty-five. The day following
this game however, we worked on our rebounding.

In addition to weak rebounding this particular game resulted in a twenty-
three percent loss of ball for us. This was reflected in our .81 average points per
possession which should have been higher considering our fifty percent shooting from the floor and excellent foul shooting with frequent use of the one-and-
one bonus.

This particular game was one of the longest games (most possessions,
run-and-gun) we've encountered in some years. If we had to point to one of the
three phases of the game (offense, defense, and rebounding), I'd say it was our
defense which won the game for us. We held them to .60 points per possession.

In Example B, we can conclude from our possession evaluation that both
the offense and defense were effective. However, we again failed to do well in
rebounding according to our one hundred six possessions to their one hundred
nine possessions. The total rebounds aren't as much misleading in this
example since the official statistics lists UNC with forty-one and the opponent
with thirty-nine.

The offense figure of .88 points per possession should be good enough to win most games. It was helped by our thirteen percent loss of ball which we consider excellent.

Defensively, we held the opponent to .63 points per possession, which is good defense. They only shot fifty-six times to our seventy-one, since we forced a very high twenty-nine percent loss of ball with our pressing defense.

Example B

UNC		OPPONENT	
71 shots for	74 points	56 shots for	52 points
21 times to foul line for	19 points	22 times to foul line for	17 points
14 loss of ball	X	31 loss of ball	X
106 possessions for	93 points	109 possessions for	69 points
93 ÷ 106 = .88 points per Possession		69 ÷ 109 = .63 points per Possession	
14 ÷ 106 = 13% loss of ball		31 ÷ 109 = 29% loss of ball	

The 1971−72 season summary chart illustrated at the conclusion of this section is rather interesting. It would appear that the 1971−72 UNC team was rather consistent offensively, dipping below .73 average points for only one game, which unfortunately was in the NCAA semifinals. Defensively, we were also consistent, holding our opponents to .77 points per possession or under in all but three games. Note that we lost each of the three games in which our opponent averaged more than .80 points per possession.

Our rebounding, as noted in the total possessions column, was not as consistent. Before this particular season, I was concerned about our rebounding. The year-end statistics proved the validity of that concern.

We have inserted the statistics of our 1976−77 and 1977−78 teams. The 1976−77 team finished second in the NCAA championship. The 1977−78 team was rated in the nation's Top Ten and won the ACC regular season championship. You will notice that fewer points are scored at the foul line in most instances with the rule change requiring out-of-bounds possession on the first six fouls.

During the past several years, I have mentioned at clinics that the best conceivable offense is one that would have the offense fouled every time down court. The statistics on possession evaluation will bear this out. Most teams average over one point per possession for each trip to the foul line. Since most teams do not average one point per possession in any one game, you can see the validity of our contention that being fouled is good offense.

Some additional possession evaluation charts are worth illustrating at this point. We have used examples from games against teams that were soundly coached. Example C is taken from our game played at Portland against the University of Oregon during the 1976−77 season.

On this particular occasion, the statistics indicate that we won the game from both an offensive and defensive point of view. Total possessions show only a difference of one. We did force Oregon into a twenty-eight percent loss of ball. High loss-of-ball percentage usually helps the offense. If your opponent loses the ball, you generally get a steal and an easy basket at the other end of the court. We think this is why pressure defense helps our offense so much.

Example C

UNC		OPPONENT	
47 shots for	60 points	47 shots for	46 points
15 times to foul line for	26 points	10 times to foul line for	14 points
18 loss of ball	X	22 loss of ball	X
80 possessions for	86 points	79 possessions for	60 points
86 ÷ 80 = 1.07 points per Possession		60 ÷ 79 = .76 points per Possession	
18 ÷ 80 = 22.5% loss of ball		22 ÷ 79 = 28% Loss of ball	

Oregon's aggressiveness did force us into twenty-two-and-a-half percent loss of ball, but we were still able to come up with 1.07 points for each possession, which is extremely high. This game is an excellent example of how good defense can make the offense effective, since we did get many fast-break baskets from steals.

I do believe our 1976−77 team was awesome at times from an offensive point of view. They failed to be above .80 average points per possession only four times. During three of those four games they played at .79 points per possession.

The chart taken from one of our games against Duke during the 1977−78 season is used as Example D. It illustrates an unusual set of possession-evaluation statistics.

Example D

UNC		OPPONENT	
66 shots for	64 points	37 shots for	40 points
13 times to foul line for	15 points	18 times to foul line for	26 points
16 loss of ball	X	25 loss of ball	X
95 possessions for	79 points	80 possessions for	66 points
79 ÷ 95 = .83 points per Possession		66 ÷ 80 = .83 points per Possession	
16 ÷ 95 = 17% loss of ball		25 ÷ 80 = 31% loss of ball	

We defeated Duke in this game 79−66 on a neutral court in Greensboro early in the year. Duke ultimately went on to become the NCAA runner-up. As you will note on the chart, each team played at .83 average points per possession on both offense and defense. I would point to the total possessions of ninety-five versus eighty as the reason we won the game. Our rebounding in this particular game was the difference. However, I was also pleased with our pressure defense, which brought about a thirty-one percent loss of ball by Duke. We played Duke two other times that year, splitting the two games. During those games, Duke was able to get their percent loss of ball down to twenty-four percent and twenty-one percent, respectively. In both games, each team played at .90 points per possession or better offensively, which is great offense.

In summarizing our 1977−78 team, we find our offense again stayed over .80 points per possession a great deal of the time. In only three games did we fail to go .80 points per possession or above. We won one of those games at .79 points per possession but lost the other two. Our defense was not as consistent as that of our 1976−77 team, but our rebounding appeared to be better.

The trend in recent years appears to be that teams in general are taking better shots and consequently the number of possessions seems to be declining. If we think we are the better team, we like to have over 100 possessions for that game. Should we ever be a huge underdog, we prefer a 60 possession game. This will be covered in greater detail in Chapter 1, *Philosophy of Defense*.

In a final update we have included the possession evaluation chart for the 1978−79 season. As we indicated, the trend in college basketball is to better shot selection, which usually consumes more time on offense. Therefore, the total possessions of each game tends to be less than it was several years ago. During the last five years, most teams also have used a zone defense against us. Generally, we do have patience against a zone and this is reflected in the lower number of possessions during the 1978−79 season. If teams use better shot selection against us and score from the field, our number of possessions will decline, since we don't have the opportunity to fast break on a made shot. During this particular season, our steals were up due to the outstanding defensive ability of Dudley Bradley.

UNIVERSITY OF NORTH CAROLINA – POSSESSION EVALUATION   YEAR: 1971-72

GAME	CODE	SCORE UNC	SCORE OPP	OFFENSE UNC	OFFENSE OPP	DEFENSE UNC	DEFENSE OPP	TOTAL POSS. UNC	TOTAL POSS. OPP	DIFFERENCE	% LOSS OF BALL UNC	% LOSS OF BALL OPP	MISC.
UNC vs. RICE	H	127	69	1.10	.59	.59	1.10	1.16	1.16	0	.26	.14	
UNC " PITT	A	90	75	.84	.72	.72	.84	1.08	1.05	+3	.28	.25	
UNC " PRINCETON	A	73	89	STATISTICS NOT AVAILABLE									
UNC " V.I.P.	H	93	60	.76	.54	.54	.76	1.22	1.12	+10	.16	.25	
UNC " WAKE FOREST	N	99	76	.86	.65	.65	.86	1.18	1.17	+1	.21	.13	
UNC " N.C. STATE	N	99	68	.89	.64	.64	.89	1.11	1.06	+5	.17	.28	
UNC " HARVARD	N	96	78	.81	.60	.60	.81	1.19	1.30	-11	.23	.19	
UNC " ST. JOSEPHS	N	93	77	1.00	.77	.77	1.00	.93	.90	+3	.15	.12	
UNC " BRADLEY	N	75	69	.85	.75	.75	.85	.88	.92	-4	.18	.28	
UNC " FURMAN	H	118	66	.85	.77	.77	.85	1.39	1.29	+10	.24	.23	
UNC " CLEMSON	A	81	61	.89	.73	.73	.89	.84	.85	+4	.22	.29	
UNC " VA.	A	85	79	.82	.72	.72	.82	1.03	1.10	-7	.23	.19	
UNC " WAKE FOREST	H	92	77	.79	.77	.77	.79	1.17	1.09	+8	.17	.22	
UNC " DUKE	A	74	76	.78	.88	.88	.78	.94	.85	+9	.18	.21	
UNC " MARYLAND	H	92	72	.92	.63	.63	.92	1.02	1.15	-13	.18	.20	
UNC " WAKE FOREST	A	71	59	.79	.70	.70	.79	.90	.84	+6	.23	.29	
UNC " N.C. STATE	H	101	78	.88	.62	.62	.88	1.15	1.24	-9	.16	.22	
UNC " CLEMSON	N	73	50	.74	.52	.52	.74	.99	.95	+4	.17	.27	
UNC " GA. TECH	N	118	73	1.00	.66	.66	1.00	1.18	1.10	+8	.19	.21	
UNC " MARYLAND	A	77	79	.74	.81	.81	.74	1.04	.97	+7	.22	.16	
UNC " NOTRE DAME	N	99	74	STATISTICS NOT AVAILABLE									
UNC " GA. TECH	H	87	66	.79	.65	.65	.79	1.17	1.14	+3	.24	.20	
UNC " VA.	H	91	78	.98	.73	.73	.98	.92	1.07	-15	.20	.11	
UNC " N.C. STATE	A	84	85	.89	.86	.86	.89	.94	.97	-3	.17	.18	
UNC " DUKE	H	93	69	.85	.63	.63	.88	1.06	1.09	-3	.13	.29	
UNC " DUKE	N	63	48	.73	.55	.55	.13	.87	.87	0	.22	.21	
UNC " MARYLAND	N	73	64	.86	.71	.71	.86	.85	.90	-5	.16	.15	
UNC " SOUTH CAROLINA	N	92	69	.89	.62	.62	.89	1.09	1.10	-1	.16	.17	
UNC " PENN	N	73	59	.85	.67	.67	.85	.86	.89	-3	.18	.16	
UNC " FLA. STATE	N	75	79	.65	.73	.73	.65	1.16	1.09	+7	.23	.25	
UNC " LOUISVILLE	N	105	91	.89	.73	.73	.89	1.20	1.24	-4	.25	.18	

WON & LOSS RECORD 26-5

UNIVERSITY OF NORTH CAROLINA - POSSESSION EVALUATION   YEAR: 1976-77

GAME		H/A/N	SCORE		OFFENSE		DEFENSE		TOTAL POSSESSIONS			PERCENT LOSS of BALL		MISC.
			UNC	OPP.	UNC	OPP.	UNC	OPP.	UNC	OPD	DIFFERENCE	UNC	OPP.	
UNC VS. N.C. STATE		N	78	66	.79	.67	.67	.79	99	99	0	.32	.32	
UNC " WAKE FOREST		N	96	97	1.04	1.03	1.03	1.04	92	94	+2	.21	.19	
UNC " MARSHALL		N	90	70	.86	.75	.75	.86	104	95	-9	.14	.23	
UNC " MICH. STATE		A	81	58	.79	.62	.62	.79	102	93	-9	.23	.31	
UNC " A.I.A.		H	99	86	.92	.71	.71	.92	108	121	+3	.19	.11	
UNC " V.P.I.		A	81	77	.92	.84	.84	.92	88	92	-4	.17	.21	
UNC " BRIG YOUNG		H	113	93	1.06	.87	.87	1.06	107	107	0	.17	.24	
UNC " O. ROBERTS		N	100	84	1.02	.80	.80	1.02	98	105	-7	.20	.18	
UNC " OREGON		A	86	60	1.07	.76	.76	1.07	80	79	+1	.21	.28	
UNC " WEBER ST.		N	75	54	.95	.67	.67	.95	79	81	-2	.24	.21	
UNC " CLEMSON		A	91	63	.87	.55	.55	.87	105	113	-8	.17	.28	
UNC " VA.		H	91	67	1.08	.74	.74	1.08	84	91	-7	.18	.16	
UNC " WAKE FOREST		A	77	75	.83	.83	.83	.83	93	90	+3	.20	.11	
UNC " DUKE		H	77	68	.75	.66	.66	.75	102	103	-1	.23	.26	
UNC " N.C. STATE		A	73	75	.86	.80	.80	.86	85	94	-9	.19	.12	
UNC " MARYLAND		A	71	68	.93	.88	.88	.93	76	77	-1	.13	.19	
UNC " WAKE FOREST		H	66	67	.84	.82	.82	.84	79	82	-3	.18	.15	
UNC " CLEMSON		A	73	93	.82	.99	.99	.82	89	94	-5	.16	.18	
UNC " GA. TECH		N	98	74	1.09	.85	.85	1.09	90	87	+3	.17	.23	
UNC " FURMAN		N	88	71	.96	.77	.77	.96	92	92	0	.16	.22	
UNC " MARYLAND		H	97	70	.96	.74	.74	.96	101	95	+6	.13	.26	
UNC " TULANE		H	106	94	.93	.83	.83	.93	114	113	+1	.19	.19	
UNC " S. FLA.		H	100	65	1.11	.77	.77	1.11	90	84	+6	.18	.20	
UNC " VA.		A	66	64	.94	.88	.88	.94	70	74	-4	.20	.19	
UNC " N.C. STATE		H	90	73	.91	.71	.71	.91	99	103	-4	.25	.21	
UNC " DUKE		A	84	71	.88	.78	.78	.88	95	91	+4	.04	.20	
UNC " LOUISVILLE		N	96	89	.96	.97	.97	.96	100	92	+8	.15	.23	
UNC " N.C. STATE		N	70	56	.89	.65	.65	.89	79	86	-7	.19	.23	
UNC " VA.		N	75	69	.99	.85	.85	.99	76	81	-5	.18	.21	
UNC " PURDUE		N	69	66	.83	.87	.87	.83	83	76	+7	.16	.22	
UNC " NOTRE DAME		N	79	77	.92	.99	.99	.92	86	78	+8	.09	.32	
UNC " KENTUCKY		N	79	72	1.20	.91	.91	1.20	66	79	-13	.14	.13	
UNC " LAS VEGAS-NEV.		N	84	83	.86	.84	.84	.86	98	99	-1	.30	.17	
UNC " MARQUETTE		N	59	67	.79	.96	.96	.79	75	70	+5	.20	.16	

WON & LOST RECORD 28-5

UNIVERSITY OF NORTH CAROLINA – POSSESSION EVALUATION   YEAR: 1977-78

GAME	COURT	SCORE UNC	SCORE OPP	OFFENSE UNC	OFFENSE OPP	DEFENSE UNC	DEFENSE OPP	TOTAL POSSESSIONS UNC	TOTAL POSSESSIONS OPP	DIFFERENCE	PERCENT LOSS OF BALL UNC	PERCENT LOSS OF BALL OPP	MISC.
UNC vs. OREGON ST.	N	94	63	1.04	.81	.81	1.04	90	78	+12	.14	.30	
UNC " OREGON ST.	H	90	64	.91	.65	.65	.91	98	98	0	.23	.36	
UNC " DUKE	N	79	66	.83	.83	.83	.83	95	80	+15	.17	.31	
UNC " N.C. STATE	N	87	82	.96	.90	.90	.96	91	91	0	.18	.20	
UNC " WM.& MARY	A	75	78	.83	1.08	1.08	.83	90	72	+18	.15	.18	
UNC " ROCHESTER	H	101	43	.90	.45	.45	.90	111	94	+17	.19	.39	
UNC " CINCINNATI	N	67	59	.79	.77	.77	.79	85	77	+8	.21	.21	
UNC " TULANE	A	108	103	1.00	.99	.99	1.00	107	104	+3	.20	.24	
UNC " BYU	N	94	81	.97	.82	.82	.97	97	99	-2	.29	.29	
UNC " TEXAS TECH	N	88	76	1.01	.96	.96	1.01	87	79	+8	.16	.16	
UNC " STANFORD	N	92	61	1.00	.74	.74	1.00	92	82	+10	.14	.28	
UNC " CLEMSON	A	79	77	.81	.88	.88	.81	97	88	+9	.23	.22	
UNC " VIRGINIA	A	76	61	1.07	.73	.73	1.07	72	84	-12	.29	.18	
UNC " DUKE	A	84	92	.94	.98	.98	.94	89	93	-4	.22	.24	
UNC " WAKE FOREST	H	71	69	.82	.86	.86	.82	87	80	+7	.19	.21	
UNC " N.C. STATE	H	69	64	.89	.80	.80	.89	87	80	+7	.19	.15	
UNC " MARYLAND	H	85	71	.89	.67	.67	.89	95	102	+7	.20	.29	
UNC " WAKE FOREST	A	62	71	.63	.83	.83	.63	98	86	+12	.19	.30	
UNC " CLEMSON	H	98	64	.96	.69	.69	.96	101	92	+9	.19	.24	
UNC " MERCER	H	73	70	.85	.80	.80	.85	86	87	+7	.17	.24	
UNC " FURMAN	N	83	89	.90	.89	.89	.90	94	93	+6	.21	.20	
UNC " VA. TECH	N	101	88	1.07	.86	.86	1.07	94	102	-8	.21	.12	
UNC " MARYLAND	A	66	64	.88	1.08	1.08	.88	72	61	+11	.17	.10	
UNC " RUTGERS	A	74	57	.85	.67	.67	.85	87	85	+2	.17	.25	
UNC " PROVIDENCE	A	59	61	.84	.81	.81	.84	70	75	-5	.29	.16	
UNC " KENT STATE	H	92	59	.93	.64	.64	.93	97	90	+7	.18	.17	
UNC " VIRGINIA	H	71	54	1.00	.86	.86	1.00	71	83	-12	.16	.21	
UNC " N.C. STATE	A	67	72	.94	1.00	1.00	.94	71	72	-1	.18	.13	
UNC " DUKE	H	87	83	.96	.90	.90	.96	90	92	-2	.19	.21	
UNC " WAKE FOREST	N	77	82	.80	.90	.90	.80	96	91	+5	.13	.22	
UNC " SAN FRANCISCO	N	64	68	.78	.82	.82	.78	82	83	-1	.19	.22	

WON & LOST RECORD: 23-8

UNIVERSITY OF NORTH CAROLINA - POSSESSION EVALUATION   YEAR: 1978-79

GAME		COURT	SCORE		OFFENSE		DEFENSE		TOTAL POSSESSIONS			PERCENT LOSS OF BALL		MISC.
			UNC	OPP	UNC	OPP	UNC	OPP	UNC	OPP	DIFFERENCE	UNC	OPP	
UNC	vs NORTHWESTERN	A	95	67	.98	.70	.70	.98	96	95	+ 1	.20	.26	
UNC	" WAKE FOREST	N	73	55	.84	.70	.70	.84	87	78	+ 9	.20	.23	
UNC	" DUKE	N	68	78										
UNC	" DETROIT	H	93	76	.84	.89	.89	.84	105	95	+10	.20	.16	
UNC	" JACKSONVILLE	H	85	56	.88	.61	.61	.88	97	92	+ 5	.24	.28	
UNC	" MICHIGAN ST.	H	70	69	.90	.80	.80	.90	88	76	+12	.14	.28	
UNC	" CINCINNATI	A	62	59	.76	.75	.75	.76	81	78	+ 3	.16	.18	
UNC	" DARTMOUTH	N	86	67	.88	.76	.76	.88	97	88	+ 9	.22	.22	
UNC	" NIAGARA	N	121	67	1.08	.67	.67	1.08	112	102	+10	.15	.23	
UNC	" CLEMSON	N	90	68	.99	.69	.69	.99	92	98	- 6	.20	.24	
UNC	" VIRGINIA	H	86	74	.96	.89	.89	.96	90	95	- 5	.23	.15	
UNC	" WAKE FOREST	A	56	59	.86	.89	.89	.86	63	66	- 3	.20	.22	
UNC	" DUKE	H	74	68	.86	.84	.84	.86	86	81	+ 5	.16	.23	
UNC	" ARKANSAS	N	63	57	.88	.84	.84	.88	70	68	+ 2	.18	.20	
UNC	" N.C. STATE	A	70	69	.94	.87	.87	.94	74	79	- 5	.18	.13	
UNC	" MARYLAND	A	54	53	.77	.79	.79	.77	71	66	+ 5	.18	.24	
UNC	" WAKE FOREST	H	76	69	1.00	.82	.82	1.00	77	84	- 7	.19	.16	
UNC	" CLEMSON	A	61	66	.76	.85	.85	.76	80	78	+ 2	.29	.26	
UNC	" FURMAN	N	70	83	.84	1.10	1.10	.84	83	74	+ 9	.14	.9	
UNC	" VIRGINIA TECH	N	92	80										
UNC	" MARYLAND	H	76	67	.97	.81	.81	.97	78	83	- 5	.16	.28	
UNC	" PROVIDENCE	N	89	55	.94	.65	.65	.94	95	84	+11	.19	.26	
UNC	" WM. & MARY	H	85	60	.99	.76	.76	.99	81	79	+ 2	.13	.30	
UNC	" VIRGINIA	A	66	57	1.06	.81	.81	1.06	62	70	- 8	.17	.23	
UNC	" N.C. STATE	H	71	56	1.04	.82	.82	1.04	72	75	- 3	.15	.19	
UNC	" DUKE	A	40	47	.93	1.20	1.20	.93	43	39	+ 4	.7	.25	
UNC	" MARYLAND	N	102	79	1.09	.71	.71	1.09	94	99	- 5	.18	.18	
UNC	" DUKE	N	71	63	.99	.82	.82	.99	72	77	- 5	.8	.19	
UNC	" PENNSYLVANIA	N	71	72	.94	.87	.87	.94	84	83	+ 1	.20	.20	

WON & LOSS RECORD 23-6

11

legend

○   OFFENSIVE PLAYER, WITH A NUMBER INSIDE, DENOTES SPECIFIC SHUFFLE POSITION.

X OR ⊗   DEFENSIVE PLAYER.

◐ OR ◯◄   OFFENSIVE PLAYER WITH BALL.

◯◄   PLAYER WHERE READER SHOULD BEGIN TO INTERPRET PLAY IN THE DIAGRAM.

<   "TURNING" AND FACING"; USUALLY ASSOCIATED WITH A PLAYER'S ACTION WHEN CATCHING, PASSING, OR SHOOTING.

- - - - →   PASS. ARROW SHOWS DIRECTION OF PASS.

——→   PLAYER MOVEMENT.

∿∿→   DRIBBLE.

———⊣   PLAYERS MOVEMENT ENDING IN A SCREEN.

············   FLIGHT PATH OF SHOT TO THE BASKET.

R   REBOUNDER.

→   DIRECTION OF PLAYER AFTER PLAY--FOUND IN DRILL DIAGRAMS TO SHOW WHERE PLAYERS FILL AFTER ACTION IS COMPLETED.

offensive

basketball

1

philosophy of team offense

The objective of any basketball offense is to score as often as possible on each possession.

Obviously, few coaches would take exception to the above definition. Determining how that objective is best accomplished is another matter, however. There are as many different philosophies underlying offensive basketball strategy as there are coaches in the profession.

Success has not been reserved exclusively for proponents of any one approach. Outstanding records have been compiled by coaches whose offensive philosophies vary considerably.

system versus flexible approach

A coach usually arrives at his own philosophy of offense based upon tempo and style of play, both of which may be effected by the personnel on hand. Some coaches continue to use the same system of play year after year. These coaches are referred to as *system-type* coaches. The *system* coach will make adjustments based upon the talent on hand, in order to get maximum efficiency out of the system he uses exclusively.

Other coaches will change their system from year to year, adapting almost exclusively to the talents of the players. These coaches can be termed *flexible-type* coaches.

SYSTEM-TYPE COACHES

The college coach whose teams won more games than any other in history can safely be classified as a system-type coach. I'm referring, of course, to Adolph Rupp, former coach of Kentucky.

If there was any dramatic change in the fashion of Coach Rupp's teams from the 30s to the 70s, it was evident only in the style of their uniforms. Kentucky teams throughout the Rupp era exercised similar set plays, looked for the fast break in the same manner, and were extremely aggressive offensive rebounders. They possessed one other common ingredient as well—they won!

We can assume that part of Coach Rupp's success was due to his ability to make adjustments to his system based on the talents of his players.

Two other notable and highly successful coaches I would place near the system end of the pole would be former coach of UCLA, John Wooden, and Bob Spear, former coach of the Air Force Academy.

Coach Wooden was extremely methodical and precise in his approach to every aspect of the game. His teams always projected much the same style, with the possible exception of the Lew Alcindor (Kareem Abdul-Jabbar) seasons from 1966–67 through 1968–69. It appeared to me that Coach Wooden did make a distinct change in his high post offensive attack to take advantage of Alcindor's tremendous size and talent. Upon Alcindor's graduation, however, Coach Wooden returned to his system and continued his amazing success until his retirement in 1975.

Coach Bob Spear, whom I assisted at the Air Force Academy, became a system coach out of necessity. The Academy was rarely in a position to recruit highly sought-after athletes. As a result, Air Force teams consistently lacked the advantage of overall height and quickness. Coach Spear consequently employed the shuffle system, which does not require a big front line. His ingenuity and effectiveness resulted in a winning record for the Academy throughout his thirteen years as coach, even though his teams were outmanned 90 percent of the time.

FLEXIBLE-TYPE COACHES

At the other end of the pole are the *flexible-type* coaches who will make major changes annually based upon the caliber of their personnel. These are coaches who may highlight a set offense one year and revert to free-lance the next; emphasize the fast break one season and play ball control the following year. The flexible coach may depend heavily on a high-scoring guard when he has one, or rely on the frontcourt men for scoring power when his guards are better ball handlers than shooters.

I would place two men, with whom I've had the good fortune to be associated with, in this category: Dr. Phog Allen, my college coach, who, incidentally, is the second winningest coach in history, and Frank McGuire, under whom I served as assistant for three years. Both of these outstanding coaches have been highly successful, and have won NCAA championships.

Dr. Allen's teams hardly looked the same in 1922, 1932, or in 1952, the year they won the NCAA title. Dr. Allen's assistant in 1952 was Dick Harp, who possessed a brilliant basketball mind and was a highly successful coach in his own right. Dr. Allen and Coach Harp instituted the theory of *between-ball-and-man* pressure defense. This technique brought about more steals and resulting fast breaks, which changed the tempo and style of play considerably. Dr. Allen would not hesitate to alter his offensive thinking from year to year in order to exploit new strategies and make the best use of his personnel.

Coach McGuire's 1952 St. John's team, his 1957 and 1961 teams at North Carolina, and his 1971 South Carolina team bore little resemblance to one another in terms of offensive style. All four teams, coached by the same man, were extremely effective and each was nationally ranked. The 1957 team won the NCAA championship.

The above examples of system and flexible coaching approaches should point out that there is no one concept nor magic formula designed to guarantee success. Each coach must formulate his own thinking and operate within the framework of the philosophy with which he feels most comfortable.

It should be pointed out, however, that the college or professional coach has an obvious advantage over the high school and junior high school coach. The college or professional coach is in a position to recruit personnel whose talents will blend effectively within his designated system. Secondary-level coaches must accept the talent available to them. As a result, they are usually required to adopt the flexible approach, in an effort to make the best use of their personnel.

AUTHOR'S OWN PHILOSOPHY

Most coaches would probably conclude that their own philosophy rested some where in between system and flexible. In determining my own position, I would consider myself to be very near the center, bearing slightly towards the flexible end of the pole. I would further describe my offensive philosophy as follows:

- Utilize personnel as effectively as possible.
- Encourage team play—achieve results through cooperation and unselfish effort on the part of every player.
- Look to fast break at every opportunity.
- Concentrate on the high-percentage shot with good offensive rebounding coverage.
- Multiple offense: Major emphasis on a free-lance offense, with rules along with some set offenses to make use of personnel.
- Eliminate element of surprise by having team thoroughly prepared to meet all possible defenses.
- Vary the offense throughout each game to prevent the defense from preparing too easily, or becoming accustomed to a singular style of play.

The personnel on hand during any one year will present the challenge of how best to use their strengths and conceal their weaknesses from an offensive standpoint. A coach must determine how tall and how quick his team will be in comparison to the opposition—will outside shooting or ball handling be assets to be exploited, or deficiencies to be obscured? Is there one man the team must get open, and if so—how? The answers to these and similar questions will ultimately provide each coach with his system for the season. The coach, however, must remain flexible enough to make changes as the season progresses.

If you have some relatively tall frontcourt men, you may prefer a set offense to be certain the ball goes inside to your height. With height, you want to be sure the shot is taken with your tall people near the boards. Some coaches with good frontcourt height discourage the fast break to be certain their big people are downcourt offensively when the shot is taken. Others feel the key to the fast break is the defensive rebound, and encourage its use if ball handling is adequate. Speed, incidentally, is not the essential element of the fast break. It comes after defensive rebounding and ball handling at full speed. With height, you can expect to play against a zone jammed back or a full-court press. More time must therefore be spent preparing to attack these two defenses.

If you have some quickness but very little size relative to your competition, there are other decisions to be made. Offensive rebounding will probably be a weakness. You will, therefore, have to place greater emphasis on careful shot selection, since shooting at a very high percentage will be a key factor in determining your success. This requires attention to ball-handling skills in order to maintain possession while patiently waiting for the good shot.

It is often wise for a small team, with or without speed, to *shorten* the length of the game by controlling the ball. This will not necessarily prohibit use of the fast break. However, when the defense of the taller opposition is set, the smaller team can maintain control of the ball (and the clock) until such time as it is fouled or can take advantage of the very high-percentage shot. Another means of shortening the game is through maximum use of the time allowed to bring the ball across the ten-second line, assuming the other team chooses not to press. Time can also be consumed after the other team scores through slow recovery of the ball for the offensive throw-in.

If a team does not have speed, size, or ability compared to its opponent, its only hope is to shorten the game by exercising ball control on offense. As awesome as the opposition may be, it cannot score without the ball. By way of an exaggerated example, if a high school team were to face the professional New York Knicks, it would have a remote chance of winning a game restricted to five minutes. The longer the game was played, the less chance the high school team would have to pull off an upset. By shortening the game through ball control, the "have nots" possess the chance to defeat the "haves." Proficiency at ball control, however, requires considerable practice at dribbling and passing in order to develop the poise necessary for successful execution.

Conversely, if your team is bigger, quicker, and more talented than the opposition, you probably would want to *lengthen* the game by moving up court and looking for the good-percentage shot as quickly as possible.

If a team possesses good outside shooting, they can expect to see less zone defenses. They can, therefore, devote more practice time to man-to-man and pressure defense.

The coach has the responsibility of designing an offense which will give a good shooter his shot with adequate board coverage. If the team has a good driver, the offense designed must place him in a favorable position from which to drive. Most man-to-man offensives can be structured to get the ball to any designated individual by having that player set a screen away from the ball. The screener is usually left open immediately after screening.

ball control vs. fast break

The use of *ball control* may not be restricted to a team that faces stronger opponents most of the time. Some advocates of ball control continue its use regardless of the caliber of their personnel. Although it may not often win in spectacular fashion, a ball-control team will rarely lose by a large margin. For this, among other reasons, many proponents favor it.

Although most ball-control teams do not take advantage of the fast break, neither do they risk the possibility of throwing the ball away. It is a sound philosophy and I take no exception to it. My own preference, however, is to look for the fast break from a missed shot or an interception.

The fast break is not only exciting to the players and spectators, it is a good way to pick up the high-percentage shot. The fast break often leads on a one- or two-man advantage as the offense approaches the basket. However, even if the fast-breaking team comes down the court three-on-three, the good-percentage shot should be more readily accessible since the defense is not set and waiting. Furthermore, the fewer defensive players in the scoring area, the better the chances for scoring. For example, it is much easier to score in a two-on-two situation than it is in a five-on-five situation. If you have any doubts about this theory, try playing seven-against-seven in practice to see how long it takes for a team to score compared to a normal five-against-five scrimmage.

The successful break, especially one resulting from an opponent's error, can serve to upset an opponent. This may help the fast-breaking team gain momentum at times.

Although we may lose the ball more often by fast breaking, we feel that the high-percentage shots or fouls drawn through its use more than compensate for lost possessions. For the above reasons, along with the relief from the offensive board, we always have believed in the fast break, even when we were not blessed with excellent talent.

the percentage shot

The chart at the conclusion of this chapter has been suggested as the most effective means of illustrating the results of our emphasis on intelligent shot selection. Some observers have suggested a significant relationship between our efforts at maintaining a high field-goal percentage to the measure of success we have been fortunate to achieve in recent years.

We try to promote opportunities which lend themselves to the percentage shot. We believe in getting the ball inside for the shot whenever possible. Outside shots are always available. We have no reservations about shooting from the outside. However, we prefer doing so after the ball has gone inside or to the baseline initially. We then can be more confident about our offensive rebounding. Also, we will have placed pressure on the defense to foul us while we moved the ball inside. This is vitally important. Some teams tend to overlook the importance of setting up conditions which make the defense more prone to fouling. At North Carolina, we consider this a major part of our offensive strategy.

Since we believe it is essential to move the defense before it can be penetrated, we emphasize the importance of passing several times before a shot is taken against a set defense.

How do we define a good shot? The amount of defensive pressure, length of shot, and individual player characteristics are each factors which determine what is or is not a good shot. Much depends on the shooting skill of the individual player. Each man must be aware of his percentages from various positions on the court. For some players, a lightly guarded twenty-foot jumper will be a higher percentage shot than one taken at close range among a number of defensive players. The shooter must have confidence that his shot will go in. The other four men must assume it will *not* go through the net in order to provide good offensive rebounding protection and defensive balance.

Although good board coverage is designed into all our offensive plans, I would not consider rebounding a major factor responsible for our overall high field-goal percentage. I would be more inclined to attribute it to good shot selection and our pressure defense, which gives us some easy scoring opportunities off the fast break.

team play

Team play is most certainly a vital part of our offensive philosophy. It has helped us considerably to bring about the high-percentage shot. If a young man wants to be an individual, or *gunner*, in basketball, it is difficult to find four other men who will be anxious to play with him. A gunner will ruin a team faster than any other factor. He is usually the high scorer of the team, with one of the worst field-goal percentages on the team. When this type of situation occurs, the team usually has a losing record.

We have had some individual high scoring averages at North Carolina throughout the years. In each case, however, the player was shooting at a very high percentage as well. When a team's leading scorer has the best field-goal percentage, that team is a winner.

Over the years shown on the chart, we have had the good fortune to win more games than any other NCAA team except UCLA, with Coach Al McGuire's Marquette a close third. UCLA, North Carolina, and Marquette have had few individuals, if any, among the Top Twenty scorers in the country. Each school, however, has had numerous All-Americans.

Ideally, our offense is designed to provide shots for each player. The flexibility of the system could be illustrated by our leading scorers, who have come from each of the five offensive positions. In the early seventies, those top scorers for North Carolina were as follows:

- 1970 – Charles Scott, small forward and big guard (swing)
- 1971 – Dennis Wuycik, big forward
- 1972 – Bob McAdoo, center
- 1973 – George Karl, small guard (quarterback)
- 1974 – Darrell Elston, big guard and Bobby Jones, center

Our players do tend to be unselfish. They realize that some nights the defense is keyed on them, thereby leaving their teammates open for better shots. One year (1971), we had seven players score twenty or more points in at least one game during the season.

A team with five individuals thinking *team* will defeat a group of superior individuals thinking of themselves. We are grateful to our players at North Carolina throughout the years for believing and playing with this concept in mind.

arriving at an offense

Teaching his players offensive basketball fundamentals is a major responsibility of every coach. It matters little what offense is used if it is not executed properly. Therefore, the decision as to how much offense can be absorbed and well-executed by the players should determine the amount of offense offered.

All-purpose offenses are becoming more prevalent. In each of my years as head coach, we have always had some offense which could be used with equal effectiveness against both zone and man-to-man. I also consider it important to be prepared with a zone offense against *all* types of zones as well as a full-court press offense to be used against *all* types of full-court presses. I do not think there is enough time for our players to learn an unlimited number of custom-tailored offenses designed to counter every conceivable defense.

At the same time, the coach must expose his team to all possible defenses. The element of surprise should be eliminated by working against the full range of defensive alignments in practice.

The proper use of practice time to accomplish this and other offensive objectives is covered in a later chapter devoted to practice planning.

We do believe in multiple offense to the extent that we don't want our opponent to be able to prepare too easily against us.

A checklist is prepared each year to determine all that must be covered from an offensive standpoint prior to the first game. Our initial emphasis is placed on the basic half-court attack against a set defense. The half-court attack is used at our offensive end of the court after we have thrown the ball in bounds in the back court. Therefore, we assume, the defense will be set up.

Our quarterback, or point man (we do believe in a one-man front), indicates which of our offenses is to be executed. He does this by signaling the appropriate number with his free hand while dribbling across the ten-second line. Incidentally, our contentment with five offenses against the set defense is purely coincidental to the shortage of six-fingered quarterbacks.

A complete chapter is devoted to each of these five offenses as well as our method of teaching them. The following will serve as a brief description along with our reasons for using them in our multiple offense.

HALF-COURT OFFENSES

1. *One-Four Game* This offense utilizes our personnel at special functions that take advantage of their strengths. We use it against man-to-man defense primarily. At times, however, we have used it against zones, particularly match-up zones. Having a screen at the point of the ball, and making use of the *mismatch*, are two of its strengths. The One-Four game is structured to bring about a good shot quickly. If the scoring opportunity does not occur, our continuity takes us into the Passing Game (Offense #3).

2. *T Game* The T Game is designed as an inside attack. It is used as an all-purpose offense against any half-court defense. The T Game can be varied depending upon the personnel on hand. It can be used as either a single- or triple-post attack. As an inside attack, it lends itself to the high-percentage shot, strong board coverage, and a greater opportunity to place the opponent in foul trouble. The T game is our only continuity-type offense.

3. *Passing Game* Our Passing Game is another all-purpose offense used against *any* type of half-court defense. It serves as our high–low post free-lance offense. It is a simple offense to learn and serves to increase overall offensive skills through its execution. We would, therefore, highly recommend its use as a primary, if not exclusive, half-court offense to secondary-education-level coaches. The Passing Game is the half-court offense we use most frequently.

4. *Four Corner Delay Game* We do believe in a delay game from which we can continue to score through lay-ups or foul shots. Our Four Corner delay game was established to control the ball as well as to score if the defense chooses to come out and chase us. It is usually (though not necessarily) used in the late stages of the game. The Four Corners require only three ball handlers instead of the four required by most other delay games.

5. *Basic Cut Movement Game* This game may be superfluous, but still remains on our list of offenses. In all my years of coaching, I have always found good reason to incorporate the Basic Shuffle Cut, from the *Shuffle Offense*, into our attack. During years we lacked height or great quickness, we used the entire Shuffle Offense (explained by Coach Bob Spear in Part 2 of this book) as our primary offense. The Basic Shuffle Cut comes after an entry from the One-Four set. Hopefully, we have disguised it in this manner. Much movement on the part of all

our players is generated, and after one Basic Cut, we move into the Passing Game as continuity. We use this offense against man-to-man defense only.

Our master offensive checklist incorporates the following techniques in addition to our half-court attacks:

- *Fast-Break Offense* – The fast-break offense begins with a defensive rebound or an interception. We cover the beginning of the break, the transition from defense to offense, taking the ball downcourt, and the scoring area at the end of the break. At this point, the secondary break comes into focus. This takes us into our Passing Game, referred to earlier.
- *Full-Court Press Offense* – Our full-court press offense has been designed to counter all types of presses, since some teams (our own included) like to change their presses throughout the game. This offense is designed to take us to the *baseline* rather than just across the ten-second line. From the baseline we can move into our secondary break, or set up into any of our half-court attacks.
- *Offensive Rebounding* – For emphasis, offensive rebounding is listed separately on our check list, although it is an integral part of every offensive attack previously mentioned.
- *Out-of-Bounds Situations* – Time must be spent to insure possession of the ball in bounds from any point on the court. Possession, rather than scoring from an in-bounds pass, should be the major consideration.
- *Jump-Ball Situations* – Although jump balls are discussed from both offensive and defensive viewpoints, we want it on our offensive checklist. Possession gained from a jump ball requires readiness and organization for offense.
- *Foul-Shot Situations* – Our first goal is for the foul shooter to believe he is going to make the shot and for the other four players to think he is going to miss it. Secondly, we want to be prepared to set up our press for the seven out of ten foul shots the shooter is likely to make. However, we would also like to regain possession of as many of the misses as possible.
- *Last-minute situations* – This category is used to cover every possible occurrence related to the unusual or to the clock. Unique situations usually come about late in a very close-scoring game. This part of the offensive checklist is vitally important since, obviously, many games are won or lost during the closing minutes.

Through the use of our master offensive checklist, we hope to cover all possible defensive tactics that can be used against us during the season. We then decide the amount of practice time to be devoted to each area listed. The implementation of our overall philosophy, the execution of each phase of offense listed, in addition to much work on individual fundamentals, should prepare us adequately as an offensive basketball team.

To better understand our diagrams and play descriptions relating to North Carolina offense, it would be helpful to know the method used in the numbering of our players.

- **#1** — Our quarterback, generally the most capable ball handler and dribbler. He is usually the smallest of the guards.
- **#2** — Our second guard, usually bigger than #1. He doesn't have to be the caliber of ball handler or dribbler as #1.
- **#3** — Our smallest forward and best ball handler of the frontcourt men. #2 and #3 have similar roles and could be classified as *swing men.* #3 is generally bigger than #2 and smaller than #4.

Table 1–1 University of North Carolina Chapel Hill, North Carolina
Dean E. Smith, Head Coach (Atlantic Coast Conference)[1]

YEAR	FIELD GOALS MADE/ FIELD GOALS ATTEMPTED	FIELD GOAL PERCENTAGE	NATIONAL FIELD GOAL PERCENTAGE RANK	AVERAGE POINTS SCORED PER GAME	WON/LOSS RECORD	ATLANTIC COAST CONFERENCE FINISH
1979–80	838/1603	52.3%	15th	73.2	21–8	2
1978–79	861/1614	53.3%	6th	76.5	23–6	1[2]
1977–78	1008/1895	53.2%	7th	81.1	23–8	1
1976–77	1054/1961	53.7%	5th	83.6	28–5	1[4]
1975–76	966/1838	52.6%	4th	85.1	25–4	1[3]
1974–75	1037/1933	53.6%	2nd	84.6	23–8	2
1973–74	1015/1952	52.0%	3rd	87.0	22–6	2
1972–73	1150/2181	52.7%	1st	84.7	25–8	2
1971–72	1031/1954	52.8%	1st	89.0	26–5	1[4]
1970–71	1010/1935	52.2%	2nd	84.6	26–6	1
1969–70	931/1936	48.1%	19th	88.9	18–9	2
1968–69	1094/2228	49.1%	7th	88.9	27–5	1[4]
1967–68	1028/2261	45.5%	55th	83.7	28–4	1[4]
1966–67	1016/2154	47.2%	24th	82.2	26–6	1[4]
1965–66	838/1620	51.7%	1st	80.9	16–11	3

[1] The Atlantic Coast Conference has a tournament following the regular season. Thus, there is a regular season champion and a tournament champion.
[2] Won ACC Tournament Championship in addition to finishing in a tie for first during regular season.
[3] ACC Championship
[4] Won ACC Tournament in addition to finishing first in Conference.

#4 — Our biggest forward whose offensive moves are similar to those of #5. There is very little to distinguish between #4 and #5 offensively. #4 is usually quicker and smaller than #5.

#5 — Our biggest man who plays defensive center. Since we do not actually list a center for offense, we define the position from a defensive standpoint.

the free-lance passing game

The free-lance Passing Game serves as our #3 offense. The term *free-lance* describes the freedom, or latitude, permitted the players. Most set offenses give the player with the ball freedom of choice, while the man without the ball has a prescribed path to follow. True free-lance gives the man without the ball freedom as well.

Passing Game is added to free-lance to negate any notion that this offense is either a one-on-one or a dribbling type of game. We should point out, however, that we have no objections to a one-on-one move, once we have moved the defense.

More often, we refer to this offense as our Passing Game rather than free-lance offense. To many young men, the term free-lance suggests going on their own—doing their own thing. The well-executed free-lance Passing Game, to the contrary, is designed to promote cooperation and unselfish play.

Although this offense is intended to allow each player considerable freedom and spontaneity, it is not without its rules.

background and evolution

My close association with Dr. Phog Allen and Coach Frank McGuire were significant factors in the shaping of my basketball philosophy. Both are free-lance advocates. However, at the time I assumed the head coaching job at North Carolina, I felt our personnel could be utilized more efficiently through a set offense with many options.

We always encouraged our players to vary the diagrammed set play if there was a good reason to do so. Despite this urging, our game films pointed out that our men would occasionally bypass an easy-scoring opportunity as a result of being overly intent on executing the set offense properly. This motivated our search for an alternate offense which would free the player's mind to concentrate on playing basketball.

During that same period, we were using a free-lance zone offense with a high—low post, employing some of the principles used by Coach Henry Iba with the 1964 Olympic team. Larry Brown, captain of our 1963 Carolina team, played on that Olympic team. As my assistant a year later, Larry was in a position to incorporate a few of these principles into our regular free-lance zone offense.

We were pleased with our free-lance zone offense which had movement, and were looking for this same type of freedom against man-to-man. With a little experimentation, we found we could use our zone offense effectively against man-to-man by adding some movement and screens. The end result was the free-lance Passing Game, which we now use against zone, man-to-man, and any combination half-court defense.

ADVANTAGES OF THE PASSING GAME

1. Simplicity: Our Passing Game is a simple offense to learn, which provides an obvious advantage to any team. The relative ease of learning the Passing Game is demonstrated annually at our basketball camp held for young men ages 10−17. During our first half-hour session with these youngsters, the Passing Game is explained and then practiced five-against-five. By the third such session, the older boys have little difficulty utilizing it properly. By the fifth session, even the ten-year-olds are demonstrating their comprehension.

2. Early Introduction into Practice: The simplicity of the Passing Game leads to the further advantage of being able to introduce it fully during the first day of practice. This provides the offense with an organized approach to use when it comes time for us to work on team defense. Defensive practice as such becomes more meaningful as a result of encountering the variety of situations created by the Passing Game. Although our practice at this point may be defensively oriented, the offense is playing sound fundamental basketball at the same time. This helps their overall improvement as well.

3. Skill Development: Significantly, exposure to the Passing Game serves to enhance many of the skills required for efficient execution of the set game. Improved ability at *reading* the defense is one example. The experience gained in free-lance, resulting from the need to observe the defensive men prior to decision making, carries over when we run the set game.

A prevalent weakness of most players at any skill level, including professional, is their limited ability to move without the ball. The Passing Game dictates that a player *must* move without the ball. As such, he becomes more intelligent in his movements and the reasons for them. This learning experience improves the player's understanding of his patterned moves during the set offense.

As indicated earlier, one of the main reasons for using the free-lance Passing Game is the desire to liberate the player from thinking about where he must move and what he must do when he gets the ball. The experience gained through this offense helps him become less mechanical in his overall actions and consequently more fluid in his execution of the set game.

4. Effectiveness Against All Defenses: An advantage to including the Passing Game in the multiple offense is its all-purpose aspect. It can be used with equal effectiveness against all defenses. Straight zones and man-to-man are the defenses most frequently encountered. Occasionally, however, we'll find ourselves confronted with a four-man zone and one man-to-man, or a triangle zone with our two best scorers defended man-to-man. This should not present a problem. Since the Passing Game can be used effectively against either zone or man-to-man, there is no reason to find it any less efficient against combinations of both. Our confidence in dealing with all the so-called "junk" defenses is increased by working against them during Passing Game scrimmages. The free-lance aspect of the game permits the players to hunt for the open spots without being tied to thinking of specific patterns to work against them. The players really seem to enjoy the opportunity to think for themselves in these situations. It helps their confidence and increases their ingenuity.

As you will note later in the chapter, we never have the high post more than one pass away from the ball. This enables us to use this offense to excellent advantage against half-court zone traps or any other half-court pressure defense.

5. Other Uses: The Passing Game has served us well as the continuity for our 1−4 and cut-movement offenses. This will be covered in detail in the chapters relating to those offenses. Also, we have used the Passing Game from the secondary fast break, moving quickly into action before the defense can become set. In the chapter covering the fast break, we will explain how easy it is to move directly into this offense from the break, without a shot.

POTENTIAL WEAKNESSES OF THE PASSING GAME

1. Rebounding: Offensive designs should provide for adequate rebounding power in the event of a missed shot. The set offense provides an advantage in this respect. It is usually designed to enable each player to know when a shot will be taken. The set offense can often be patterned to solidify a strong offensive rebounding triangle whenever a shot is taken.

In free-lance, the players must become sharply attuned to each other's shooting habits in order to gain an edge in positioning for the boards. The emphasis we place on generating good movement and extra effort going to the board has enabled us to overcome possible problems in this area. In fact, our rebounding has not suffered with the use of the Passing Game, although logically, rebounding should be better in a pattern game. I believe the very good movement we get out of the Passing Game has enabled us to rebound even better at times. The very fact that the defense is being moved and has trouble seeing both ball and man prevents the defense from boxing out as well as it could against a pattern team.

2. Individual Attainment at Team Expense: The Passing Game is a strength to the unselfish team, but can hurt the team if individual players are overly concerned about their own scoring. In this regard, the coaching staff has the responsibility of instilling appropriate attitudes as well as placing emphasis on the importance of intelligent shot selection.

At North Carolina, we place a man's scoring average in what we consider to be its proper perspective. For our own internal purposes, our players are ranked offensively based on a *composite* rating of field-goal accuracy, free-throw accuracy, rebounds, and assists, in addition to point average. Rebounding and defensive contributions are each considered separately, but are more difficult to assess strictly on the basis of statistics.

We've often discussed the free-lance Passing Game at coaching clinics. I'll sometimes note a bit of apprehension regarding its use on the part of a coach who must work with a wide variance in the talents of his players. I usually take this opportunity to cite examples which illustrate that the Passing Game can help the team, the great player and the less-than-average player.

Bill Bradley, for example, began his career at Princeton before some of the Ivy League schools began their aggressive recruiting. Bill, with all his fantastic individual ability, initially did not have a talented group of teammates on the floor with him. Princeton (coached then by Butch van Breda Kolff) and Bradley elected to play very much as a team, however. They did not look to constantly set up the one man with proven ability. Bradley's field-goal percentage was probably more noteworthy on a consistent basis than his scoring average. The approach taken served to instill confidence in the other four men who improved rapidly as a result of playing a major role in the offense. The ultimate result hardly hurt Bradley, whose national prominence was enhanced by Princeton's 62–21 record, three Ivy League titles, and one NCAA Eastern Regional championship during his brilliant career there.

Our own Charles Scott, a great basketball player and individual talent, is another good example, even though he had more talented teammates at North Carolina than Bradley did at Princeton. Charles was also an extremely unselfish player and recognized the value of team effort. This ultimately made even Charles a better player by improving his ability to play without the ball.

We could also point to the great UCLA teams under Coach Wooden. Although these teams were blessed with outstanding talent, no individual player ever led, or even came close to leading, the nation in scoring.

On the other hand, I could cite examples of offenses that have been geared almost exclusively to the superior talents of one individual with minimal long-range success. In past years, we've seen teams with one highly skilled player scoring as many as fifty points or more on his own at times. Ironically, these same schools often have difficulty finishing anywhere near the top in their own conference.

Ultimately, even the supremely talented player may be hampered in his contribution toward the team's overall achievement if other players are not developed, nor encouraged, to supplement his scoring efforts.

If the proper atmosphere is established, the free-lance Passing Game makes a significant contribution to the multiple offense in this respect. It serves to improve the performance of lesser players and enhance the contribution of the superior player at the same time. Both objectives obviously contribute toward achieving the ultimate goal of maintaining a consistently successful basketball program.

During the past several years, many coaches have come to Chapel Hill to visit with us about the Passing Game. In addition, questions have been asked of me while lecturing at clinics about this free-lance ruled offense. Most coaches who have used this offense have found it suitable to their personnel and preferable to the set offenses they had used previously. When Coach Bob Knight visited Chapel Hill for a couple of days several years ago, he was looking to move toward more of a free-lance offense. Indiana had done extremely well with the set offense, but Coach Knight wanted to make this change nevertheless. In November of the following season, he sent me some of his practice film. I was amazed to see they had given up their set offense completely. I should add here that I think the Indiana team of 1976 executed the Passing Game better than any of our own teams. They do have, perhaps, a few more rules than we do, but they still make use of the free-lance opportunities.

Bob Boyd, former coach of USC, also was very successful with the Passing Game and was an excellent teacher. On the professional level, Larry Brown, the former head coach of the Denver Nuggets and my former assistant at North Carolina, did a tremendous job with the Passing Game as a single-post offense during the 1974–75 season. In the 1976 season, Denver had the best record of any professional basketball team. Doug Moe, a former North Carolina player who coached the San Antonio Spurs, and is presently coach of the Denver Nuggets, effectively used the Passing Game without any set offense at San Antonio.

My greatest thrill is to have many junior high and high school coaches write me after introducing our Passing Game to tell me how great a help it has been to them. With the time situation being very limited at the junior high and high school levels, practice time, I think, is best spent defensively. A coach quickly can put in a Passing Game to cover all types of defenses.

Many years have passed since we first introduced this offense in the early 1960s. If you choose to use this Passing Game with your team, I am hopeful you will find it equally successful for you.

free-lance
passing
game

   We always approach any set half-court defense in the same manner. What is done from that point on depends upon the quarterback's call. Diagram 2-1 illustrates the basic set which gave us the terminology for the T Game.

Diagram 2-1

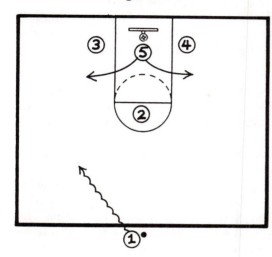

Diagram 2-2

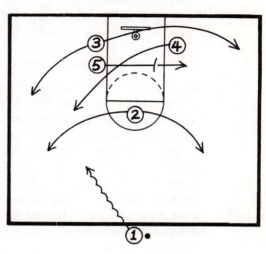

   It is not necessary to line up and have an entry to the Passing Game if the defense is not set. However, if we signal the Passing Game after our opponent has scored (and is not pressing us full-court), the defense will be waiting. We will then line up accordingly.

Diagram 2-3

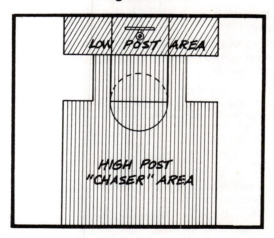

Diagram 2-2 As soon as the quarterback dribbles on the ten-second line, #2 may move in either direction for a pass from #1. #2 has considerable room to get open. Since the game is free-lance, #2 may choose to go screen for #3, #4, or #5 to get open. However, we encourage the move as diagrammed in 2-2. #3 has many locations to which he may move. His only instruction is that he move to an open area, unless #1 is double-teamed. If this occurs, we want #3 moving to the ball. We want #4 or #5 moving into the high-post area as #2 vacates it. Although we have shown #5 screening for #4 to come high, it makes no difference which of the two comes to the high post *as long as one of them does.* The screen is not essential since, in this case, #4 could sprint just as easily to the high post directly.

Diagram 2-3 Our designated high-post *chaser* area and low-post area are illustrated in Diagram 2-3. Please note that although we use the term high post, this chaser position covers a much larger area than the free-throw circle for our purposes in the Passing Game.

It is the high post's responsibility to find the open spot in that area and become a logical receiver. The high-post area is all-important, since it is a highly advantageous place to have the basketball against *any* type of defense. With the ball near the top of the key, it is difficult for the defense to determine a *weak* or *help* side. The high post is in position to pass in *all* directions. The low-post position is important as well. If one man is high, we want the other man low. Constant movement and interchanging are generated between the high and low posts against man-to-man defense or combinations.

GENERAL SCHEME

Before enumerating the rules pertaining to the post and outside men, we should cover the general scheme of the Passing Game:

1. It is not a one-three-one alignment, but could evolve as such at any stage.
2. The ball should be passed at least three times before a shot, other than a lay-up, is attempted.
3. The ball should not be dribbled during the period of the first three passes unless doing so is necessary to escape trouble, or a straight line to the basket opens up for any easy lay-up.
4. The ball *must* go to the high post *at least* every third pass.
5. As in all North Carolina offenses, #5, #4, and #3 are designated rebounders with #2 going to the board periodically. #1 is back for defensive balance when a shot is taken.

POST RULES

1. The high post remains high for no more than three seconds. If he hasn't received the ball within that period of time, he initiates the interchange with the low post—which brings the low post high.
2. If #5 gets the ball, #4 goes to the basket.

3. If #4 gets the ball, #5 goes to the basket.

4. When the high post receives the ball, he holds it *over his head* as he faces the basket. Then he looks for his low post. If he can't pass low, he looks to pass to the side *away* from which he received the ball.

5. The high post may also shoot or make a move to the basket if the defense dictates it. Some big men know their limitations and choose not to shoot even if left open at the high post. This presents no problem since the primary purpose of getting the ball high is to change the attack to the opposite side of the court.

6. The high post must always be one pass from the ball.

7. After passing the ball to an outside man, the high post must do one of the following: (a) go to the basket, (b) go screen away, (low post usually), (c) go screen for the man to whom he has passed.

8. After the high post passes the ball to an outside man, the low post may choose to set a rear screen for the high post coming low.

9. When the low post receives the ball, his first look is to score. His next look is to the high post moving to basket.

10. Both post men always work for offensive rebounds.

11. When a dribbler comes toward either post, the post man should move out to screen for the dribbler or go to the basket.

12. The low post should be away from the ball seventy-five percent of the time, generally looking to screen for cutting teammates moving to the ball.

OUTSIDE MEN RULES

1. Man with the ball:
   (a) Looks to high or low post first.
   (b) Attempts to use a screen if made available.
   (c) Uses penetrating dribble only after three passes. Does not kill the dribble without penetration.
   (d) Acts quickly, not holding the ball more than two seconds.
   (e) Does not look for the outside shot until a post man has received the ball at least once.

2. Options after passing the ball:
   (a) Pass and go to basket.
   (b) Pass and go screen away.
   (c) Pass and go screen for the man to whom he has passed.
   (d) Pass and slide along perimeter.
   (e) Pass and cut to baseline away from the basket area.

3. Man without ball:
   (a) Looks to make a move to the ball when a logical receiver.
   (b) Keeps moving. Never stands in one position more than two seconds. If possible, sets screen away from the ball, while moving.
   (c) When overplayed as logical receiver, goes to basket, or screens away.
   (d) When a dribbler approaches, sets a screen for the dribbler, or slides on perimeter (zone), or goes to basket.
   (e) Looks to use low post as screen from which he can *popout* for a shot.
   (f) Avoids *bunching up* with another man without the ball unless setting a screen for him.
   (g) Avoids top of key area, leaving that position for the high post.

As indicated earlier in the chapter, the free-lance Passing Game is an all-purpose offense. Minor adjustments or preferable option choices may be indicated, however, based upon the defensive alignment.

1. When the option is to *slide* along perimeter or to screen, the type of defense encountered will influence the choice. Screens are usually used more against man-to-man defenses while the slide is more important against zone defenses.

2. We prefer a slightly quicker movement of both ball and players when confronting man-to-man defense as opposed to zone.

3. Against the man-to-man defense, our #3 man or even our #2 man will sometimes alternate as a post man with #4 who switches to the outside spot. The change is contingent on #2, #3, and #4 having near equal ability at playing either position. The purpose of the switch is to move #4's defensive man out onto the court if he happens to be a big man. #2 or #3 would then take his smaller defensive man into the pivot. Inside scoring opportunities as well as rebounding strength are thereby improved. For obvious reasons, however, the tactic would serve little purpose against a zone.

4. We look to dribble and penetrate more against the zone than we do against man-to-man. An outside man with the ball should look to penetrate a gap in a zone defense, then penetrate to the middle, and then pitch to an open man.

5. The high–low post interchange is not done as quickly against a pure zone. The high post may choose to handle the ball twice before moving in low and letting the low post replace him.

_____SCORING SITUATIONS

The free-lance aspect of the Passing Game makes it almost impossible to outline all possible scoring situations. Many things can happen to bring about two points or a foul by the defense. We are not concerned about having our play interrupted by a foul. In fact, we will be happy to have it occur each time we come downcourt. Even with the 1972 rules change in effect, a team fouled consistently would prove to be nearly unbeatable.

As you study the material to follow, please keep in mind that the nature of the free-lance Passing Game makes it somewhat difficult to diagram. The outside men could be almost anywhere on the court other than the positions indicated in the diagram. What we have done is arbitrarily bring together some typical *individual* moves for the purpose of illustrating various scoring opportunities that could develop within the general scheme of play.

Diagram 2-4   The post action often develops into a score as shown in Diagram 2-4. Assume we have already made two passes on the perimeter by the time #2 passes to #4 on the high post. #2 then elects the screen away option. #3, on the baseline, uses this screen. When he doesn't receive a pass from #4, #3 heads for the rebound on the shot subsequently taken by #5. #4, who received the pass from #2 initially, quickly looks to the basket as #5 breaks swiftly for position toward the other side of the lane. The defense on #5 does not have much team help in most cases, and does not have that help here. #5 receives the ball in the lane and, in this instance, turns to score. #4 moves to the board for rebounding position with #5 and #3. #1 and #2 are back for defensive balance.

Diagram 2-5 #4 chose not to pass to #5 this time. Instead he exercises his second option, passing *away* from the side from which he receives the ball to #1. #4, after passing, then exercises the option of cutting to the basket. This high-post movement low initiates the post interchange. (#5 could screen for #4 and still not incur a three-second violation before moving into the high-post chaser area.) #3, coming out over #2's screen, could move out near the top of the key as the diagram illustrates, or he could screen back for #2 to come. However, it is very important that outside men *stay away* from the top of the key if a post is using that area. #1 now has all the options given to the outside man with the ball under the rules presented earlier.

Diagram 2-4

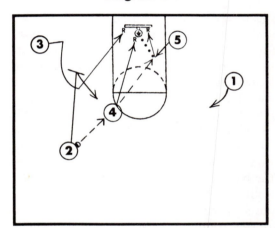

Diagram 2-5

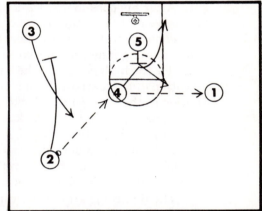

Two of many possible scoring situations are diagrammed in 2-6 and 2-7. In 2-6, we are working against a man-to-man defense. Diagram 2-7 presents a common move against the zone. Please keep in mind that we have picked up the action after three or more passes in each of these situations. The early passes serve to move the defense. I have always felt very strongly that a good defense *must* be moved before you penetrate it.

Diagram 2-6 Many quick moves are depicted in Diagram 2-6. We pick up action as #2 has the ball. #2 passes to #3 and chooses the cut to the basket option, hoping to rub his man off #5. #2 then chooses to use #4 as a screener coming out from underneath. Had #3 passed to #5, #5 could have hit #2 for a jump shot over #4. #3, however, chooses the pass to #1, after which he decides to go to the basket.

#3's decision to go to the basket may not be the best choice, since doing so will leave #1 with few outlets available. Although it may not be the best choice, I might point out that going to the basket is never really a bad choice against man-to-man.

#5, who was at the high post at the time of the #2 to #3 pass, moves into an open area for a possible pass from #3. Since #3 chooses to pass to #1, #5, who has been high long enough, should either go to the basket or screen away for #4. #4 comes high. #1 then chooses a penetrating dribble toward #4; #4 chooses to screen for him and roll to the basket. #1 may have a shot with good board coverage, as shown in the diagram, or may pass to his screener, #4, or may pass to #2 coming up to become a logical receiver. At the same time, #5 would again move to the high post since #4 rolled low.

The two passes and penetrating dribble shown in the diagram opened the door to a number of scoring possibilities, in addition to the one ultimately attempted.

Diagram 2-7 We begin with the same initial positions depicted in Diagram 2-6. This time, however, we are faced with a zone defense.

After his pass to #3, #2 chooses to slide along the perimeter. This is an effective and important move against a zone providing, of course, the designated position on the perimeter is open. #3 quickly hits #5, who has found an open passing lane. #3 then chooses a cut to baseline. #5, in keeping with the rule for the high post, puts the ball above his head and looks to #4 moving for position at the low post. If #4 is covered, #5 then exercises the second passing option of the high post by looking to the weak side and throwing to #2. #5, after passing, cuts to the basket, which again initiates the post interchange bringing #4 high. If #2 shoots, #4 moves back for rebounding position. On the #5 to #2 pass, #3 sprints baseline to become a logical receiver, utilizing a possible screen from #5 against the baseline zone man. #1 moves up to the area vacated by #3 upon #3's baseline move.

The diagrams arbitrarily combine specific choices made by the players. The individual choices depicted are very common. However, frequent repetition of similar *accumulative* choices would be highly unlikely.

Diagram 2-6

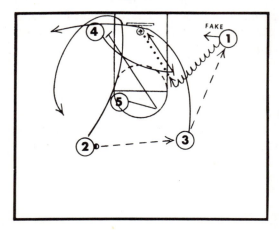

Diagram 2-7

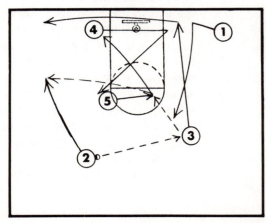

teaching the passing game

Similar to the approach used to introduce most of our concepts, the Passing Game is initially presented within the five-against-five *whole method* approach. We then rely upon the *part method* of instruction for teaching concentration. Ultimately, we return to the whole method for polishing.

Prior to the first activity, we cover the rules for post and outside men described earlier in the chapter. We then initiate the whole method approach through our *keep-away game* during which the passer may exercise only two of his options. He must either pass and go to the basket, or pass and screen away. We do not want the screen set for a man with the ball since the offense is not allowed to dribble at this point. A screen at the point of the ball would be asking for a dribble.

Since neither dribbling nor shooting is permitted, the use of a no-bounce ball serves an excellent purpose for this half-court game. Should a man attempt to dribble at this point, a no-bounce ball has a rather dramatic way of responding to the situation. Of course, a regular ball can be used as well with a dribble counting as a violation.

This keep-away game, which we use a lot at the beginning of the season, helps us teach passing and ball handling. It's main objective, however, is to generate swift offensive movement. By prohibiting the dribble, the man without the ball must move quickly to give his teammate an outlet. *This teaches the man without the ball to move.*

The coach talks to the offense constantly during the game but will not stop the action unless a serious mistake occurs.

The team completing the most number of passes without losing the ball wins the game. If the offense is fouled, an additional five passes are scored to their total and the offense takes the ball out of bounds. The losing team must run extra sprints after practice.

Generally, each team is given possession three times. During the early part of the year, the winning team usually averages forty successful passes for the three possessions.

The keep-away game with the above rules is played several times before we permit the offense its other options. The use of all other options including dribbling and shooting is facilitated during half-court scrimmage. At this early stage, however, a minimum number of passes, considerably in excess of the game rule three, is required prior to permitting a shot. As in all half-court scrimmages, the defense is instructed to fast break on a missed shot or steal. If a team scores or is fouled, it is allowed another possession. However, after the offensive team scores, it must first get back, show a defense, and pick up the other team which is taking the ball out of bounds. Once they have picked up, they are allowed another possession.

When the ball is lost without a shot, the defense goes to offense.

There are no winners or losers in the half-court scrimmage since it is designed primarily as a detailed learning experience.

Part-method drills are scheduled during practice sessions when the Passing Game receives our offensive emphasis. Our part-method drills concentrate on teaching and exercising simple, basic basketball techniques. Various techniques such as how to pass and go to the basket, pass and screen, reverse without the ball, pass and screen away, and others are taught. These drills serve to reinforce all essential movement and passing techniques, which are fundamental to any offensive basketball system.

To facilitate our part-method drills, the squad is divided equally into as many baskets (and coaches) as we have available. No defense is used initially. Within a few weeks, our part-method practice for the Passing Game narrows down to one major drill. For the benefit of illustration, let us assume our personnel consists of two coaches, twelve players and two managers. One end of the court is designated for our men who will be playing the post position. The other end is used for those who play outside. Players required to work both positions from time to time will alternate accordingly.

DIAGRAM 2-8: POST MEN DRILL

If there are five men who will play the post, two of them match-up against two others. The fifth will serve as an outside man for a few plays. He will then trade off with one of the four playing the post. A manager assumes another outside position. The outside men cannot shoot, nor are they opposed by a defensive man. They are not required to move intelligently, either.

The objective of the outside man is to pass to a post man as soon as one is open. The two post men interchange quickly and simulate a true game situation. When one post man gets the ball, he looks for the other going to the goal. *Main rule*: If he can't pass to him, he returns the ball to an outside man (on the side opposite from which he receives the pass) and then moves.

The defensive post men may do what they wish to stop the offensive posts. If one of the defensive men gets a rebound, he passes the ball out to one of the

Diagram 2-8	**Diagram 2-9**

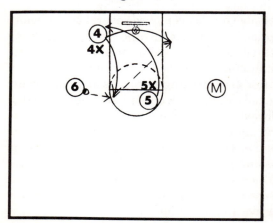

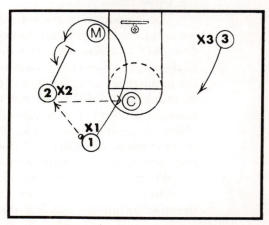

dummy outside men. The former defensive men then assume the offensive post positions. If the offense scores or is fouled, it continues on offense.

DIAGRAM 2-9: OUTSIDE MEN DRILL

At the other end of the court, a similar arrangement is implemented. In this case, however, the posts are without defense and the coaching emphasis is on the six outside men. Regular game situations are created which require the outside men to pass to the high post at least every third pass. The coach serves as the high post and remains there without movement.

This division of post-outside men and their respective drills serves as an excellent competitive vehicle for teaching the rules of the Passing Game. The drills are repeated frequently throughout the year.

Post men develop their skills at overhead passing, low-post positioning, rebounding, and appropriate movement.

The outside men improve on the skills learned during the earlier part-method drills. They become more aware of the need to pass to the high post frequently as well as the value of screening away from the ball. They also learn to use the screen of the low post, played in this drill by a manager.

We return to the whole-method through full- and half-court scrimmages during which emphasis is maintained on the rules of the Passing Game. Until we near our first game, we continue to impose an excess minimum number of passes as a prerequisite to the first shot.

The drills referred to earlier do help us. However, we find that the best way to improve our execution of the Passing Game is to scrimmage half-court, or even full-court, using different rules for different days. For instance, one day at the end of a scrimmage, we may quietly tell the #3 man on the blue team that he may not shoot. When he gets the ball he simply moves it quickly and then moves to screen. At the end of a ten-minute period we may ask him how many times he screened effectively. We will also pick out a man on the white team and ask him to do the same thing. We call these players the *sacrifice men* of the day.

During that same scrimmage, we may also tell one team that they must make seven passes against a set defense before they can shoot unless it is a wide-open lay-up. The other team may have to make five passes before a shot. By doing this we are encouraging screening, movement, and perhaps even being fouled, which is good offense. We are also guaranteeing the chance to change the sides of the floor of attack at least twice.

It is important to emphasize that we do not require any number of passes before a shot on a secondary break when the defense is not set. The fact that we do average a high number of points would indicate that we are not a control-type offense, yet neither are we a run-and-gun team.

The players usually pick up the rules of the Passing Game with little difficulty. It then becomes a matter of putting it all together. The more our men play the free-lance Passing Game, the better they like it. The initiative exercised at finding their own ways to counter all possible defenses probably accounts for much of the satisfaction.

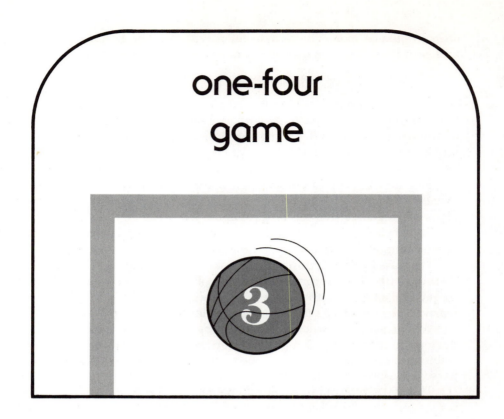

one-four
game

Perhaps no other offense in our system has served as many purposes for us, at different times, as the One-Four game. We have used this effective and somewhat unique alignment to accommodate a variety of changing needs ever since we stumbled on it in 1961.

We first observed the One-Four as it was used by Coach Leon Brogden's Wilmington, North Carolina high school team. We were immediately impressed with the potential of Coach Brogden's formation in terms of our own needs at the time. We experimented with the alignment and made some major adjustments. Coach Brogden had his wing and post standing near each sideline. We moved the posts to where the foul line and circle meet. The One-Four soon became the basis of a very effective delay offense for us. We later used it as an entry to the full shuffle continuity and subsequently took advantage of its value as a sound *all-purpose* offense. During recent years we've gone to the One-Four primarily to utilize our personnel strengths.

Although it no longer serves exclusively as many purposes for us as it did in the past, our One-Four game is still a part of our offensive design for a number of reasons. One of the primary advantages of the alignment is that it provides a team with a quick-hitting attack. There are few wasted passes and a good shot can be taken quickly, with excellent board coverage.

Having a half-court alignment which enables the offense to go to the basket quickly is an obvious advantage when a team must play catch-up ball.

We therefore go to the One-Four when we are behind by a number of points, and battling the clock late in the game. If a good shot is not available out of the One-Four game, our continuity takes us into our Passing Game described in the preceeding chapter.

Perhaps the most significant advantage of the One-Four is its effectiveness as a means of combatting pressure. Most teams predicate their pressure defense on the premise that defensive help is available from the weak side. The one-four alignment, however, spreads four logical receivers over the width of the half-court. The formation thereby eliminates a weak side for defensive help if each potential receiver, one pass from the ball, is being pressured.

A tight man-to-man against this alignment also removes defensive help from the basket area. This allows the offense to utilize its personnel, exploit the mismatch, and go backdoor for the lay-up. At the same time, a one-man front cannot be pressed as easily as a two-man front. The offense is not likely to run into the *trap press*, which is often used against the more traditional two-guard front. The One-Four alignment (regardless of the specific plays a coach decides to build into it) is *designed* therefore to combat half-court pressure, and serves an extremely valuable purpose under these conditions.

As indicated earlier, the One-Four can be used as an all-purpose offense. During my early head coaching years, the trend of defensive basketball was in the process of swinging to alternating defenses as well as increased use of pressure. We felt the need for an entry to our offense against man-to-man, zone, press, or any combination defense. The One-Four served this purpose for us and was effective as an entry against all types of defense on the principle that, once the defense is moved, the offense can attack and penetrate easily.

During those early years, we also used the One-Four formation to in-bound the ball against a full-court press as well as in out of bounds throw-in situations from the sidelines. This helped us to cut down on the amount of offense we had to teach, which was a big help to us in those days. The One-Four was therefore multipurpose for us during those years.

In the late 1960s, however, we reserved the alignment primarily for use against pressure man-to-man defense. Although the One-Four is effective against the zone, it does lend itself to the quick shot as we indicated earlier. We therefore use it against a man-to-man *or zone* when we want to get off a fast shot in special situations—such as the closing seconds of the first half. Under normal conditions, however, patience and a number of quick passes are the two most effective weapons an offense can use to *widen the holes* in a zone and then penetrate it. We therefore rely more heavily on our other zone offenses such as our T-game and Passing Game to accomplish these two objectives for us.

One final advantage of the One-Four (although admittedly a minor one) is that the alignment is not as commonly observed as the more traditional *two-guard—two-forward—center* formation. This gives our opponents a little extra to prepare for, and is in keeping with the philosophy and purpose behind our multiple-offense system.

We do use the identical One-Four alignment as an entry into our Basic Cut Movement game (Offense #5), which features the basic cut from the Shuffle Offense. In this case, the use of *similar* entries is designed to prevent the defense from knowing with certainty which of the two offenses to anticipate from the same One-Four alignment. We might point out that since they are generated from similar alignments, our Offense #1 and Offense #5 are compatible, and can merge into a single half-court attack by combining the preferred options of both games. We have done this ourselves during seasons we wished to cut down somewhat on the quantity of offense our players had to learn.

DIAGRAM 3-1: BASIC ALIGNMENT

The basic one-four alignment is illustrated in Diagram 3−1.

Diagram 3-1

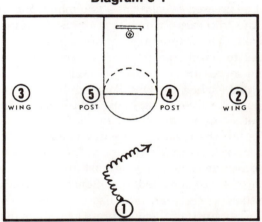

As the quarterback signals Offense #1, the offense is keyed out from the baseline into the One-Four alignment. #4 and #5 take post positions parallel to the foul line just outside the circle. #2 and #3 move into wing positions at the foul line extended, close to the sidelines. All four logical receivers are facing the quarterback as he dribbles the ball into the offensive half-court. The quarterback has the extremely important responsibility at this point of eliminating a possible weak side from which defensive help might come. In most cases he does this by tying the defense down on one side initially. He then reverses his dribble quickly to the other side before setting the intended play in motion.

The three basic plays built into Offense #1 are the post option, wing option, and dribble option. Since each of these plays are executed on the left or right side of the court, the quarterback has six possibilities open to him initially. His decision may be influenced by the strategy of the moment, such as the desire to exploit a particular mismatch, or the need to draw a key opposing player into foul trouble. These possibilities are covered often at regular quarterback meetings and during time-outs. Ultimately, the decision will be determined by reading the defense. For example, if the quarterback sees #2 on the wing being overplayed, he will attempt to get the ball to #4 on the post. His reasons for exercising the post option in this situation are illustrated in diagram 3-2.

Diagram 3-2

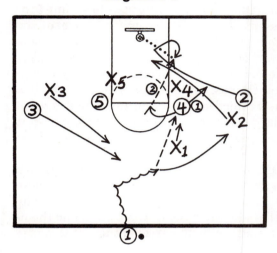

Diagram 3-3

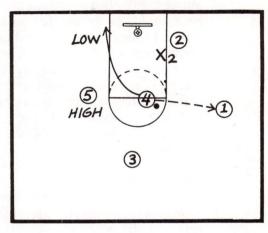

Diagram 3-2   The post option is one of our most effective plays, and we've used it to great advantage for many years. #1 sees X2 pressing #2 and passes to #4 on the post. #2 goes very hard backdoor and looks for a left-handed bounce pass from #4. If #2 does not receive the ball as he approaches the lane, he button-hooks away from the basket or into the lane if the defense is waiting for him. This backdoor sprint and button-hook is very difficult for X2 to cover. It is important to note that if #4 cannot make the left-hand bounce pass to the cutter #2, he looks for #2 button-hooking by turning toward the basket *in the direction of #5 to his immediate right*. #4 must use his *right* foot to pivot as he makes this turn.

#4's right-foot pivot and move in this direction is essential for three reasons. First, by turning his back on X2, the defender has the tendency to let up once he stops the backdoor. This helps make #2's button-hook all the more effective. Secondly, the move minimizes the effectiveness of X1, who will tend to jam back on #4 when #1 moves to the wing after passing. Finally, #4's pivot in the direction of #5 pins X5 to #5, away from the basket area in anticipation of a possible #4 to #5 pass.

#1 moves into #2's wing position after passing to #4. #3 brings X3 out with him as he moves to fill #1's spot. All these moves are designed to give #2 a wide area under the basket in which to operate one-on-one.

The identical post option can be exercised on the other side of the court. If #1 throws to #5 initially, #3 moves backdoor. In this instance #5 uses his *left* foot to pivot and make his turn in the direction of #4.

Timing is obviously an important prerequisite to effective execution of the post option, and is given considerable attention during a special drill designed for this purpose in practice. This drill is covered later in the chapter.

DIAGRAM 3-3: TRANSITION INTO PASSING GAME

In the event #4 does not pass to #2 backdoor or button-hooking, we are automatically in our Passing Game (Offense #3). If #4 passes to #3 or #5, or back to #1, he breaks low to assume the initial low-post position in the Passing Game. #5 is already high as the transition to the Passing Game is made. Diagrams 3-2 and 3-3 illustrate one of the fundamental concepts underlying our offensive philosophy. The One-Four is designed to alleviate pressure and make effective use of personnel. The post option is exercised to accomplish both objectives. The play is obviously intended to result in a score or defensive foul. Simultaneously, however, the defense is being moved, which makes it vulnerable to penetration as the continuity takes us into our free-lance Passing Game.

The post option is also designed to place a good scorer in a position to make use of his ability. We have had many great athletes at North Carolina whose size placed them in the *swing* position. Outstanding players such as Bobby Lewis, Larry Miller, Charles Scott, and Walter Davis would often find themselves at the better end of a mismatch and make excellent use of this post option.

The play was actually designed for Bobby Lewis, our All-American in 1966. Bobby was an excellent post man in high school. At 6′3″, we often had him at the guard spot and moved him low on the post option to take advantage of a shorter opponent. Larry Miller, A.C.C. Player of the Year in 1968 and concensus All-American, was a master at getting the ball in low, and either scoring or drawing the foul. Charles Scott, an outstanding *swing man*, could take a smaller guard into that position to exploit a mismatch. The same was true of Walter Davis, who at 6′6″ was able to use his height advantageously for the same purpose. Steve Previs, known mostly for his great defensive ability, seemed to like the play as well. However, when Steve had the ball inside, he would still look to pass off to a bigger man coming to the basket. Steve may have been overly unselfish at times; however, his great spirit and leadership permeated the entire team during the 1971 and 1972 years.

DIAGRAMS 3-4 AND 3-5: DRIBBLE OPTION (QUICKIE)

We commonly refer to the dribble option of Offense #1 as the *quickie*. It is designed for a good quarterback to come off a screen and put up a fast shot. However, it is also intended to free one of the post men inside and we often go to it to capitalize on an opponent's big man in foul trouble.

#1 staggers his dribble to signal that he will dribble in, rather than pass at the outset. Both posts, #4 and #5, set screens. In diagram 3-4, #1, knowing that X4 is in foul trouble, chooses the right side and dribbles off the screen set by #4. (Note: One advantage of the play is provided by having #4 screen the smaller X1. If X1 and X4 switch, it results in a mismatch that the offense is in an excellent position to exploit as the play unfolds.) #2 goes hard in the direction of the basket, but stops before he gets to the lane if he doesn't get the pass. He then backs off to the corner. #3 floats to the left corner. As #1 comes off #4's screen, #4 rolls to the goal. #1 may go for the Quickie by taking the shot off the screen. However, if the object of the play is to exploit X4 in foul trouble, #1's first look will be to #4 rolling to the basket. #1 could pass to #2, who could also hit #4. One of the most effective methods of getting the ball to #4, in the event #4 is fronted by the defense, is illustrated in Diagram 3-5.

Diagram 3-5 This is a continuation of diagram 3-4. As #1 dribbled right initially, X5 would likely have given ground on the weak side in an effort to lend defensive help. #1, seeing #4 fronted, quickly reverses pivot and throws back to #5. #4 holds off defensive man X4 on the #1 to #5 pass. He then steps in for the pass from #5 and is generally free for it. Note that #4 (low) and #5 (high) are in perfect position for our Passing Game in the event the dribble option does not fulfill the objective.

Diagram 3-4   **Diagram 3-5**

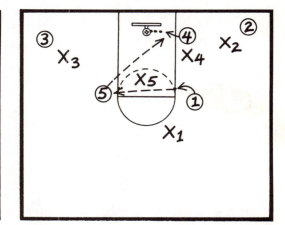

DIAGRAMS 3-6 AND 3-7: WING OPTION

The wing option is designed to make use of our personnel. In this case the play is aimed initially at getting the ball to a big man inside under pressure. However, it is really designed for a close range shot off a screen for an outside threat positioned on the wing. Outstanding board coverage off the outside shot is a key feature of the play.

Once again the selection of the play is determined by the game situation and the action of the defense. X4 has dominated the boards, but is in foul trouble. #1 sees that #4 is being fronted. #2 however has worked himself free for the pass. As the ball is passed to #2 on the wing, #4 releases to the basket and looks for the pass from #2. If #4 doesn't get the pass in the lane, he looks for it as he moves to the opposite side of the basket. Since defensive help is drawn away from the basket by #1, #3, and #5, #2 may throw a lob pass to #4 if necessary. The principle scoring possibility off the wing option is illustrated in Diagram 3−7, which completes the action of Diagram 3−6. The same outstanding players mentioned earlier in relation to their wing responsibility on the post option, were outstanding shooters as well. Therefore, we had fine shooters putting the ball up with good board coverage.

Diagram 3-7 On the initial #1 to #2 pass, #5 sprints to the ball, taking X5 with him. #2 may pass to #5. However, the *primary* objective of #5's sprint is to set a screen on X2 and prevent X5 from lending defensive help as #2 dribbles off the screen for the shot. #5 rolls to the basket after screening. X5 is generally prevented from lending defensive help, since he is more concerned with beating #5 to the ball. Consequently, he is not prepared to help out on #2, as #2 dribbles off the screen set by #5. #3 pounds the board on the shot, joining #4 and #5 for an ideal offensive rebounding triangle. #1 returns for defensive balance. The rebounding protection is further solidified as X5 attempts to help out on the screen. The result is a screen at the point of the ball, a 15- to 17-foot shot for a good shooter, and outstanding board coverage.

In the event neither of the two scoring opportunities diagrammed in 3-6 and 3-7 are exploited, #2 could pass to #3, who might have a good shot. #3 might also be able to hit #4 on the low post. If not, #4 would then come high as the initial high post in the Passing Game.

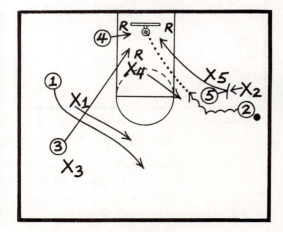

Diagram 3-6 **Diagram 3-7**

THE ONE-FOUR AGAINST THE ZONE

As we pointed out earlier, we have not used the One-Four against a zone defense in recent years, except when we have needed a good shot quickly. However, I think the One-Four could have value as a primary zone offense if a coach chooses to attack the zone with little patience.

Regardless of how often the One-Four is used against the zone, we always want our players prepared to make the necessary adjustments. This preparation becomes especially important when the One-Four is used for catch-up purposes, since many defenses will go to the zone with a sizeable lead late in the game.

Actually, with some minor exceptions, each of the three options of the One-Four is executed in much the same manner against the zone as against man-to-man. When we speak about preparation for the zone what we refer to is knowing which options are more effective against a particular zone alignment. Against match-up zones, all the options appear good to us. The post, quickie, and wing options tend to vary in usefulness against a particular type zone. For example, the post option is very effective against an odd-man front zone such as a one-two-two, one-three-one, or three-two zone. The wing option serves best against a two-man front zone, such as the two-one-two or two-three, although you could easily screen the match-up zone with the wing option as well. The quickie does a good job at breaking down the half-court trap zone. It is also useful against the odd-man front zone, particularly the one-two-two.

DIAGRAMS 3-8 AND 3-9: POST OPTION AGAINST THE ZONE

To illustrate the post option against a zone we have chosen a one-three-one defensive alignment. You will note by a comparison of diagrams 3-2 and 3-8 that the assignment of the post who does *not* receive the pass (#5 in each diagram) represents the only variation from man-to-man execution of the post option. Against man-to-man, #5 simply holds or widens his position. Against the zone, illustrated in Diagram 3-8, he slides down the lane looking for a pass from #4. #2 moves in a straight line to the basket on the pass from #1 to #4 just as he does against man-to-man. #1 fills #2's position. #3 moves slowly in the direction of #1's old position searching for a hole in the zone.

Diagram 3-8	**Diagram 3-9**

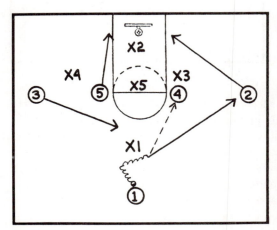 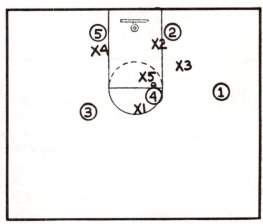

In Diagram 3-9, its easy to see some scoring opportunities if #4 reads the defense correctly. We have also moved the one-three-one zone defense as it adjusts to the pass from #1 to #4.

#4 may have a short jump shot as he receives the ball or he may pass low to #2 or #5 as he pivots in on his right foot. #4 must read X4 as he turns. Generally, X4 moves low to prevent the pass to #5, which leaves #3 wide open for a jump shot. If #3 shoots, #5, #4, and #2 are in good rebounding position. #1 will be back on defense.

If #3 doesn't shoot, we are automatically into our Passing Game, which is all-purpose, and our most frequently used zone offense. #4, after passing to #3 or #1, then comes into the high-post chaser position. #2 moves out from the basket in either direction to assume his free-lancing in the Passing Game.

DIAGRAMS 3-10 AND 3-11: DRIBBLE OPTION AGAINST THE ZONE

As one might surmise, the quickie is a good option to exercise against a one-man front, since the quarterback has essentially one defensive man playing him. The quickie is also effective against the half-court zone press, with the offense beginning farther out on the court. Against the one-two-two zone, the quickie is run exactly as it is against man-to-man, although #5 may have to step higher to receive the pass from #1.

Diagram 3-10　　　　　　　　**Diagram 3-11**

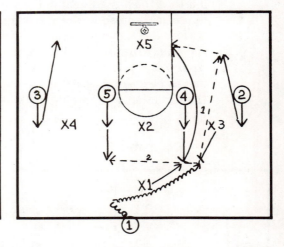

#1 chooses to drive off #4's screen. #1 probably is picked up by X2. He then looks for #4 sliding down the lane or #2 in the corner. If #1 passes to #2, #2 could look for #4 low. More likely, #1 will fake to #4 and pass to #5 on the opposite post. #5 looks quickly to #4 underneath, who has held off X5. If #5 can't pass to #4, he may throw to #3. #3 may hit #4 low, or take the shot with #4, #5, and #2 on the offensive backboard. If #3 doesn't shoot, we are in our Passing Game, with #5 and #4 already situated in the post positions of that offense.

In Diagram 3-11, the defense is set in a one-three-one half-court zone press, which keys the offense to move out higher on the court in the One-Four alignment. #1 still gets a screen from #4 or #5, which prevents the quick double-team. #1 could pass quickly to #2, or even to #5 before the screen is set by #4. A good shot could become available as soon as the ball gets to the baseline. Sometimes the shot is taken at the baseline on a pass from #2 to #4. Generally, however, if #5 gets the ball, #3 or #4 will be wide open. If the pass goes to the baseline, a good shot often presents itself as the pass returns out. Once again, we move into the Passing Game after this initial movement is completed.

DIAGRAM 3-12: WING OPTION AGAINST THE ZONE

The wing option against the zone provides us with the quickest transition into our Passing Game. It is generally used against a two-man front zone, such as the two-one-two. However, it can also be used against a one-three-one or a one-two-two.

Diagram 3-12

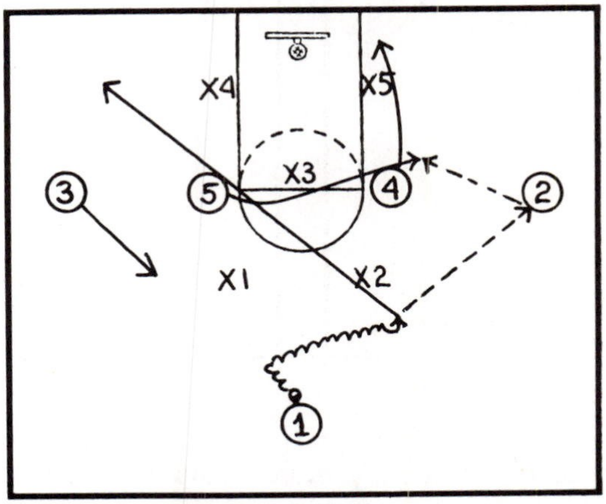

The variation in our execution of the wing option against the zone pertains to the post men. On the pass to #2, #4 goes low, but does not back out to the side of the ball as he would against man-to-man. #5 moves across in the direction of #2 as he does against man-to-man. Against a one-man front such as a one-three-one or a one-two-two, #5 might look to screen the wing man zoning #2. However, against the two-one-two zone depicted in diagram 3-12, #5 looks for an open spot from which to receive the pass from #2. If #2 has difficulty getting the ball to #5, he could choose to penetrate dribble toward the middle, and then pass to either #3 or #1.

In diagram 3-12, #2 passes to #5. #5's first look is to #4 low, then to #3 or #1 on the weak side. At this point, we are already in our Passing Game. The quick transition into the Passing Game is a key feature of the wing option.

This is why we still occasionally use the One-Four as an entry to the zone. The wing option can be exploited for a quick score. Primarily, however, it serves to give the defense another look.

teaching the one-four offense

In keeping with our overall teaching approach, the One-Four offense is initially taught five-against-five through the whole-method approach. The squad is then divided into two groups of six players for part-method drills at each end of the court. Initially, the part-method drills may be worked without defense. Thereafter each six-man group is divided into offense and defense as illustrated in **Diagram 3-13.**

Diagram 3-13

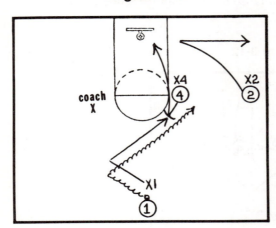

Diagram 3-14

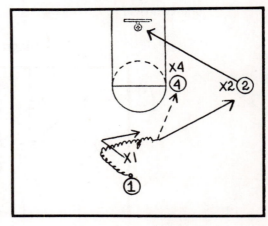

The offense consists of a quarterback, a wing man, and a post man. The defense may do anything they wish to stop the offense. We alternate between the right and left side of the half-court. However, if we run the quickie option on the right side, as in diagram 3-13, the quarterback is free to drive all the way to the left side in order to keep X1 honest. What we concentrate on mostly during this drill is a good screen required of #4. #1 can look to hit #4 on a screen-and-roll, or he may pass to the coach standing in the other post position. #1 could also pass to #2, who then would try to hit #4 in a low position.

Diagram 3-14 illustrates the three-on-three drill used to teach the post option. It is during this drill that we stress the forced-foot work discussed earlier in the chapter. The timing of the play, as well as the wing's ability to get free underneath, is also emphasized during this drill.

When we work on the wing option, we want #4 positioned on the *far* post as shown in **Diagram 3-15**. This gives us the opportunity to drill on the two-on-two situation that is set into motion when #4 moves across the screen X2. Since #2 knows the screen is coming, we want him to fake very hard to the baseline to set up X2 for the pick.

One final drill we use to teach the 1-4 offense is shown in **Diagram 3-16**. It is a warm-up and alternates as such with our three-lane fast-break drill early in practice. The drill requires two balls.

A line forms at the quarterback position. A player is positioned at each wing and two men take the posts. #1 starts the drill at the line by faking to #2 and passing to #4. #2 sprints backdoor and takes a left-handed bounce pass from #4 in for the lay-up. #4 rebounds #2's shot and fires an outlet pass to #1, who has moved to #2's former position on the wing. #1 then throws back to #7 in the middle of the line. #2 moves to the back of the quarterback line after shooting the lay-up.

Diagram 3-15   **Diagram 3-16**

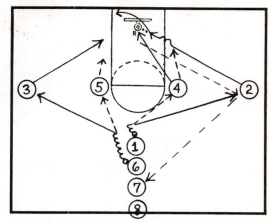

After #2's lay-up is made, #6 begins his dribble to the left side with the second ball and the identical manuever is repeated by #6, #3, and #5 on the left side of the half-court. The only difference, of course, is that #5 will make a *right*-handed bounce pass to his cutter #3. #6 subsequently passes to #8 at the line. #7 then begins the play on the right side again. #1 who started the drill on the right side is now at the wing, and is keyed backdoor on #7's pass to #4. After about twenty lay-ups, #4 and #5 go to the line at the quarterback spot and are substituted for by two other post men.

This drill serves many purposes for us aside from improving our overall execution and timing. The repetition at the post position is especially helpful in teaching our post men to make the bounce pass, turn, and go for the rebound. Lay-up shooting and several different types of passes are also practiced. The drill requires much running as well.

The whole-method approach is eventually reintroduced through half-court scrimmages concentrating on the One-Four offense. We often require both teams to run the same option a number of times to determine which team can score the most points off the same play. We do this with each of the options of the One-Four from time to time as a means of further improving our execution.

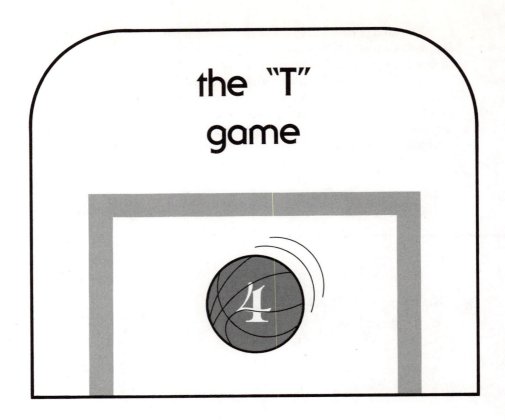

the "T" game

The T Game is an all-purpose offense which can be used against both man-to-man and zone defenses. In addition to its versatility, the T Game provides several additional advantages.

First, it is designed as an inside attack. Any inside attack lends itself to the high-percentage shot and a greater opportunity to place the opponent in foul trouble. As a football offense works to establish its running game first, we attempt to initially establish our inside game. When the defense adjusts to offset our inside attack, easy outside shots with good rebounding position become more readily available.

Offensive rebounding power is another advantage of the T Game. Any offensive design should provide for adequate rebounding strength. In the T Game, the bigger people (forwards and center) are never too far from the basket. Their rebounding paths are patterned to provide a strong offensive rebounding triangle.

A third feature is continuity. Although I agree that a continuity offense is not always essential, it is helpful to have at least one offensive set which provides continuity. Continuity gives a team the opportunity to control the ball in an organized manner while working for the good shot.

Flexibility is a fourth feature of the T Game offense. Adjustments can be made from year to year to suit your personnel. We have used it as a single– as well as triple-post offense. We have also devised it as a double-post offense, although the needs of our personnel have not dictated that use to date.

We first employed the T Game for our freshman team during the 1965–66 season. We were looking for some type of inside-oriented offense, since for the first time during my tenure as head coach we were blessed with a man over 6'7" who was a natural post man. Rusty Clark (6'10"), a young man we were fortunate to recruit from Fayetteville, North Carolina, was an outstanding passer and shooter. He possessed intelligence and basketball savvy. (Rusty, incidentally, turned down a lucrative pro contract after his graduation in order to pursue a career as a thoracic surgeon.) We needed an offense to make use of Rusty's strengths, but since he was not exceptionally quick, we wanted this offense geared to keep him within fifteen feet of the basket.

Bear in mind that we were playing against other centers 6'10" and up. At the high school level, therefore, the same needs could apply to a 6'5" young man with minimal speed, who would be opposing players of comparable height.

The summer before Rusty's freshman season, I discussed our problem with my good friend, Ted Owens, coach at the University of Kansas. Ted was using a single-post offense at the time, and I was impressed with the continuity. We had also observed the efficient use Kansas State teams under Jack Gardner and Tex Winter made of the lob pass when the post defense was playing in front. Combining these two concepts, we put together our T Game with a single post, using it primarily against a man-to-man defense at first. We later made a great many adjustments, in order to utilize our personnel more efficiently as well as to make it more effective against a zone defense. The triple-post continuity we now use as our Offense #2 is the end result of those adjustments.

the single post "T"

The "T" formation shown in diagram 4-1 illustrates the name designated for the offense. This is the basic beginning set of our T Game.

Diagram 4-1   Post man #5 positions himself at either side of the lane. Ultimately, he moves to the same side to which #1 dribbles, thus creating the strong side to the left. If there is pressure, #5 comes to the high post, and then reverses to the goal on the quarterback's pass to the corner.

Diagram 4-2   This shows the move of our T Game to a standard two-guard front with two forwards and a center in the usual single-post set. Since #1 dribbled to his right, #4 becomes his primary outlet. #4 must time his *up-and-out* break to be open for the pass when #1 picks up his dribble. #5 has elected to come high initially, to offset pressure defense. He will move to the low post on the #1 to #4 pass coming up in Diagram 4-3.

Diagram 4-1   **Diagram 4-2**

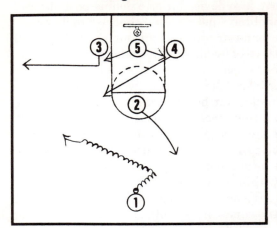
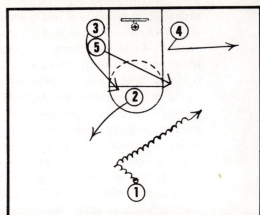

BASIC SCORING OPTIONS

The basic scoring options are relatively simple. Much depends on the ability of #4 to read the defense.

DIAGRAM 4-3: FIRST SCORING OPTION

#4 receives the pass from #1 and looks immediately to #5, who is moving from the high post into a good low-post position. If X5 is behind #5, as illustrated, #4 passes to #5, who turns either way to score. Most young men can be taught inside moves (to score or be fouled) from the low-post position (presuming they are the same relative height as their opponents).

Other essential moves in this basic scoring option are as follows:

- #3, who moved to a high-post position on the pass to #4, quickly returns to the weak left side for board coverage on the #4 to #5 pass. Should X3 leave #3 unguarded to work on #5 with the ball, #3 would be open for an easy scoring opportunity.
- #4, after passing to #5, *chops* his steps waiting on #5's move to the basket. Should #5 move toward the foul line, #4 then moves quickly for rebound coverage along the baseline. Should #5 move to the baseline side with the ball, #4 would cover the possible rebound in front of the basket.
- #1, after passing to #4, crosses over to the weak side, taking a path between the basket and #3, who is also moving. Should X1 jam #5, #1 would be free for a scoring opportunity on a pass from #5. #1 is in position to resume defense once a shot is taken.
- #2 moves to serve as an outlet from #4. When the #4 to #5 pass is made, #2 may approach the offensive board for a long rebound, or one which has been batted away.

DIAGRAM 4-4: SECOND SCORING OPTION

This illustrates the second basic scoring option. We use this option when the opponent defends the low post between #5 and the ball. This defense is used more often against us than one in which the opponent elects to play behind our post man. In this situation, #4 upon receiving the pass from #1, looks inside to see if X3 stays in the lane or moves to the high post with #3. If X3 follows #3 to the high post, #4 attempts an *over-the-top* pass to #5. By over-the-top, we are referring to a two-handed overhand pass designed to bypass X5's deflection. If the overhead pass is successful, #5 is usually able to score. Although we usually do not require rebounds on a lay-up shot, #4, after passing to #5, moves toward the basket for that purpose. #3 also approaches the basket down the strong-side lane on the #4 to #5 pass.

Diagram 4-3   **Diagram 4-4**

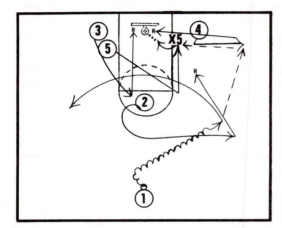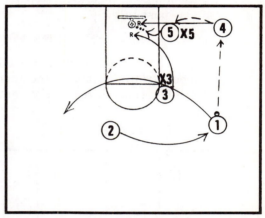

DIAGRAM 4-5: THIRD SCORING OPTION

If X3 stays in the lane to prevent the over-the-top pass to #5, #4 then passes to #3, who is open at the high post. #3 could score, or pass to #5, holding off X5 underneath. If #3 decides not to take the shot or pass to #5 underneath, he may pass to #1 on the weak side. #1 may shoot or begin the pattern again.

Diagram 4-5

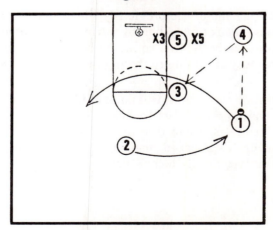

Let us assume that none of the options described above are exercised. Instead, #4 passes to #2. Although an alert defense will usually not overplay #2 when #4 has the ball and his dribble is alive, the offense should be prepared for such an opportunity. If this occurs, #4 drives to the middle and #3 could screen for him. #4, #3, and #5 could play three-against-three, which would lend itself to many scoring opportunities. Should #4 pass back out to #2, two more scoring options are set in motion.

DIAGRAM 4-6: FOURTH SCORING OPTION

#2 passes to #3 at the high post. #5 is attempting to get good position at the low post. He takes a step in the lane and looks for a pass from #3. #3 could also pass to #1.

DIAGRAM 4-7: FIFTH SCORING OPTION

The scoring option is especially effective against a zone defense. #2 makes a penetrating dribble to the middle. #1 floats to the weak side. #3, seeing the dribble, sets a screen for #2 and rolls to the basket.

Diagram 4-6

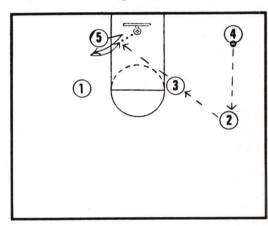

Diagram 4-7

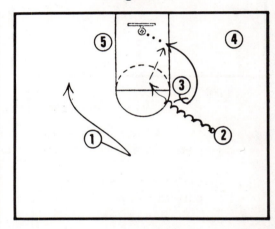

Diagram 4-8 If none of the previously illustrated scoring opportunities are open, #2 passes back to #4, thereby setting up the same basic scoring options described previously. At this point, #3 becomes the initial low post and #5 assumes the duty of coming to the high-post position. #2 proceeds as #1 did initially.

The question comes up at this point as to what alternatives are exercised if #1 cannot pass to #4 to start the offense. Generally, proper timing between #1 and #4 enables #4 to free himself for the pass. However, additional alternatives are established insuring open receivers for #1. We will cover these alternatives briefly before moving on to the continuity portion of the game.

Diagram 4-8

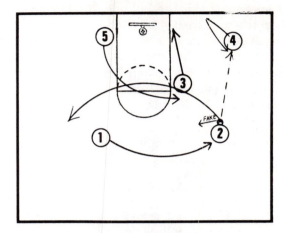

Diagram 4-9 #1 may pass directly to #5 (over the top if #5 is fronted by the defense) as illustrated in Diagram 4-9. #1 also might throw to #2 stepping out, which simply moves the initial attack to the left side, establishing #3 as the corner man. A third possibility is for #1 to pass to #3 stepping to the ball, which sets up a diagonal backdoor cut. If all four receivers are overplayed, the lack of defensive concentration around the basket lends itself to a backdoor pass to one of the logical receivers.

Diagram 4-9

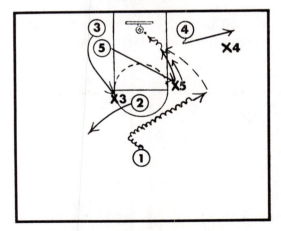

SINGLE-POST CONTINUITY

Diagram 4-10 The continuity of our "T" Game is established when the attack moves from one side of the court to the other. The #2 to #1 pass keys the change of sides continuity. #3 moves around #5's screen to his initial forward position. #4 moves hard to the foul line on a diagonal cut. #1 dribbles quickly to his left on the pass from #2.

We are now in the exact position on the left side of the court as we would have been if #1 had dribbled left to start the offense. On the pass from #1 to #3, we are once again set for our basic scoring options. Against pressure defense, #5 usually moves to a high post until this #1 to #3 pass is completed and then moves low for position.

Diagram 4-10

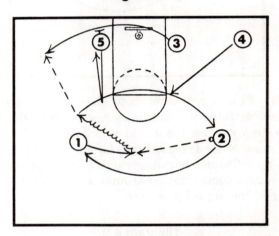

Diagrams 4-11 and 4-12   Diagrams 4-11 and 4-12 illustrate another change of sides to the original positions established in Diagram 4-2. The movement here permits #5 to set a screen for #4 circling around him. This gives #4 a better

Diagram 4-11

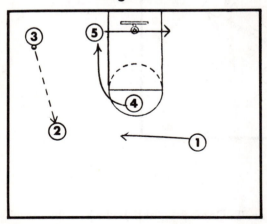

Diagram 4-12

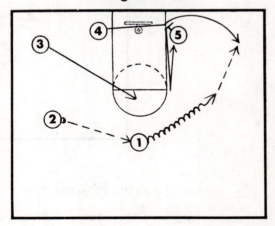

opportunity to be open for the pass from #1. #5 may again pop into a high post after screening and then move low on the pass from #1 to #4.

THE TRIPLE-POST CONTINUITY

The single-post continuity was used during the years we found it necessary to keep our #5 man at a low post. The triple-post continuity was experimented with at the freshman level during the 1967–68 season. It has proven most effective for us. In all probability, we will remain with the triple-post continuity (in lieu of the single post) unless our #5 man could not pass the ball well, or would not be a shooting threat from the corner.

Flexibility is its prime advantage. The triple-post continuity permits us to freely interchange our frontcourt men between the corner, low, and high posts. It is an excellent offense for a team with three forwards and no true center. If, for example, our corner man is pressed, he reverses to the low post and lets the low post assume his corner position. Equally important, if our man in the high post, or corner, has a height advantage over his opponent, he can exploit this mismatch by sliding into the more advantageous low post. We simply want the three spots filled—a passer in the corner, a low post, and a high post.

The triple-post continuity is illustrated in Diagrams 4-13 through 4-17.

Diagram 4-13 On the pass from #4 to #2, #5 moves to the other side of the lane. #3 remains high. #1 comes across to meet the pass from #2.

Diagram 4-14 The #2 to #1 pass signals the attack to the other side of the court. After #1 receives the pass from #2, he takes it on the dribble as shown in the diagram. #5 moves out to become an outlet for #1. #3 moves across the high-post area, preparing to go low when #1 passes to #5. #4 moves along the baseline.

Diagram 4-13   **Diagram 4-14**

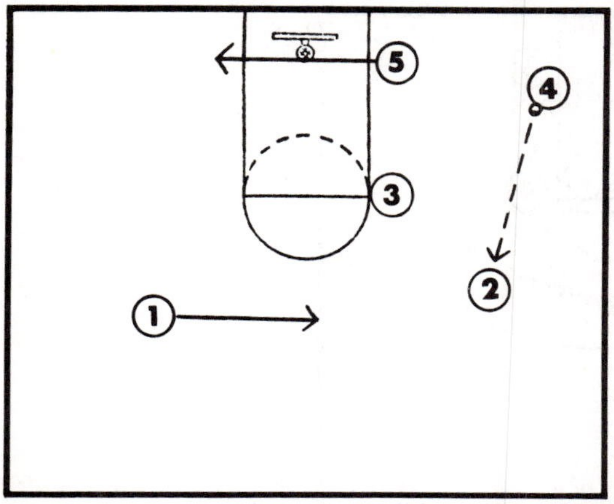

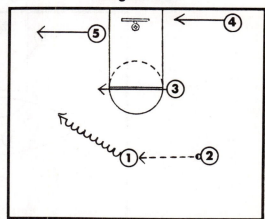

Diagram 4-15 #1 passes to #5 in the corner. #3 goes low. #4 moves to the high post. #1 and #2 interchange positions.

Diagram 4-16 On #5's return pass to #2, #3 backs out, and #4 remains high. #1 comes across to meet the pass from #2.

Diagram 4-15

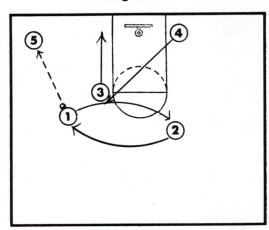

Diagram 4-16

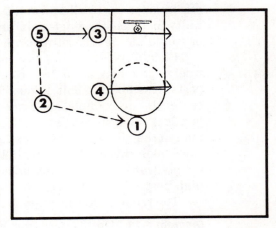

Diagram 4-17 #1 dribbles over. #3 moves to the corner for the pass from #1. On the #1 to #3 pass, #4 goes low and #5 comes high.

Diagrams 4-13 through 4-17 show the frontcourt players in each of the positions of the triple post. This is illustrated in the chart below for quick reference.

Diagram 4-17

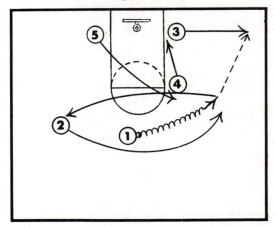

Player	High Post	Low Post	Corner
#3	Diagram 4-13, 14	Diagram 4-15	Diagram 4-17
#4	Diagram 4-15, 16	Diagram 4-17	Diagram 4-13
#5	Diagram 4-17	Diagram 4-13	Diagram 4-15

THE T GAME AGAINST ZONE DEFENSE

Early in this chapter, the T Game was referred to as a multipurpose offense, meaning one which could be used effectively against any defense. Only one major variation from the previously described patterns would be required to implement the T Game successfully against zone defenses. That variation would require the guards to remain on their respective sides once the offense was initiated.

Diagram 4-18 #1, upon passing to #3 in the corner, maintains his position on the right side, instead of cutting through and interchanging with #2. We suggest this variation against zones to insure a quick outlet back from #3, in the event #3 is double-teamed. Furthermore, since the interchange of guard positions will not alter a zone defensive alignment, the move becomes superfluous. The guards also can penetrate dribble to the middle on a pass from the baseline, somewhat more frequently against a zone than they do against man-to-man. However, one of the most important considerations in the use of the T Game against the zone is illustrated in diagram 4-19.

Diagram 4-18

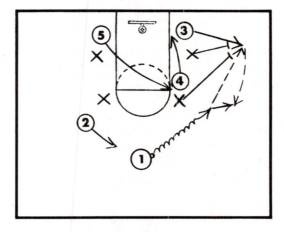

Diagram 4-19 We like to see the pass going from the corner to the high post. The high post would then look to the low post or to the weak-side guard. If the corner throws back to the guard (#3 to #1), we then like to see the guard pass

to the high post, who looks to the weak-side guard, or to the low post on the other side of the lane.

Diagram 4-19

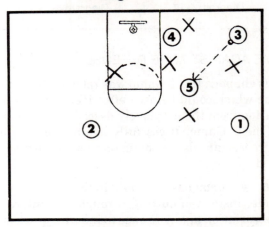

Excellent rebounding is one of the main features of the T Game, regardless of whether it is used against man-to-man or zone defenses.

The T Game is perhaps most effective against the one-two-two and three-two zone defenses, although we use it against a two-one-two zone as well. We have experienced good success with it against all zones when applied in conjunction with our Passing Game. The principles of both games are similar, although our T Game is patterned and the Passing Game is not.

teaching the "T" game

Similar to our approach used to introduce most concepts, the T Game is first presented within the five-against-five whole-method approach. We then focus our attention on the three post men.

PART-METHOD APPROACHES

Our part-method approach is facilitated sometimes through individual work with the frontcourt men prior to practice. When our frontcourt, three-on-three drills are used during regular practice sessions, the backcourt men are usually working on the skills required of them, such as ball handling and working against the press.

DIAGRAM 4-20: DRILL ONE

#4 is instructed to make a two-handed overhead pass to #5. #5 is taught to score, or draw the foul upon receiving the pass from #4. At the same time, he is taught how to position himself against X5. #3 is taught to react to the basket on the #4 to #5 pass, as well as the value of working for offensive rebounding position. Should #5, with the ball, be bothered by X3, he would pass to #3, who would break toward the basket. The triple post is practiced by rotating each man to the corner passer, high, and low-post positions. The continuity is anticipated by exercising the drill on the left as well as right side of the court.

Diagram 4-20

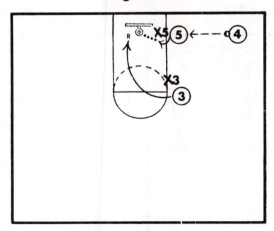

DIAGRAM 4-21: DRILL TWO

This is the drill used primarily to perfect the over-the-top pass. Each of the three frontcourt spots is filled in order to create a game-like situation. The corner and low-post men have defensive players working against them, while a student manager plays against #3 who moves to the high post. The defense is instructed to front the low-post man. The T Game's basic scoring options start upon the coach's pass to #4. If you recall, earlier in the chapter, we emphasized the importance of #4 reading the defense correctly before passing. This drill is keyed on #4's execution, based on his observation of the manager. If the manager follows #3 to the high post (and we instruct him to do so most of the time), we want #4 to throw the over-the-top pass to #5, or pass to #3, if the manager doesn't come with #3. #3 would then dump off to #5 underneath.

Once again, all positions are rotated (except the manager and coach) and both the left as well as right side of the court is used.

DIAGRAM 4-23: DRILL THREE

Our most effective part-method drill is one which has three offensive men working against three defensive men in the frontcourt positions. Two guards without defense run the entire T Game. The guards are restricted to outside shots. These shots may be attempted if a post man, going for a shot, pitches out to them. The post men then work on positioning and offensive rebounding. We should point out that if a shot comes from the corner, the new high post must rush to the weak side for rebounding.

The drill is made competitive by keeping score. The offense maintains possession when fouled, or upon scoring. The defense may work either man-to-man, or zone. This drill improves execution, strengthens rebounding ability, and builds confidence. Its competitive aspect allows us to make defensive adjustments as well.

Diagram 4-21   **Diagram 4-22**

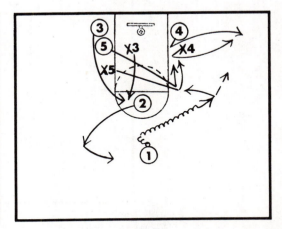

WHOLE-METHOD APPROACHES

Half Court Games   In addition to the part-method drills described above, the whole-method approach is implemented during half-court games. These games are designed specifically to improve our execution of the T Game against any possible defense. I might mention at this point that the defense is instructed to fast break on all missed shots during all our half-court games. Turns are taken on both offense and defense, and the game is scored differently to encourage the continuity. If the offense scores or is fouled, they receive two points. Three points are awarded, however, if the offense has initiated two or more court side changes in the interim. An assistant coach is assigned to the defense, which is deliberately varied from pressing man-to-man, sagging man, to all types of zone alignments.

Scrimmages   Ten minute scrimmages, during which the offense is restricted exclusively to the T Game, are also employed. Regular scrimmages, as well, are utilized towards perfecting the T Game.

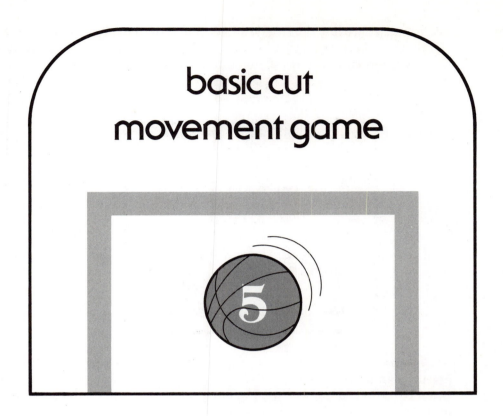

basic cut
movement game

Our Offense #5 derives from the basic option of the Shuffle Offense. I first learned to respect the Shuffle and its Basic Cut as a player at Kansas University during the year we won the NCAA championship. The problems Dr. Phog Allen and his assistant coach Dick Harp anticipated defending the shuffle required us to spend more time preparing for one team than all others. That was Bruce Drake's Oklahoma team, which used the Shuffle Offense.

This respect was heightened during the time I served as assistant to Coach Bob Spear at the Air Force Academy. Coach Spear's teams employed a well-executed shuffle to frequently defeat opponents with far superior individual talent. The complete Air Force shuffle offense is described in detail by Coach Spear in Part 2 of this book.

During my early head coaching years at North Carolina, we used the full Shuffle continuity until we were fortunate to recruit a pure center. If the team were ever again in the position of having to go with a small center, I wouldn't hesitate using the Spear Shuffle as an alternate offense to the Passing Game. I probably would use the One-Four alignment as an entry, since it camouflages the Basic Cut so well and can surprise the defense. We still use the Basic Cut from the Shuffle in our offensive design and probably will continue to do so.

Diagram 5-1 The Shuffle Basic Cut, referred to by Coach Spear as "the heart and primary threat of the shuffle offense," is good sound basketball. There is always the chance for an easy lay-up, and the play serves to move the defense. This makes the defense more vulnerable to continuity of offense.

Diagram 5-1

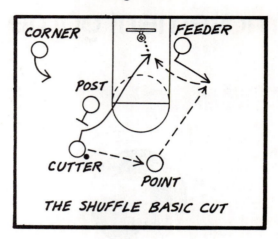

THE SHUFFLE BASIC CUT

When run in a surprise situation, the well-executed cut is most difficult to defend man-to-man. For this reason, we try to disguise it within the same One-Four entry alignment used in our Offense #1. The similar formations prevent the defense from knowing with certainty which offense to anticipate.

Our Offenses #1 and #5 are compatible offenses since they generate different movements from the same One-Four alignment. One year, in fact, we combined both offenses, running the post option from the One-Four and the Basic Cut from our #5 offense. We merged these offenses in an effort to cut down on the quantity of offense our players had to learn. In retrospect, this was probably unnecessary, since our players in recent years have had little difficulty learning to execute both offenses efficiently. The additional offense in our multiple system thereby serves to add an extra wrinkle for which our opponents must prepare.

DIAGRAM 5-2: ONE-FOUR ENTRY TO THE BASIC CUT (WING OPTION)

This illustrates the One-Four alignment used to disguise the Basic Cut from our Offense #1.

Timing on the change from the One-Four entry positions into the shuffle alignment is very important. Since we don't want the wing holding the ball, the other four men must move very quickly into position on the quarterback pass to the wing. #2, the weak-side wing, must anticipate the pass going to #3, and start moving off #4 to the post position. #1 sprints to the basket off #5 and may be open for a scoring opportunity. #5 goes to the corner as soon as #1 cuts off, or sets a screen for #3, the cutter. We show both possibilities in the diagram. After screening for #2, #4 moves to the point for the pass from the cutter, #3. To better #4's chance of being clear for the pass, we want him setting a good screen on #2's defender.

DIAGRAM 5-3: SHUFFLE POSITIONS

Our One-Four entry line-up takes into consideration the positions that must be filled in the Shuffle alignment on the initial pass to the wing. We want the cutter, who is a wing, or quarterback, to be an outside scoring threat, in order to be respected from the cutter's spot. The post (who is a wing) should be a good outside shooter as well, since is usually open at the top of the key after screening for the cutter. The feeder should have good passing ability. The feeder position is filled by our quarterback regardless of the side he chooses to run the wing option. Since it is important that the point man is not pressed, we fill this position with a post man. Post defense does not usually press as well outside. The corner position is filled by #5, who becomes the high-post chaser in our Passing Game if the Basic Cut does not produce the lay-up.

Diagram 5-3 shows the wing option to the left, which places #3 as the cutter, #4 at the point, #1 as the feeder, #2 at the post, and #5 at the corner. If the quarterback runs the wing option to the right, #2 would be the cutter, #5 would be the point, #3 the post, #4 the corner, and #1 would still be the feeder on the other side.

Diagram 5-2

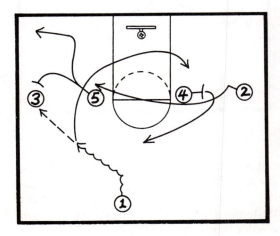

Diagram 5-3

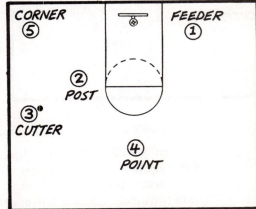

DIAGRAM 5-4: BASIC CUT

This again illustrates the Basic Cut after the break from the One-Four alignment. The cutter, #3, passes to the point, #4, and begins his cut around either side of the screen set by the post. The point, #4, puts the ball above his head quickly and swings it to the feeder, #1, who in turn makes a bounce pass to the cutter for a lay-up.

DIAGRAM 5-5: TRANSITION TO PASSING GAME

We don't consider the play completed until the feeder is provided additional outlets in the event the lay-up is unavailable. This is similar to the full Shuffle's change of sides.

After passing to #1, #4 moves to screen #2's defender, which gets #2 open at the top of the key. #5 comes up the sideline (or stays in his screener's position) on the #3 to #4 pass. He begins his move to the post position on the #4 to #1 pass. These moves take us to the end of the Basic Cut and into our Passing Game, if the cut is not open. Any pass #1 makes to his teammates at this point initiates the Passing Game. He has three near outlets to choose from in #3, #5, or #2. Note that #4 and #5 end their moves in perfect position to begin the Passing Game's high-low post interchange. Since the defense has already been moved, no minimum number of passes is required prior to shooting.

Diagram 5-4   **Diagram 5-5**

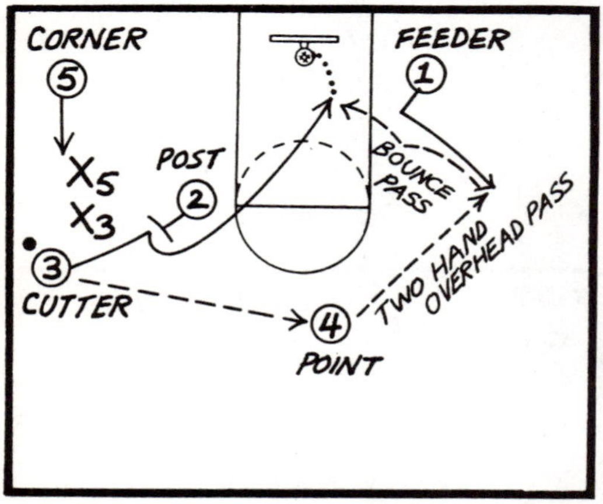

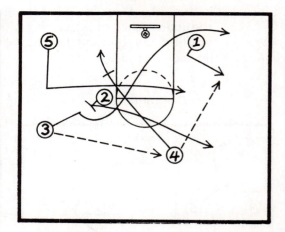

DIAGRAM 5-6: REVERSE PASS TO FEEDER

Options off the Shuffle alignment are necessary in the event the point has difficulty passing to the feeder off the lane. The point's first alternative would be to pass to the feeder reversing to the basket for a lay-up. We want our point man to quickly take the ball over his head on the pass from the cutter. He then can make the reverse pass to the feeder more easily, if it is called for.

DIAGRAM 5-7: POINT OPTION

The second alternative is referred to as the point option. #4 fakes to the feeder, and then kicks back to #5 coming up out of the corner or holding as screener. #4, after passing, cuts around #2 toward the basket. He then button-hooks in the low-post position if he doesn't receive a pass back from #5. #2 begins by screening for #3 on the basic cut. He then starts to the top of key, but notices that #4 did not pass to the feeder. #2 then sets a rear screen for #4 and pops-out to be the outlet for #5. When #1 does not receive the pass from #4, he returns to the lane to set a screen for #3. For timing purposes, #3 goes back to set a screen for #1 on the lane. Therefore, when #2 pops-out to receive the pass, he has a choice of passing #4 button-hooking on the low post, or passing to #1 coming back off a screen set by #3. After #2 makes his pass and a shot is not taken, the point option is completed. We then move into our Passing Game. #4 is already at the low post as the point option terminates. #5 quickly moves to the high-post area to put us in position for the Passing Game.

The point option completes our plays which are keyed by the initial pass to the wing. Obviously, the same plays would be used if #1 threw to #2 on the right wing. The only change that would take place would be a shift in duties between #2 and #3 and likewise between #5 and #4.

Diagram 5-6　　　　　　　　　　　**Diagram 5-7**

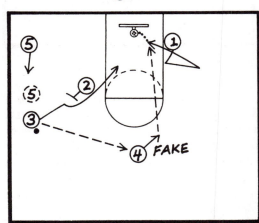　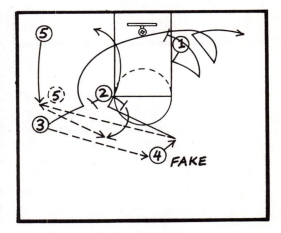

DIAGRAMS 5-8 AND 5-9: DRIBBLE OPTION

The move we refer to as the dribble option can be exercised in lieu of the wing option, to bring us into the Shuffle alignment. If #1 has difficulty passing to the wing, he simply dribbles hard toward the wing, who reverses to the basket. Occasionally, a bounce pass to the wing reversing will result in a lay-up.

The moves to these Shuffle positions shown in diagrams 5-8 and 5-9 are identical to those of the wing option illustrated initially in Diagram 5-2 and 5-3, except for the interchange of position between the quarterback and the wing. If the quarterback dribbles toward #3, the left wing, #2, #4, and #5 move exactly as they would on a pass from #1 to #3. #3, however, reverses to the basket to become the feeder, while #1 assumes the cutter's role on the dribble option left.

All subsequent options from the initial Shuffle positions are identical whether the alignment is keyed by a pass to the wing (wing option) or dribble to the wing (dribble option).

Diagram 5-8

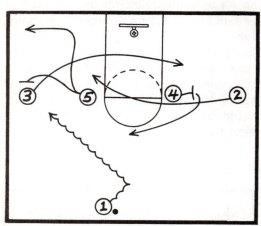

Diagram 5-9

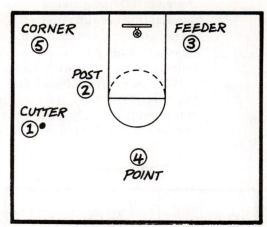

DIAGRAM 5-10: POST OPTION

The post option from our One-Four was designed primarily to create a good, quick scoring opportunity. The post option of the Basic Cut, however, generates different movement from the One-Four alignment. We use it essentially as an entry to the Passing Game. Again, bear in mind that the different moves made from the same One-Four alignment, depending on the offense we're running, makes the offense more difficult to defend. Although our Basic Cut post option serves the prime purpose of bringing us into our Passing Game, it does lend itself to one possible scoring play.

Diagram 5-10

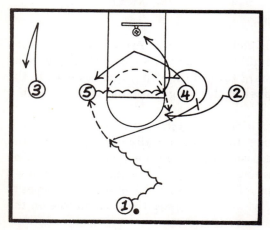

Diagram 5-11

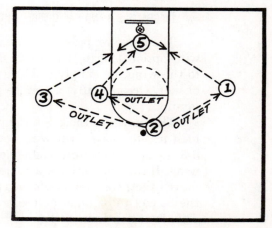

#1 begins this post option by passing to #5. As #5 receives the ball, his first look is for a bounce or over-the-top pass to #4, breaking to the basket. #3 (who breaks to the basket in our One-Four offense) moves to the corner this time and then back to the wing. #1, after passing to #5, moves to screen away for #2, who is coming out. #5 dribbles to the other side of the foul line hoping to hand off to #2. #5 hands off, and gets a rear screen from #1 as he sprints to the basket, looking over his left shoulder for an over-the-top pass from #2. #4, who went low initially, begins back to #5's original position on the handoff to #2.

Diagram 5-11   If #2 does not throw the over-the-top pass to #5, he has three near outlets in #1, #3, and #4 to begin our Passing Game. Since X5 has been moved, we are in a good position to work the ball in low to #5 at this point, as the diagram demonstrates. Therefore, although the pass from #2 to either #1, #3, or #4 puts us into the Passing Game, the receiver is instructed to immediately look low to #5 getting position.

Note that each of our diagrams has the quarterback attacking the left side of the court. This has been done only to maintain sequence and clarity for the book. Keep in mind, however, that the offense is *mirrored*. Should #1 pass to the right side, the play would be identical with positions and paths reversed. The Basic Cut post option aims primarily at working on a particular defensive man guarding one of our posts. If, for example, X4 is a poor defensive player or in foul trouble, the quarterback calls this offense and exercises the post option by passing to #4. We know that the play ultimately results in a screen for #4 who ends up low for a possible feed.

teaching the basic cut movement game

We begin our instruction in the Shuffle alignment from which the Basic Cut is taught. This is run for two or three days as dummy offense. We then put the Basic Cut into a four-man passing and shooting drill to perfect execution. The team is divided into two groups. The four men assume the Shuffle alignment positions without a corner man. Later, the coach may assume the corner spot when the point option is incorporated into this drill. If seven men were at each end of the floor, four fill the spots and three wait to rotate in. Wings and quarterbacks must learn the cutter, feeder, and post position of the Shuffle. The post only needs to fill the top of the key in this drill.

Diagram 5-12   The cutter begins with the ball. He passes to the point and then breaks to the basket on either side of the screen set by the post. The point must quickly swing the ball to the feeder using an over-the-top pass. The point then moves down to screen an imaginary defense on the post-screener's defender. The feeder starts out from the lane when the point receives the ball from the cutter. The feeder then receives the ball about six feet from the lane, and makes the bounce pass to the cutter for a lay-up. The feeder may choose to fake the pass to the cutter and feed the post, #2, coming to the point for an outside shot. As shown in the diagram insert, the feeder also has the option of reversing to the basket if he is overplayed.

Diagram 5-12

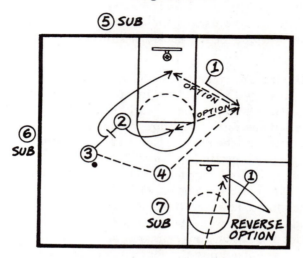

The rebounders are the initial point man and the initial cutter. The rebounder makes an outlet pass to #6, the substitute cutter coming on the court to start the drill over again. The cutter, #3, now becomes the feeder, and is the only player to run the drill twice in succession.

After a few minutes of overload on the left side of the court, we move the overload to the right side.

We exercise each of the Shuffle options in the whole-method without defense. We then move to the four-man drill for the purpose of teaching each position. We do not go over the One-Four entry to the Shuffle alignment until the options from that alignment can be well-executed.

DIAGRAMS 5-13 AND 5-14: POINT OPTION DRILL

The point option is taught through this drill in the same manner, with the coach moving up from the corner on the pass to the point. As soon as all of the options are learned from this Shuffle alignment, they are executed when running the drill. The coach, or manager, assumes the corner spot to facilitate the point option. He moves up on each cutter to point pass when this option is exercised.

We introduce later the One-Four entry to the Shuffle positions by passing or dribbling. The whole-method approach then is implemented within half-court scrimmages, alternating between the Offense #1 and Offense #5 One-Four alignment games. The whole-method is used also to teach the post option of the Basic Cut.

Diagram 5-13

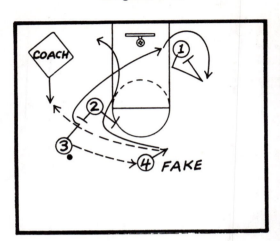

Diagram 5-14

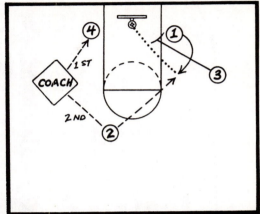

four corners
offense

Our move into the Four Corners delay offense is usually greeted by loud cheers when we use it at home and equally loud boos when we run it on our opponents home court. If our fans somehow interpret our Four Corners as a sure sign of victory, that conclusion is never quite as obvious to our coaches and players, who know we must execute well to win.

Our fans' enthusiastic confidence in our Four Corners probably stems from the fact that we have used this delay offense with a lead in 107 games between 1966–1972 with the good fortune to win 105 of them. We have also increased our margin from the time we began our delay to the final buzzer in eighty-one percent of those games. The latter statistic at any rate supports the premise that a delay is not a *freeze*, but a style which consumes time while drawing the opposition into defensive errors resulting in a score or a foul shot for the offense.

Some coaches do not use a delay game. If their team has a three-point lead with forty seconds to play, they believe the twenty foot jump shot will go in. I admire their confidence but question their percentage thinking. I am inclined to assume the shot could be missed, and therefore believe in the merits of a delay game if it can be effectively handled.

use and choice of delay game

Any type of delay game is probably difficult to execute at the junior high level. The limited ball-handling skills usually prevalant at this age level make this kind of game somewhat vulnerable to aggressive defense.

The same problem is not as relevant at the high school level. The smaller court might make it a little more difficult to spread the defense if this kind of tactic is used. However, many high school coaches have written to me that they have used our Four Corners on their 84′ × 50′ court for long delay with excellent results. Our own 1972 North Carolina team played and won an international tournament in Madrid on a court *less* than regulation width and length than the one to which we were accustomed. We managed to use our Four Corners successfully. Although the limited space gave us less room to operate, our players eventually adjusted quite well to the situation. Later in this chapter we will discuss how we used the Four Corners in conjunction with the 30-second clock during this same tournament.

Regardless of the specific type of delay game selected by a coach at any level, our own experience suggests the use of one which can be employed against all defenses with very few adjustments. During my early head-coaching years, we used one type of delay against a half-court zone press and another against man-to-man. We later discovered that our Four Corners could be used effectively against any type defense. In addition to cutting practice time, the change to a single delay game helped us concentrate our efforts on building confidence through improved execution. The player's confidence in the delay is an *absolute prerequisite* to its use. The unusual amount of faith our players have in the Four Corners is the prime reason we use it frequently and without hesitation.

WHEN TO DELAY

The next important decision a coach makes regarding a delay game is when to use it. Most coaches who use a delay look to it only towards the end of a game. Although we have called on our Four Corners more frequently during the latter stages of a game, we won't hesitate using it over longer periods of time if necessary. There are several factors which govern the use and timing of our delay game, which we'll describe at this point.

1. Strength of Opponent   Our knowledge of the opposition often helps us anticipate the appropriate timing of our delay. As discussed in our earlier chapter on Philosophy of Offense, it is wise to shorten the game through ball-control tactics when you are obviously outmanned. The opponent's rebounding strength relative to ours is the key factor in making this determination. If we expect to get only one shot to their very possible two each time down the court, we do not hesitate using our delay very early in the game with any kind of lead.

When badly outmanned in a key game back in 1966, we started our delay at the opening tip-off. Although we eventually lost by a single point, our delay kept us in the game down to the final second. Anything could have happened during the closing minutes to change the result. Had we not used the delay, the eventual outcome would probably have been determined at some point during the first half.

Only once did the overwhelming strength of an opponent cause us to stay in the delay although behind. This was against the 1968 UCLA team in the NCAA finals. Not only did UCLA have Alcindor (Abdul-Jabbar) at center, but many great players, such as Lucius Allen and Mike Warren, in strong supporting roles. In my opinion, this was the best college team of all time. In addition, we were facing them before their home crowd in Los Angeles.

We started in delay hoping to establish control and upset them mentally. We wanted to keep them on defense for as long as possible, and bring Alcindor out from under the basket at the same time.

With the score 8−6 in favor of UCLA early in the game, we decided to hedge somewhat on our slowdown approach. After delaying with each possession to erase thirty seconds off the clock, we moved into our regular zone offense. If I had that particular decision to make over again, I would have kept our team on straight delay, hoping the score would still be 8−6 at halftime. As it was, we controlled pretty well and played excellent defense during most of the game. The score was 38−32 UCLA with seventeen minutes to play in the game when our big forward, Bill Bunting, got into foul trouble trying to help Rusty Clark on Alcindor. When we tried to run and catch up during the last ten minutes, they blew us out 78−55.

2. *Score, Time Remaining, Bonus Foul Situation* The score and time remaining in the game obviously has much to do with the decision to move into the delay. If we continue to maintain a very comfortable margin against a team we should have little difficulty beating, we do not go into our Four Corners just for the sake of exercise. However, even against a team we should beat, we will go to delay inside three minutes remaining if they are within some degree of reach. For obvious reasons, we like to be in the one-and-one bonus situation when we do so. However, the 1972 rule change allowing for retained possession in lieu of the one shot foul allows for an earlier delay game. The change prevents the risk of giving up two points in exchange for one at the foul line. I consider the rule a good one, since possession is worth more than a one shot foul. At the same time, the bonus foul penalty prevents a smartly-coached team from arbitrarily fouling for profit.

3. *Momentum* Momentum of the game is another factor determining our move into delay. If, for example, our opponent suddenly cuts our twenty-point lead in half with seven or eight minutes remaining, we may use our delay to cut their momentum. Conversely, we often switch to delay against a strong opponent after momentum helps us overcome a big deficit to take the lead late in the game. Some might say that by slowing our pace we're cutting our own momentum. That may be true. However, I believe that momentum often has an uncanny way of shifting once a team has come from behind. There is that tendency for the team that has just pulled ahead to breathe an understandable (although premature) sigh of relief. Simultaneously, the opponent's adrenaline flow usually begins to surface with the realization that the lead must now be recaptured rather than merely protected.

One such experience which reinforced by *alternating momentum* theory occurred in 1966 against a good Virginia Tech team. Our team was down fourteen points with eight minutes to play. We recovered to go ahead by two and had possession with 3:30 left on the clock. I had a hunch to go into our delay, but didn't want to halt our momentum. We eventually lost the game as the momentum switched hands. From that point on, we made it a practice to go into our delay after coming from far behind late in the game to earn the lead and the ball.

This idea held us in good stead a couple of years later against a nationally-ranked Utah team in the semi-finals of the Far West Classic in Portland, Oregon. Utah led by seventeen points with nine minutes remaining. We caught up gradually by pressing on defense and scoring most of the time we had the ball. At the 3:32 mark on the clock, we went up by one point. Utah came up the floor and missed a shot. At that point, I signaled the Four Corners to our quarterback. (We never call time-out to move into the delay). With a lay-up after delaying for a minute, and some clutch foul shooting, we won the game 86 to 84.

4. The Foul Situation   The situation on both teams dictates, to some degree, the point we move into our delay. If some of our key players are in foul trouble, we may delay earlier than usual, since very few fouls occur on offense, particularly on delay offense. On the other hand, if our opponents are in foul trouble, we prefer to keep pressure on the defense and will avoid shortening the game through delay. If delay seems indicated despite our opponents foul trouble, we may attempt a moderate delay hoping to kill some time without entirely easing the pressure off the defense.

evolution of the four corners

During my first two years as head coach, we needed to make much use of the delay game. We used the One-Four post option as our basic scoring play. Continuity resulted from running this post option continuously. This was our man-to-man delay. To delay against a zone press, we passed the ball around Four Corners, using our best ball handler in the middle. Many teams used the Four Corners against a zone press, although most placed their post man in the middle.

The change to a single delay game we use against any type of defense came about late in the 1963 season. It resulted from somewhat of a fluke occurrence during a practice session, as we were working on our zone press delay.

Larry Brown, our great 5'10" senior quarterback, was doing his usual fine job as the chaser in the middle. The defense was having no success getting the ball. I called the defense together, suggesting they begin in a zone press and then switch to a man-to-man press. I was looking for Larry to spot the switch and move the offense into our man-to-man delay. Larry missed the change, however, He simply drove around his man to the basket and passed off to our 6'4½" sophomore center, who was left open for the lay-up when his man came out to stop Larry. That 6'4½", 175 lbs. sophomore, by the way, turned out to be one of the great college and pro players of all time. I'm referring, of course, to Billy Cunningham who continued to grow in college, and graduated at 6'6", 218 lbs. Some nine years later, incidentally, Billy and Larry teamed together once again (as player and coach, respectively) to help carry the professional ABA Carolina Cougars to its most successful season.

Most defenses, behind in the late stages of a game, generally line up man-to-man and then double-team the dribbler. That one simple play in practice made it suddenly clear that we could use our zone delay equally well to spread man-to-man coverage, thereby allowing us to operate one-on-one.

We were further encouraged in this direction by observing Chuck Noe, the outstanding coach at South Carolina at the time, who used his *Mongoose* as an effective man-to-man delay. The *Mongoose* had three men stationed across the ten-second line and two men playing two-on-two inside.

We finally went to the Four Corners as our only delay game in 1966. As indicated earlier, this change to a single delay game allows us to devote more time to perfecting execution and building confidence in the Four Corners.

Most teams in our Atlantic Coast Conference accustomed to seeing our Four Corners have begun to defend it almost exclusively man-to-man in the corners and six feet off the middle dribbler. I was a member of the 1971 National Rules Committee when the regulation preventing a closely guarded dribbler from controlling the ball was passed. I voted in favor of the change for the betterment of basketball, although at the time I thought it would mean the end of our Four Corners. As it turned out, we were able to maintain the effectiveness of the offense by making one minor adjustment which will be described later on in the chapter.

During the 1971 ABA play-offs, the Virginia Squires used the Four Corners to defeat the New York Nets. I was quite surprised to read about the Four Corners in pro ball. I called Charles Scott, our former All-American, who played the middle of the Four Corners for the Squires. Charles indicated that the rule in the ABA required the defense stay within a number of feet of his own man. Charles and Doug Moe, another North Carolina All-American, and one of the smartest basketball players I've ever known, suggested the Four Corners to Coach Al Bianchi. Al wisely put his two biggest men (though smaller than the Nets) in the mid-court corners, Charles in the middle, and two great shooters at the baseline corners. Charles then would dribble around looking for an opening. Since no one could stop Charles one-on-one, defensive help had to come from the corners. Charles then either would pass to the shooters for a short jumper, or go all the way to the basket for the score or foul.

Of course, the pros and foreign teams working with a 30-second clock adjust their game accordingly. During the previously mentioned Madrid International Tournament, we were faced with a similar requirement. When we used the Four Corners, we stayed in it for twenty seconds and then popped into our One-Four alignment which quickly gave us a good shot with strong board coverage.

BASIC ALIGNMENT

We move into our Four Corners out of the One-Four alignment when the defense is set. If we come up court in our full-court press offense or on a controlled fast break, either offense takes us to the baseline. We then move to the Four Corners positions directly from the baseline.

Diagram 6-1   We move from the One-Four alignment into the Four Corners. As #1 crosses the mid-court line, #2 and #3 move to the mid-court corners (leaving approximately six feet to the sideline and six feet to the mid-court line). Notice that #5 delays his move to the baseline corner until #1 passes the ball. If #1 dribbled left, #4 would delay his move to the corner. This is done to insure four possible outlets for #1, the quarterback.

#1 attempts to dribble by his man until X2, or some other defender moves to help on #1. If we're facing a zone press, #1 dribbles the same way and passes as the second defensive man approaches him. We want #1 to pass off *before* a double-team occurs. Even if #1 cannot get rid of the ball prior to the double-team occurring, the principle is not to panic, but continue looking for the open man. We rather take the jump ball than throw the ball away at this point.

We were fortunate to have a great quarterback in the late 1960s by the name of Dick Grubar. Dick seemed to enjoy being double-teamed, then picking out the open man. Dick was a very talented ball handler, but his daring here gave us some very nervous moments.

One of the reasons we spread out is to avoid double-teaming. Once that first pass is completed, we consider ourselves in excellent position, since each player who then receives the ball can pass as well as have his dribble alive.

Diagram 6-2   Diagram 6-2 is a continuation of Diagram 6-1. Keep in mind that since we are in a free-lance situation, the action diagramed represents possible, rather than patterned, moves. Here, however, #2 has the ball. #1 is the chaser. The chaser *always* positions himself one *near-pass* from the ball. In this instance, he is at the sideline when he receives the pass from #2. #1 turns to drive the middle, which brings X3 up to stop the penetration. #1 then throws to #3. #3 returns the pass to #1, who moves to get open again one near-pass from the ball. #1 then penetrates the left side this time. When X5 moves to stop the penetration to the basket, #1 throws to #5, who takes a quick look to #4 breaking underneath. The rule here is that when one post receives the ball, the other post goes to the basket. If #4 does not break to the basket, #5 would have difficulty passing to the corner. In this situation, however, #5 chooses to pass back out to #3.

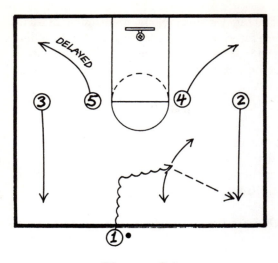

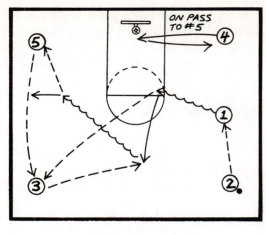

Diagram 6-1   **Diagram 6-2**

Diagrams 6-3 and 6-4 The method used to change the chaser is illustrated in Diagrams 6-3 and 6-4. #1 may grow tired of chasing or have trouble getting open as #3 has the ball. The mid-court corner man (either #2 or #3) may also elect to take the middle if he is having difficulty finding the open man. In this case, #3 dribbles into the chaser's area and #1 circles out to the vacated corner. With the Four Corners, it is ideal to have three players (#1, #2, and #3) who are adept at ball handling and foul shooting. Since most delay games require four men handling the ball, this is an improvement. If #3 is not a good dribbler, he should attempt to get the ball to the other mid-corner man, who will take it to the middle. The posts #4 and #5 (who do most of the scoring) do not have to dribble the ball, except in emergency.

Diagram 6-3   **Diagram 6-4**

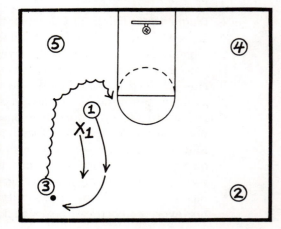

After controlling the ball through several passes and penetrations, the opponent usually begins to wonder if we ever will shoot or give up possession without their fouling. This is often the point at which we can penetrate for a score. We usually score in one of the following ways:

1. *Foul Shots*: When the opponent is anxious to get the ball, it often leads to a foul. We probably score more through foul shots during delay than we do through field-goals.

2. *One-on-One Drive by Chaser*: The one-on-one drive to the basket usually makes things happen. Most teams, however, use their defensive men on the posts to help out against this drive and prevent the lay-up. The chaser then may pass off.

3. *Penetration to Goal and Pass to Corner Moving In*: We probably score most of our field-goals when our dribbler, stopped by a defensive post man, passes off to our post moving to the basket. The rule for our post men is to go to the basket if his defender moves to help on the dribbler.

4. *Post-to-Post Against a Zone Press*: Against a zone press, the score usually is made through a pass from our chaser to one post who passes underneath to the other post.

5. *Back Door Reverse to Basket*: The back door play was initiated as a result of the 1971 rule change mentioned earlier in the chapter. It is an adjustment against the defense which trys to cover both the four corners tightly and the chaser loosely, yet in a closely-guarded position (within six feet according to the rule).

Diagram 6-5   The rule is for the post men to come up the sideline to the foul line extended when the chaser must pick up his dribble to avoid a five-second count. If #1 pivots and faces #5 coming to the ball, #5 reverses to the basket. #3 and #2 move only in an emergency to help a player who uses up his dribble.

Diagram 6-6   We have found that the post reverse isn't needed often, since the posts' defenders usually trail their men to the ball on the sideline. When #1

Diagram 6-5

Diagram 6-6

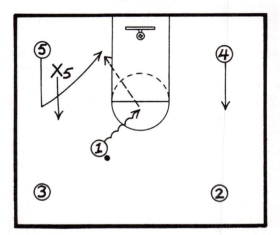

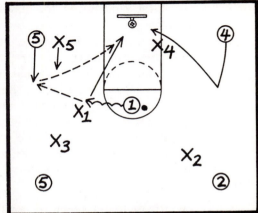

passes the ball to #5 in this position, X1 attempts to keep #1 from getting the ball again. Therefore, #1 reverses to the basket. #4 moves in for board coverage, or a pass from #1 should X4 move to help on #1.

Since the players are faced with very few rules, many different types of scoring opportunities develop. We do prefer the lay-up or foul shot. We take a wide-open jump shot if we have taken time off the clock, teased the defense, and have more than a three-point lead. We have been tempted to add some specific scoring plays against a man-to-man defense, but felt that doing so would destroy the simplicity and freedom of the offense.

There is little difference between attacking the zone press and the man-to-man press. Against a zone press, we pass the ball more than we dribble since the players are more frequently open for the pass.

teaching the four corners

All of our teaching effort relating to the Four Corners is handled through the whole-method approach. Our first job is to teach our players the relative few rules, while we build their confidence in the delay game. This is done by placing our second-team ball handlers and first-team post men together on offense. Our first-team ball handlers (the #1, #2, and #3 positions) along with our second-team post men comprise the defense and are faced with the challenge of getting the ball. We huddle the offense together and tell them how easy it is to keep the ball away from the defense. We suggest they "smile at the poor, frustrated guys who'll be knocking themselves out trying to get the ball." We play half-court only, and do not permit the defense to fast break should they steal the ball. Since the zone press is not as effective against the Four Corners, we deliberately use that defense initially, in order to build confidence in the offense.

After ten minutes of chasing the ball, we ask the defense if they would rather play offense. The enthusiastic "yes" we invariably get marks the first step we've climbed towards building confidence in the offense.

After continuing the half-court work for a week (always late in the practice session), our next step is to make a game of it. The offense is given a three-point lead with two minutes to play. We keep the scoreboard operating and start with a typical score, such as 76–73. The defense is given one point each time they gain possession. When the offense scores, they receive two points; if fouled, they shoot the foul shots. The defense is given one point on each score since they would normally obtain possession after a score.

We tell our student referees to be certain to call the fouls closely on the defense. Again, our major objective at this point is to build confidence in the delay game more than to simulate a real-game situation. Later in the year, we will use *six* men on defense when working against a zone press.

Overtime Scrimmage   At the end of most practice sessions, we play a five minute overtime scrimmage. (The high school coach, incidentally, may wish to make this a three-minute game to correspond with the duration of the high school overtime.) A tie score, such as 70–70, is set on the board with five minutes left on the clock. Both teams are placed in the bonus foul situation. The quarterback on each team decides when to move into the delay game.

It is interesting to note that the quarterback invariably moves into the Four Corners as soon as his team gets the lead and the ball. Occasionally the quarterback, particularly if his team is the underdog, moves into the delay with the score tied. We vary the reward and punishment to the winners and losers. Sometimes after practice, sodas are withheld from the losers, with the extra soft drinks going to the winners. We usually add sprints for the losers, or eliminate some sprints from the winners. It makes for a highly competitive contest.

The game also provides us with the opportunity to handle last-minute situations, which are covered in a separate section in the book. With the exception of calling the delay game, all other decisions relating to these last-minute situations are made by the coach during the overtime scrimmage.

Since this was first written we have had tremendous success in the Four Corners using a young man who played the chaser at North Carolina during each of his four years. His name is Phil Ford, a first-team All-American and a starter on our gold-medal-winning 1976 Olympic team. With his fantastic individual ability with the ball, in addition to his passing talent, the Four Corners became even more of a scoring-type offense and one that was most difficult to defend.

Even during the Olympics, with the thirty-second clock, we were able to go to the Four Corners late in the game, spreading out the defense and moving in for the score. Of course if we could not get the lay-up, we looked for an open jump shot after twenty seconds. We were fortunate to have the pure shooting ability of Scott May, from Indiana, on the Olympic team. Scott was so consistent from fifteen feet, he made that jump shot almost as "automatic" as the lay-up.

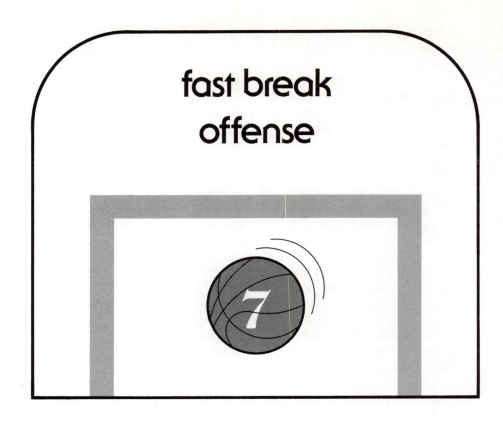

fast break
offense

The fast break often is associated with run-and-gun teams. Admittedly, the offense lends itself to more loss of possession. Acknowledging this, and considering what has been written to this point about our high-percentage thinking, you might wonder initially how the fast break fits into our scheme.

The fast break merely doesn't fit into our scheme. It is a major theme. The break has been an integral part of our offensive design at North Carolina ever since I've been head coach. It not only is compatible with our philosophy, but one of the major reasons we have enjoyed our high field-goal percentage over the years.

When the break, and its *aftermath* (our secondary break), is used to create and exploit opportunities for the high-percentage shot, it helps fulfill our major offensive purpose. We look for it at *every* opportunity.

When the fast break is misused as license for reckless passing and indiscriminate shooting, it fits the definition of run-and-gun basketball. Our teams at North Carolina have never been known as run-and-gun teams, nor will they ever be as long as I'm head coach.

In addition to giving us the high-percentage shot, the fast break makes for exciting basketball. Our players thoroughly enjoy it, as do the spectators. Although a coach's first responsibility is to design a system that will win basketball games; it is helpful when the players happen to like the system under which they're playing. Basketball players, similar to individuals in all walks of life, tend to work harder and excel at efforts they enjoy.

Our normal game at North Carolina is to fast break from every missed shot and any time we do not have to make the throw-in from out of bounds. At the end of the break, we look for the percentage shot. If it is not there, we swing the ball in our *secondary* break. If the shot still isn't there, we fall into our Passing Game without setting up. The *ultimate* objective *always* is to get the percentage shot. Since the break often results in the percentage shot, I can't remember any day I told our team *not* to look for it.

Some coaches avoid the fast break in an effort to make certain their big man is under the board when a shot is taken. Our feeling is that if the percentage shot is not available at the end of the break or secondary break, the ball won't go to the basket anyway until we're into our Passing Game. By that time, of course, our frontcourt men are in good position to give us our offensive rebounding protection.

Even in the few instances when we are employing ball-control tactics, we will fast break for the high-percentage shot from an interception or a defensive rebound. If the shot off the break isn't available, we then set up the time-consuming ball control.

The fast-breaking team often begins to gain its offensive advantage even before it has the ball. The very threat of the break aids us in defensive rebounding. Our opponents must hesitate to jam the offensive board if they know a fast break is imminent. Furthermore, by moving downcourt quickly, we often get one of our bigger forwards matched against one of the opponent's smaller guards. The defense must stop the break first, *then* go to their respective men or zones.

Our secondary break extends this advantage for us. During my first two years as head coach, prior to developing our secondary break, we would set up our half-court offense immediately if the shot off the fast break wasn't available. When we did this, we gave the opposition an equal opportunity to organize their man-to-man or zone defense. The secondary break, on the other hand, swings us from the primary break into our Passing Game without pause. While doing so, it affords us many excellent scoring opportunities by delaying our opponent's intended defensive alignment against our half-court attack.

There are disadvantages to the break, but it is our belief that the advantages gained far outweigh the drawbacks.

One disadvantage can result from players becoming too dependent on the fast break and finding themselves in a game with few such opportunities. This could occur, for example, against a team that is successful in its effort to counteract our break by setting a slower tempo. If our opponent's ball-control tactics enable them to maintain possession until they manage the high-percentage shot, it results in fewer defensive rebounds for us. When a fast-breaking team must make the throw-in from out of bounds, it destroys the effectiveness of the break as we like it. It is then that we must be able to attack the organized defense, work harder, and execute well to create the high-percentage scoring opportunities which come more easily off the break.

As indicated earlier, more frequent loss of ball can be considered another disadvantage. Handling the ball at near top speed as opposed to a much slower pace is bound to result in more turnovers. However, by referring back to our *possession evaluation* analysis covered in a previous chapter, we should be able to put this factor in its proper perspective. The important statistic regarding loss of ball is not the number but the percentage of times the ball is lost without a shot compared to total possessions. A fast-breaking game will usually result in more overall possessions than one which is shortened by ball control. The percent loss of ball, however, may not be necessarily higher. When it is, this factor then can be considered a disadvantage of fast breaking for a particular game.

We feel, however, that since our field-goal percentage is substantially increased through the high-percentage shot gained from the fast break, we can afford the percent loss of ball to be a shade higher.

fast break organization

When playing man-to-man defense, a team can not predetermine where each of its players will be as the defensive rebound comes off the board. It is difficult to fast break unless the team plays good defense to force the missed shot and then rebound well on the defensive backboard.

Our fast-break organization begins with the rebound. We use two methods to initiate the break. The rebounder may either pass to an outlet man, or explode downcourt with one or two quick dribbles. Since the big man usually has more trouble putting the ball on the floor, he is encouraged to use the outlet pass. The rebounder who can dribble well is encouraged to use the explode dribble method of initiating the break.

We want all *five* of our rebounders checking their respective men to keep them from getting inside on their offensive board. Consequently, our guards do not move downcourt on the shot. Since the offensive backcourt men rarely go to the offensive board, the defensive guards are free to attempt to box out a big man and retrieve some long rebounds. Our guards are responsible for filling the outlet zones and insuring the safety of the outlet pass once the rebound has been taken by a teammate. The outlet zone is anywhere to the side creating a passing lane. If the opponent is pinching outlet passes, the guard comes toward the opponent's basket. If there is no danger of an interception, the guard approaches half-court.

If the rebounder initiates the break by dribbling, the outlet guards start downcourt and the responsibility of the successful pass is then on the shoulders of the rebounder.

IMPORTANT RULE: As the break is initiated, our guards are responsible for the ball handling along with the rebounder. Nonrebounding frontcourt men do not concern themselves with handling the ball until they are in our offensive half-court. They simply run a foot race to our end of the court.

Diagrams 7-1 and 7-2 demonstrate the two methods of initiating the break.

Diagram 7-1   **Diagram 7-2**

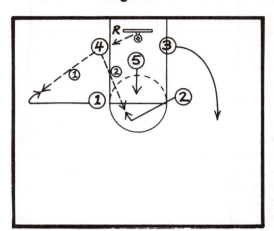   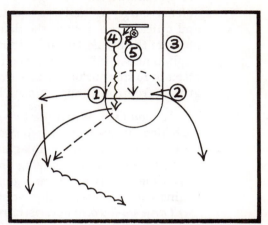

Diagram 7-1 #4 gets the rebound. His first option is to #1, who must be facing *in* as he receives the outlet pass. #4's second option is to #2. #3 and #5 (the nonrebounding frontcourt men in these diagrams) have no responsibility other than to sprint toward our basket once the rebound is secured by a teammate.

Ideally, we want three lanes filled quickly with the ball in the middle. Presuming #1 receives the outlet pass, he should pass immediately to #2 in the middle. If #2 is not open, #1 can begin dribbling toward the center court jump-ball circle. #2 would then fill the wide lane going either in front of or behind #1, the dribbler. The other outside lane is filled by either #3 or #5, depending on which of the two gets there first.

Diagram 7-2 #1 and #2 fill the outside lines as #4 dribbles to start the break. #4 should pass downcourt to #1 or #2 and follow his pass. The guard to whom he passed would take the ball to the middle on the dribble.

Should the rebound fall toward the middle of the court, both guards clear outlet zones to each side giving the rebounder two quick outlet pass choices. If the pass goes to one guard, the other guard does not move downcourt, but comes toward the ball. This gives the receiver the opportunity to pass to the middle where we want the ball.

If #1 or #2 gets the rebound, we encourage him to explode downcourt on the dribble. Should either of our guards intercept a pass, he would begin the break with a fast dribble downcourt. If a pass is intercepted by one of our frontcourt men, the guard *waits* for the outlet pass as he would after a rebound, unless there is no opponent player back on defense.

To repeat again, we want our guards handling the ball, and our frontcourt men sprinting to the basket as the break is set in motion.

Once the three lanes are established and the break is under way, we allow some freedom insofar as advancing the ball. One of the guards will generally bring it toward the scoring area in a high, fast dribble unless confronted by a defensive man around mid-court. When this occurs, he should pass to a wing and quickly run around the defender, looking for a pass back. During this phase of the break, the important rule for the man advancing with the ball is to pitch ahead if he sees an open man ahead of him downcourt. When teams attempt to stop our break as we move downcourt, the pitch ahead rule usually gives a frontcourt man an easy lay-up.

Two-on-One: When the two-on-one advantage occurs around mid-court, we believe in the use of rapid two-hand chest passes between our two men as they move in for the lay-up against the one defender. By using this passing method, as opposed to having one man control the ball, the defense doesn't have time to play a guessing game with the offense. The two-on-one usually begins with an interception or steal, as opposed to a rebound.

Three-on-Two: There is hardly a *typical* three-on-two situation in the scoring area. Nonetheless, we will cover the three-on-two situation in terms of the guidelines we provide our players.

Diagram 7-3 #2 is the middle man in this instance. He approaches the scoring area with the ball. We would like him going to the foul line and taking the jump shot, if he is not challenged. The diagram, however, indicates that in this situation #2's shot might not be the best option. By the time #2 gets to the foul line, #1 and #3, in the wing positions, have hit the foul line extended for the forty-five degree cut toward the basket. #2 attempts to read the defense and passes to either one. When in doubt, we like to have our biggest wing receiving the pass. When the wing gets the ball, he has several options open to him. He may pass to the other wing for a lay-up if X1 hasn't moved back quickly. He may return the pass to #2, who has moved off-center after passing. He may pull up for a jump shot off the board, or he may fake a jump shot and drive to the basket. This drive is very effective for a wing man with ability. First, the defensive men back in a break situation are usually the smaller guards. Secondly, there is much operating room near the basket, without big men there to block shots. The foul can also be drawn more easily since the defense is not stationary, and must move out to play the wing.

Occasionally in a three-on-two situation we'll find the two defenders lining up parallel to the baseline rather than in the tandem defense illustrated in Diagram 7-3. When this occurs, #2 will usually have an easy jump shot from the foul line with excellent board coverage from our wing men and trailers. Should one of the two defenders choose to come up and play #2 at the foul line, one of our wing men will be open for the lay-up.

Many times our middle man will pitch ahead to a wing, who then dribbles to the middle. The former middle man then moves to the vacated wing. This gives us all of the same options described earlier. The wing dribbles to the middle, however, *only* if there are two defensive men back. If there are three defensive men back, the wing dribbles to the baseline which activates our secondary break.

Three-on-One: The three-on-one situation is just about the ultimate advantage afforded the fast-breaking team. It seldom occurs, however, against good opponents. When we do find ourselves with this advantage, we should have little difficulty scoring or drawing the foul ninety-five percent of the time.

Our middle man has the simple task of passing to either of the wings. The pass should be made early but timed so that the wing need not dribble to score. As he receives the ball, the wing begins the one-and-a-half steps for a lay-up. If the defense is in his path, the wing simply passes by the head of the defender to the other wing for a lay-up.

Diagram 7-3

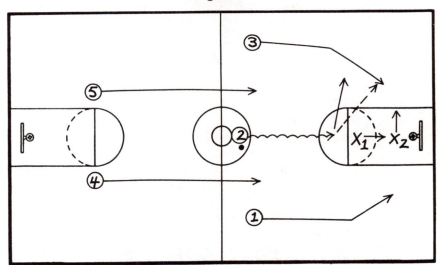

SECONDARY BREAK

The secondary break is most important to us in view of the relatively conservative method we use to initiate the break. As you have noted by now, our guards have some important responsibilities to fulfill before they can break downcourt. Consequently, the fast break will not always result in the two-on-one or three-on-two advantage. When these advantages are not apparent as we approach our scoring area, the secondary break comes into focus.

As illustrated in Diagrams 7-4 and 7-5, our move to the secondary break can be made regardless of whether our middle man or wing has the ball.

Diagram 7-4 Our middle man, #1, has the ball. As he approaches the scoring area, he sees three men back on defense. We might compare this to a traffic light directing our break changing from green to amber. #1 then puts the secondary break into motion by dribbling slightly one way or the other (here going left). This keys the wing to hit the baseline, and back-off to the corner for a pass from #1. #2 receives the pass and takes a quick look to #3, the opposite wing moving under the basket. If #2 can't hit #3, he passes back to #1. The ideal timing on this pass has #3 moving back out of the low post as #5, the fourth man downcourt, moves into a medium post. #4, the last man down the court, moves off center opposite #1 and serves as the key player in swinging the ball from one side to the other. As #4 receives the ball, we officially have moved into our passing game without pausing to shift gears.

#2 generally will cut off #5 after passing back to #1. #1 will move also after passing to #4 as he would in the Passing Game. The last man downcourt is usually one of our post men, and for all practical purposes, he assumes the initial role of high post in the Passing Game. In the event #3 is one of the trailers, he assumes one of the posts of the Passing Game, until the ball is taken to the opposite side. He then vacates the post for either #4 or #5. The move to our Passing Game's low- and high-post areas point out the need to have our two trailers come down the middle of the court on each break.

Diagram 7-5   This diagram illustrates the move to the secondary break after the middle man has pitched ahead to a wing. Here it is the wing who sees three defensive players back, which is the signal for us to move into the secondary break. #2 then dribbles to the baseline, looking for #3 coming underneath. At this point, the move into our Passing Game are similar to those illustrated in diagram 7-4.

Our players are allowed considerable freedom during the secondary break. They often take the shot on the swing of the ball since the defense is caught off balance in their transition between stopping the break and moving into their organized defense. If the intended half-court defense is a zone, some of the defensive players may be caught out of their assigned areas. If it is man-to-man, they may not as yet have picked up their designated men. As a result, the secondary break presents a great opportunity to get off an easy shot.

Diagram 7-4   **Diagram 7-5**

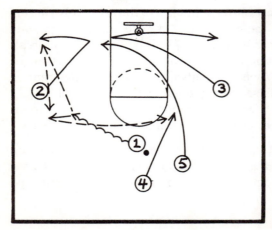
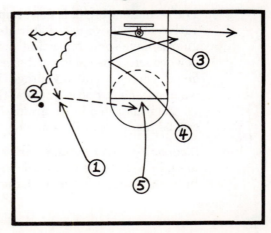

teaching the fast break

We begin teaching the break with the five man organization exclusive of defense. Most of our emphasis at this point centers around the proper methods of initiating the break and advancing the ball to the scoring area. Once the scoring area has been covered, we move into the part-method of teaching the three-on-two, three-on-one and two-on-one. Once a week, we may play the three-on-two continuity game that many coaches use.

Early in the season, we use a three-on-one half-court drill. The one defensive man attempts three things: to keep the three-man offense from scoring, make them use three passes prior to scoring, draw the charging foul. When he succeeds in accomplishing one of these objectives, he may quit defense. The extent of the three-on-one advantage usually is demonstrated by the approximately fifteen attempts it normally takes before the one defender is successful.

FAST-BREAK DRILL

Another drill we use at least every other day as well as during our half-court pre-game warm-up is described in Diagram 7-6. This is a multipurpose, two-ball drill in which the entire squad participates. It provides running, assists the fast-break organization, and develops ball-handling ability at top speed. It also aids execution of the two-hand chest pass on the move, the bounce pass, the lay-up, the overhead outlet pass, and the baseball pass. Although this one drill is designed to sharpen most of the skills required for the fast break, it is not difficult to run. We use it at our summer camp and all our youngsters, including the ten-year olds, run it daily.

Diagram 7-6 #3 begins the drill on the side as though he had just received the outlet pass. He passes the ball to #1 on the move. #1 returns the pass to #3, who chest-passes the ball back to #1. Before #1 hits the top of key, he dribbles to the foul line and bounce passes to either wing for a lay-up. (The lay-up incidentally keys #4, #5, and #6 downcourt with the second ball.) #1, after pausing at the foul line, moves out in the direction to which he passed to serve as the new outlet man.

Note the position of #1 as he completes his move from the foul line to serve as the new outlet. *Coaching point:* Be sure the initial outlet never loses sight of the rebounder and *turns in* so that he can see the entire court.

#3 rebounds the made lay-up and makes an overhead pass to #1 in the outlet zone. #1 throws a baseball pass to #8, the next man in line on the far side. #1 hustles to the line to which he passed. The shooter, #2, continues to the opposite wing line. The rebounder, #3, goes to the middle line.

If a frontcourt man is in the middle line, he follows his first pass to the wing. The wing then dribbles to the middle to assume the middle man's role while the big man takes the wing spot.

We look to generate a lot of enthusiasm and good execution when we run this drill. If a player makes a bad pass or misses a lay-up, he must run up the auditorium steps and back.

Diagram 7-6

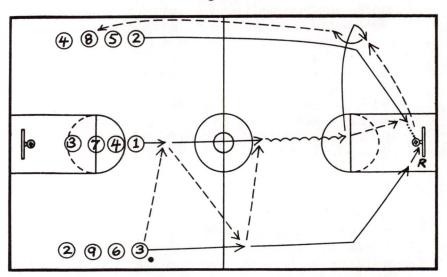

SECONDARY BREAK DRILL

The drill we use for our secondary break simulates an actual game situation and always gives us excellent results. It becomes a highly competitive contest which helps our primary break in the scoring area, as well as our secondary break. When a shot is missed, the drill helps us practice our counter break as well.

The squad is divided into two teams. Presuming the squad consists of fourteen players, the sixth and seventh members of each team stand on the sideline and substitute themselves into the game each time the ball is dead. A manager is posted on the baseline at each end of the court.

Diagram 7-7 The O's are given first possession. The manager passes the ball (as though it were a rebound) to either #3, #4, or #5. In this instance the pass goes to #4. When #4 gets the ball, X5 and X3 must first touch the baseline, two steps away, before they may spring back on defense. These extra two steps simulate a game situation for the fast break. Since X4's man receives the pass, he is not required to come baseline. He may either bother #4 directly or sprint immediately downcourt on defense. X1 and X2 may do anything they wish to stop the break. They may attempt to steal the outlet pass or move downcourt immediately on defense.

With the one exception of requiring two of the defending three frontcourt men to touch baseline initially, the drill becomes a regular scrimmage situation. Neither the guards nor the frontcourt man defending the rebounder are required to touch the baseline. When, on occasion, the first pass from the manager goes to #1 or #2, none of the defending men are required to take these extra steps back.

If the O's come downcourt and score or draw the foul, they get one point. After scoring, they get the first pass from the manager at that end of the court and proceed on offense again. If the O's miss a shot and the X's rebound, the X's move back downcourt on offense. If they score or draw the foul, they will get the initial pass on court.

The action is re-set only on the referee's whistle, a field-goal, or the ball going out of bounds. If it is the O's ball out of bounds, they set up underneath as in Diagram 7-7. Foul shots are taken only when they could result in the winning basket. We usually play that approximately six baskets win, depending upon the amount of time we wish to devote to the scrimmage.

In addition to the specific drills and scrimmages described, much of our preparation for the fast break is accomplished through the work we do on *all* our half-court offenses and defenses. During most our practice sessions, regardless of the emphasis, the defense is usually expected to break.

Through repetition, we become accustomed to quickly changing from defense to offense and offense to defense. Instinctive readiness for this all-important transition is fundamental to the success of any basketball team. It is an absolute prerequisite, however, to the success of the fast-breaking team.

Diagram 7-7

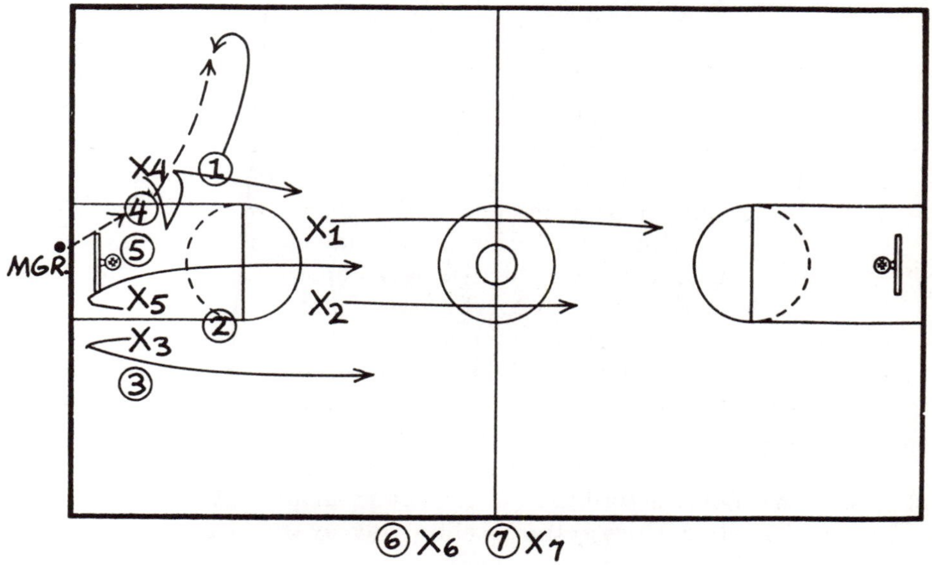

full-court press offense

For many years, full-court pressure tactics were reserved by most teams for the waning moments of a game when there was little choice but to gamble for possession. Recently, however, more coaches are recognizing the value of aggressive multiple defense. The trend appears to be in the direction of the full-court game, and the press is no longer reserved exclusively for catch-up basketball. Some teams, ourselves included, wonder if the offense should ever be allowed an easy time getting the ball out of their backcourt. As this trend continues, it becomes increasingly important for a coach's repertoire to include an effective full-court press offense.

The press offense is not as much a method of scoring as it is a means of successfully advancing the ball into the offensive half-court. Once this is accomplished, most teams usually revert to their half-court attack. Our full-court press offense, however, is designed to take the ball through to the *baseline* of our offensive half-court against any full-court press. By designing the offense accordingly, it gives us a valuable option which is exercised at our discretion. Once at the baseline, we may treat the situation as we do the fast break *or* we may pass back out into an organized half-court attack. The decision rests with the coach, and usually is made before game time. Much depends on the team we're playing, the objective of their press, the tempo we wish to set, and the time on the clock.

When we faced UCLA's full-court press in the 1968 NCAA Finals, we decided to take the ball through to the baseline and then come back out to set-up our half-court offense. This decision was based upon what we believed were UCLA's reasons for pressing as well as our desire to shorten the game in view of their superior board strength.

We felt the primary reason for their press was to speed tempo and give us the open eighteen foot jump shot with Alcindor (Abdul-Jabbar) under the board. They did not appear to be overly intent on stealing the ball and were successful in so doing only twice with their full-court press.

During one game in 1972, as an example in the opposite direction, we set a North Carolina scoring record of 128 points against a team that used its full-court press throughout the game.

Most teams, including the one used in the latter example, have run the press against us when they were behind in the game and gambling to catch up. If the team using the press for this purpose isn't clearly superior in board strength, we try to make them pay for gambling with so many of their men in the backcourt. We do so by taking the ball to the baseline and treating it as a fast-break situation. If the good shot is not available, we look for it as we move into our secondary break before swinging into our Passing Game.

If we are in our delay game when pressed, we take the ball through to the baseline looking for the lay-up. If it isn't there, we will fall into our Four Corners and chaser positions.

MAN-TO-MAN VS. ZONE PRESS

At North Carolina, we do not have a separate press offense for each pressing defense. We have one alignment with a few rules.

When faced with a man-to-man full-court press, most teams simply give the ball to their best dribbler and let everyone else clear out. When the dribbler crosses mid-court, the offense then runs its half-court game. This is usually an effective means of dealing with the man-to-man full-court press. However, most press defenses today are seldom straight man-to-man. They are usually a combination of zone and man-to-man. We believe it is important to prepare for the zone press first and then adjust accordingly when confronted with the man-to-man press. Our press offense is designed in this manner.

ATTACKING THE ZONE PRESS

One of the first problems to be resolved when developing an offense against the zone or combination press is the number of offensive men needed backcourt to begin the attack. Obviously, the less defensive men backcourt, the easier it is to break the press. A one-on-one situation in our backcourt, for example, gives us our most effective press offense. The press increases in difficulty in direct proportion to the number of additional defensive men used backcourt.

Diagram 8-I Since the zone press usually places four men in our backcourt, as illustrated, we feel we need four men there also. We prefer less than four, but three offensive men backcourt does not help us since X5 can play two men all the way downcourt.

The full-court zone press makes the offense use more than one ball handler, unless that one man is so skilled he can dribble around four defenders. Although the zone press is basically a weak defense against good ball handling, it serves the purpose of making the offense use four men capable of advancing the ball downcourt.

Regardless of the type of zone press alignment used against us, we want the initial receiver in bounds (#1) to have three near-outlets about fifteen to twenty feet apart. We want a fifth man all the way down-court to tie down one defensive man, thereby enabling us to play four-on-four.

Diagram 8-1

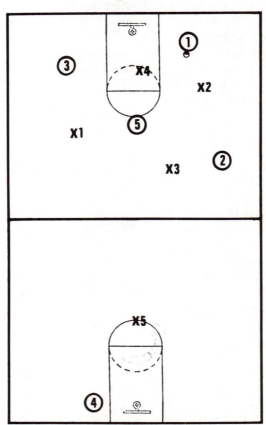

SETTING UP OUT-OF-BOUNDS

The next question to be decided is whether it is best to get the ball in bounds quickly or organize at the same time the defense is setting up. Initially, we took the latter approach by setting up our offense before picking up the ball after an opponent's score. We then realized that, by designating a player close to the board to throw in *quickly*, we could gain a valuable jump on the defense and still organize our press offense effectively.

After an opponent's field-goal, we can quickly put the ball into play without difficulty. After an opponent makes a foul shot, with their players in designated spots, it is more difficult, but still very possible, to in-bounds.

When the quick throw-in method is used, it is best to designate one man (or position) for the job. Pre-selecting the player responsible for the quick throw-in eliminates the possibility of time consuming hesitation, which would defeat the purpose of the approach. A frontcourt man is suggested since he is usually near the defensive board when the opponent scores. The tallest frontcourt man (our#5 man) might not be the best choice. Requiring the big man to run baseline to baseline can wear him out, as well as delay his progress to the half-court attack and the all-important offensive board. By process of elimination, we come down to the #3 and #4 men. We make our selection on the basis of superior passing ability, which is an obvious asset for the job of throwing the ball in bounds. Also, you would want your best shooter at the end of the break (or press offense).

THE NORTH CAROLINA PRESS OFFENSE

Our press offense is illustrated in the remaining diagrams and descriptions.

Diagram 8-2   We diagram our transition from defense to offense in our effort to throw the ball in bounds quickly after our opponent's field-goal. Bear in mind that since we may have been playing man-to-man defense, our initial positions in the diagram represent *possible*, although not highly unlikely, starting points.

#3 rushes for the ball as it drops through the net. He may move to his right or left along the end line. #1 and #5 have the responsibility of getting open quickly to become outlets for #3. #1 generally moves in the same direction as #3 in an effort to become the first outlet. #2 goes to mid-court. Although it has not been necessary for us, #2 can return if he is needed as an outlet for #3 should #1 or #5 have difficulty getting open. #4's only responsibility is to get downcourt and then serve as an outlet for a teammate who eventually gets the ball near mid-court. #4 and #5 are interchangeable, with the better passer in the backcourt.

Diagram 8-3   #3 throws to his first outlet, #1. #3 must throw the ball in bounds with two hands unless he passes to #4, going to the basket. On the #3 to #1 pass, #5 quickly *posts up* or button-hooks into a post position. #2 moves to the sideline in the direction that the ball is passed. #3 slides away from his pass but remains behind #1 in relation to our basket. We are now in our basic shell, from which #1 may pass short to #5, #3, #2, or long to #4. If #1 is double-teamed at this point, one of the other four will be left open for the pass. However, by quickly throwing the ball in-bounds initially, we seldom will be double-teamed since #1 will have passed the ball to the next outlet before a double-team can occur. *Note*: It is important for the initial outlet (#1) to receive the pass a minimum of fifteen feet away from the sideline.

Diagram 8-2　　　　　　　　　　　　　　　**Diagram 8-3**

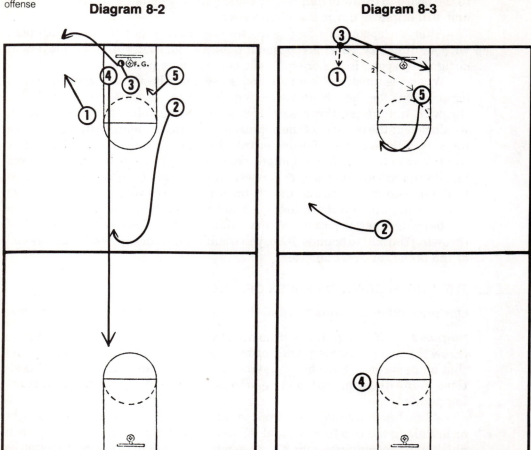

Diagram 8-4　#1 chooses the pass to #5, which we prefer. With the ball in the middle, our options are maximized. We can go left, right, forward, or even backwards if necessary. #1, after passing, cuts hard to fill the lane on his side. #2 posts up quickly. #3 fills the other lane, but moves more slowly to be sure that #5 will have an outlet.

Diagram 8-5　#2 in the middle, becomes #5's initial outlet. #1 is his second option. As #5 passes to either #2, #1, or possibly even #3, #4 comes into the action. #4 must provide an open passing lane to the receiver of the pass from #5. We instruct #4 to be in a line with the ball parallel to the sideline. This allows the passer to know where to look for him. #4 has some flexibility to vary this line depending on the defense. We prefer that he not vary it greatly, however. Before discussing #4's next move, let's go back for a look at some additional backcourt options.

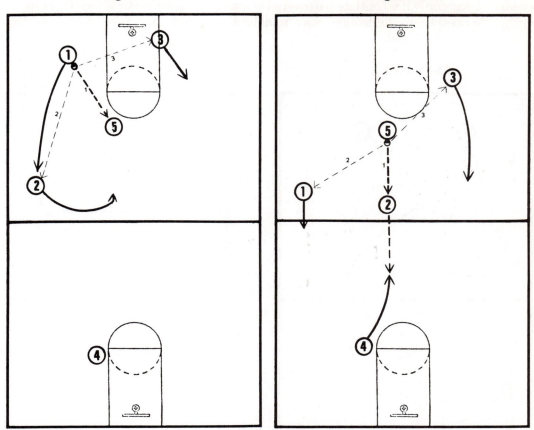

Diagram 8-4   **Diagram 8-5**

Diagram 8-6 #1, the initial receiver of the in-bounds pass, has difficulty getting the ball to #5 in the middle. #1 passes to #2 instead and moves to fill the middle lane as #5 takes the far lane. #2's first look is to #4, who is usually open. If #4 is not open, #2 may pass to #1, or across to #5, or back to #3. If the pass is made to #3 deeper in our backcourt, #5, #1, and #2 must button-hook as receivers in their respective lanes.

Diagram 8-7 #1 returns the initial in-bounds pass to #3 and slides down the outside lane. #5 spreads wide and #2 posts up as logical receivers for #3. If #3 passes to #5, #5 looks for #4, but still has #2 or #3 as outlets. Usually, if two passes have been made successfully in the backcourt, the press has been broken down to the point where the offense should be in complete control. If #3 passes to #2, #4 posts up for #2. #2 can then pass ahead to #4 or to #1 or #5 in the outside lanes.

The above options from our basic shell have all been passing options. We also will pass the ball upcourt against a man-to-man press, if these passes are open. However, since they are not open often in a man-to-man press, we usually find ourselves bringing the ball up the court on the dribble in this situation.

We now must cover the situation requiring #1 to dribble. This is necessary only if all outlets are covered or a soft zone press is employed. This type of
press keeps the defense away from the man with the ball, thereby encouraging
him to dribble.

Diagram 8-6   **Diagram 8-7**

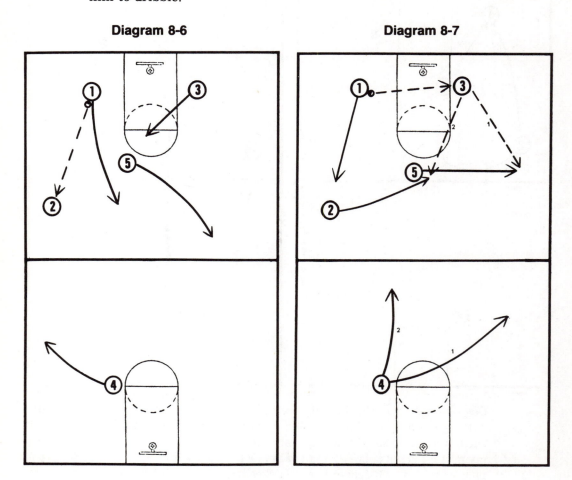

Diagram 8-8 Each man is defended tightly. #1 has no outlets. He begins a
controlled dribble after waving his teammates downcourt. They do not leave
quickly, but keep the same proportionate distance to #1 as he dribbles. The
rule for our outlets in regard to clearing is to come back to the ball if their
defensive men leave them. If no one runs at the dribbler, he simply crosses the
mid-court line and calls our half-court offense.

Diagram 8-9 We show X2 moving back on the dribbler for a double-team. #2
must come back also as an outlet. #5 returns to post up as well.

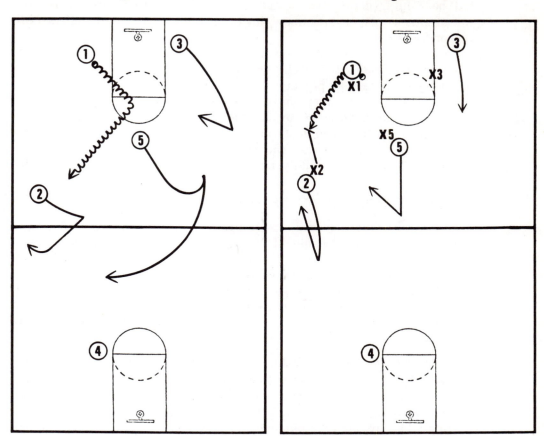

Diagram 8-8

Diagram 8-9

The post up against the press is not new. Dr. Allen used it at Kansas back in the 1920's, and it was part of our press offense at Kansas in 1952. I believe a free-lance press offense is possible if each player knows the value of posting up.

In all of our diagrams to this point, we have taken the ball as far as a pass to #4 downcourt. When #4 receives the ball, our offense should have gained the advantage. Our players continue at this point as they do when the ball reaches our half-court during our fast-break offense. #4 should have an outlet as the players move in from our backcourt.

If no outlet is available, #4 may dribble the ball to the baseline which sets up the secondary break and takes us into our Passing Game. If #4 is not a good dribbler, he is encouraged to look for one of the guards to set up the half-court offense.

Of course, as indicated earlier, our game plan may *call* for us to bring the ball back out from the baseline and set-up the half-court attack. If this is our intention, our players will know this prior to the game and the offense will respond accordingly.

At this point, we should mention that a very simple alternative press offense is available to the coach who is pressed for practice time. If the team is a fast-breaking team, it probably can employ its fast-break organization as a press organization. In other words, instead of rebounding the ball and looking for the quick outlet as he does on a missed shot, the defender takes the ball out of the net (after the field-goal), jumps over the line, and throws the quick outlet pass from out of bounds. The rest of the press offense is run identically to the break. This is effective if the ball is gotten out of bounds quickly enough.

PRESS OFFENSE AFTER MADE FOUL SHOT

The foul-shot situation presents a bit more difficulty since the defense can move into their press more quickly than they can after a successful field-goal.

We use the same press offense described earlier once the ball is in bounds. Prior to the foul shot, however, we want one of our men going downcourt to help relieve any defensive pressure which might be applied if the foul shot is successful. With one of our men downcourt, the defense must have one of their players back to cover him. This could delay their moves into their respective press positions.

Diagram 8-10   We like to vary the man we send downcourt. Consequently, #1, #2, and #3 remain three feet or so in back of the lane in the direction of the sideline. This delays our opponent's knowledge of the man designated for the downcourt assignment. Our quarterback sets the play in motion by signalling. He may, for example, call "31." This will key #3 to take the ball out-of-bounds and pass to #1 in the familiar outlet zone. #2 goes downcourt since his number wasn't called. He leaves just before the referee hands the ball to the shooter. If the call is "12", #1 takes #3's position and throws it to #2. #2 takes #1's position and #3 moves downcourt.

Diagram 8-11   This is a continuation of Diagram 8-10 on the "31" signal after the successful foul shot. #3 is three feet in back of the lane behind #4. He moves in to grab the ball and rush it into play. #1 must block out the shooter and go to the side elected by #3. #4 blocks out X5 and sprints to our basket. #5 moves fast to post up. #2 returns to our backcourt on the side chosen by #3. We are now in the exact positons illustrated initially in Diagram 8-3 on the in-bounds pass. The assignments would, of course, vary somewhat if #1 or #3 were signaled downcourt in lieu of #2. As such, #1, #2, and #3 must learn each other's positions.

If the foul shot is missed, we are in excellent position to fast break since we already have a man downcourt. The rebounder must look to the man blocking out the shooter for the outlet (#1 in Diagram 8-11) who will move to the side in the direction of the rebound.

Diagram 8-10 **Diagram 8-11**

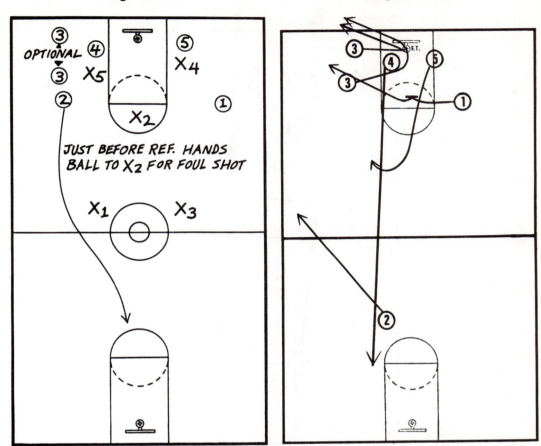

Just before ref. hands ball to X₂ for foul shot

THROW-IN AFTER TIME OUT

We must also prepare for a throw-in on the baseline after a time out, as well as any other situation which prevents a quick throw-in. The formation used is similar to the press alignments previously illustrated.

Diagram 8-12 The adjustment made in this instance effects #4. He is the first man in action the moment the referee hands the ball to #3. #4 peels off the screen set by #1 and races all the way downcourt. #1 then moves to his usual position. #5 goes to the other side, setting a screen for #2 and moving to an outlet position. #2 holds his middle position until the ball is thrown. He then comes to the side where the ball is located. We are now in the same press alignment positions as before.

At this point, it probably is evident that one of the purposes of using a *single* press alignment, adjusted for varying situations, is to maintain simplicity. The easier it is for our players to remember their respective responsibilities, the quicker we should be able to execute against the press.

Diagram 8-12

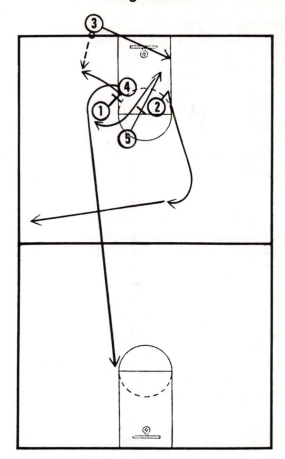

teaching the press offense

We begin teaching the press offense in the whole-method without defense. We then move to the part-method approach, concentrating on one-on-one, three-on-three, and four-on-four situations.

Once the rules of the press offense are perfected, we attempt it against six-man defense. Our teams always moves through the press easily in practice. The sixth defensive man is used to cancel the crowd noise and counteract the adrenalin in the defense at game time.

Eventually, we return to the whole-method approach through regular full-court scrimmages as well as the use of a press offense-defense game our players enjoy.

To begin, we run our press offense in the same drill used for our fast-break organization. The coach throws the ball up on the board and the fast break begins. When the shot is made off the primary or secondary break, our #3 man jumps out of bounds with the ball. We now run press organizations back down the court without defense. The press offense takes the team into the secondary break and then into the Passing Game, unless the quarterback calls another half-court offense. The next team then moves to the court and repeats the procedure. We want the players exercising a different option each time we run the press organization during this drill.

During part-method drilling, much work is done with our backcourt men on one-on-one, two-on-two, and three-on-three situations while the frontcourt men are working on drills appropriate to their needs.

The one-on-one drill is exercised by dividing the backcourt in half with a line from the basket to the center circle. The guard is challenged to advance the ball mid-court in the limited space allotted. If he can do so within the restricted area, he should have an easy time when the entire backcourt is available to him.

Three-on-three work is done at the same time. With one less player in the backcourt, the three-man offense attempts to get the ball in bounds and advance it against both zone and man-to-man pressure. Attacking the double-team also, as well as clearing out and circling back for the dribbler, is practiced during this drill.

Four-against-four press offense *and* defense are practiced competitively while another group of four is shooting at the other end of the court. During this drill, the press organization is matched against every possible form of full-court pressure. A manager assumes #4's role downcourt. The offense may not pass to the manager until the ball has been advanced close to mid-court. The teams alternate on offense and defense. The winner is determined by the number of successful passes made to the manager.

Work against our opponent's foul shot is practiced when the press offense is listed separately on the practice plan. During these drills, six defensive men are used in alternating zone, man-to-man, and combination presses.

We return to the whole-method through regular game-type scrimmages. The press offense usually comes into play as well during the last five-minute game which concludes daily practice.

PRESS OFFENSE—DEFENSE GAME

Our press offense-defense game is alternated with the secondary break game every other day before our water break. Since we have several press defenses, it makes for an interesting game and helps both the offense and the defense. One team begins with the ball at the endline as the quarterback on the opposing team secretly calls one of our defenses. From that point on, it is a regular scrimmage situation.

If the offense scores, they again take the ball out of bounds and the defense calls another press. If the defense gains possession on a rebound or steal, they fast break and continue on offense. A foul counts as a basket for the team fouled.

When the ball goes out of bounds, the team awarded the throw-in sets up its press offense again at the endline and the game continues. Substitutes enter the game after each score.

We usually play the game to between five and ten baskets, depending on the amount of work required on either press offense or press defense. The usual extra soft drinks or fewer sprints serve as reward to the winners.

Our North Carolina teams have rarely been pressed full-court except when our opponents have been behind late in the game. Nonetheless, we feel it is important to prepare our team to cope with any defensive maneuver which could be employed against us at any time by our opponents.

the shuffle

offense

2

Coach Bob Spear (left), Bob Beckel (center), and Coach Dean Smith (right). This shot was taken while all three were at the Air Force Academy. Bob Beckel played varsity from 1956—59. He was the AFA top individual 3 year career scorer with 67 games, 1528 points, and a 22.8 point average. He was named to the second team of the Helms-All American in 1959. He is presently Brigadier General Commandant of Cadets, USAFA.

introduction

BY DEAN E. SMITH

If I had to list my personal selection of the most outstanding basketball coaches in America, the name Bob Spear most certainly would appear close to the top. During his sixteen years as head coach of the United States Air Force Academy, Coach Spear managed the near impossible by compiling a winning record against odds that were consistently overwhelming.

As a specialized military school, the Academy was never in a position to recruit competively. Air Force teams have always consisted of young men who attended the Academy exclusively for the purpose of pursuing a service career. Under Coach Spear, the basketball program was predominately put together with young men who received no NCAA Division I scholarship offers prior to coming to the Academy.

The schedule, however, made up primarily of schools with excellent reputations in college basketball, was always brutally tough. Playing against such teams as Marquette, Colorado State, Wyoming, Colorado, and Texas Western, the Academy almost always entered their games as decided underdogs. Despite the odds, they won more games than they lost. They did it with the Shuffle Offense and good pressure defense, under the expert direction of Coach Bob Spear.

I first met Bob Spear while serving in the Armed Forces in Germany after my graduation from Kansas. I was slated to return to the University of Kansas in a new position as second assistant coach after completing my military obligation. In the interim, Bob, who was retiring from the Air Force as a Lt. Colonel, was named head basketball coach of the new Air Force Academy. He asked me if I would reconsider my plans and join him as his assistant at the Academy. Bob said the situation would not be an easy one. It was a new school and a new program. We also would be lucky to average 6'1" in the front line.

I accepted it as a challenge and an excellent opportunity. I spent the next three years learning the coaching ropes from one of the finest basketball teachers I've ever known. As I think back to that experience, I can't help but wonder what Coach Spear would have accomplished in terms of national prominence had he been in the position to recruit his players as do most Division I schools.

Bob wasn't inaccurate about the height disadvantage we would be up against. Only one of our starting players topped the yardstick over 6'1". He was 6'4". We had to come up with an offense that would give us a fighting chance against the tall, strong teams we would be facing.

I told Bob that we spent more time in defensive preparation for Bruce Drake's Oklahoma Shuffle teams than any other team during my playing years at Kansas. Bob went to work studying the Shuffle and soon he was a bona fide expert on the offense.

In the years that followed, no coach ever looked forward to playing against Coach Spear's teams, despite the fact that *on paper* they were invariably outmanned and appeared to be a cinch to beat. The Shuffle was executed brilliantly by Air Force teams. They used the offense expertly to control tempo and force their opponents to stay on defense until they could break free for the lay-up or a high-percentage shot.

The Spear Shuffle is a disciplined set offense which varies from the original Bruce Drake version in that options off the basic, such as the *split* and *rotation*, are run in set combinations with the basic play. It thereby provides for great continuity going from one option to another. It is a very effective attack as a whole, yet a coach also can take one or two options and incorporate them into his offense.

Coach Spear's outstanding success with the offense was the primary reason we went to the full Shuffle continuity ourselves during my early head coaching years at North Carolina. Although we departed from the full Shuffle continuity when we were fortunate to recruit our first pure center in 6'10" Rusty Clark, the Basic Shuffle Cut is still a part of our offensive design as we indicated earlier in the book. There are free-lance possibilities off the Shuffle which provide both the advantages of a free-lance passing game as well as a highly basic set offense.

For these as well as other reasons, I feel the Spear Shuffle is important reading for any coach, and might be considered required reading for those who are aspiring to enter the coaching profession for the first time.

Coach Spear, regarded by his peers as a coach's coach, describes the Shuffle in the following chapters as well as he demonstrated its effectiveness from the bench prior to his retirement. It makes for a most significant contribution to this book.

introduction

BY BOB SPEAR

When Dean Smith joined me in 1955 to begin the new Air Force Academy basketball program, we were faced with an exciting, yet unique challenge. Desiring a competitive but realistic approach to the game, we wanted to build a program with ongoing momentum, one which would eventually permit us to compete with the ranking powers in the country on a balanced schedule. With this goal as our main objective, we needed a vehicle to propel our philosophies of solid, fundamental basketball into action.

The Air Force Academy was founded not as an athletic proving ground, but as a university oriented toward high scholastic achievement and in-depth military training. Thus, in terms of pure basketball talent, we were forced to adhere to player restrictions not associated with the normal major college basketball program. Consequently, we would be playing teams comprised of individuals possessing better raw skills, and in all probability, would be outmanned physically. Naturally, if we were to satisfy our goal, these disadvantages had to be overcome.

In the early 1950's, Bruce Drake, the basketball coach at the University of Oklahoma, utilized an offensive system based on a continuous series of plays and constant player movement known as the "Drake Shuffle." This offense, designed to use all players in a rotating pattern, must be credited for its substantial contribution to the game of basketball. The Shuffle Offense is predicated on the team concept, on ball control and player movement, and upon a flow of play which provides many opportunities for scoring. Coach Smith, after playing against it while at Kansas, suggested we incorporate the Shuffle into our basketball program. In the years to follow the Shuffle was to become the foundation for our success.

Though our players did lack the size and innate ability of those now classified as superstars, they did possess intelligence and dedication, and perhaps most importantly, an unselfish quality which fueled team play. Also they were excellently conditioned athletes who came to play. As their coach, I was proud to watch them reach their potential in our program, which combined the Shuffle with an aggressive man-to-man team defense, and an organized fast break. This balanced attack became our reward and many opponents' downfall.

The Shuffle Offense has not been immune to criticism and cycles of popularity. Many people, whether coaches, players, or fans, have voiced their opinions on the merits of this team offense as being too mechanical, or as an excuse to stall and keep the ball away from high-scoring opponents, or as an offense which should only be implemented when a coach finds himself saddled with a team of misfits. I take strong exception to these labels. After teaching this approach to the game for many years, I feel I have become an authority on its advantages and its adaptability to any situation. The system will work whether you have less talented players or very exceptional players, and will work proportionately to their caliber. The offense's true positive aspects, though, are its action, its constantly changing appearance, and its confusion and frustration for the opponent.

I would be naive to espouse the Shuffle as the only way and demand that every coach should use it. But believe me, it is a worthy option, an offense which carries with it the entire spectrum of the game. The Shuffle relies on basic fundamentals—the art of passing, catching, positioning, moving without the ball, one-on-one skills, and the sense of team play. It lends organization to your game and gives every player responsibilities and identification. It demands of your program comprehensive attention to strategy, and makes its mark on both ends of the court. As you begin to study the Shuffle's patterns, you may think the offense is complicated, but keep in the back of your mind this fact: every motion, every adjustment, is a simple basketball move which has been in the books from the very beginning. Instead of hapazardly employing them on the court, the shuffle allows you as the coach, and your players on the floor to blend them together in a common thrust to victory.

In the following two chapters, I will present the mechanics of the Shuffle Offense. I will dissect its parts into workable entities which can be understood by you as coach, player, or merely a student of the game of basketball, and then join these parts into the whole where you can see the beauty of its overall concept. I will provide suggestions on how to teach it during practice—specific drills where the players will not only be practicing the offense but sharpening their skills in fundamentals as well. It is extremely important for players to set their thinking in the ways of the offense, to become comfortable with its movement and also to know where their best scoring opportunities are to be expected. And during the practice sessions, these drills will demand improving individual skills.

Finally, as the coach, I hope to offer you insights into game strategy centered around this very effective offensive system. Though every game has its own personality, similar situations will arise which are common to all games, and to which a shifting of gears in the offense can be applied most effectively. This discussion will hopefully allow you to see the many facets of the Shuffle and show its varying degrees of tempo under actual game conditions.

As you read my descriptions, especially in the initial section on mechanics, attempt to visualize the action as it would happen on the court. Remember, as we talk about one segment of the offense, action is simultaneously occurring with other players. Everyone is doing something positive for the offense at all times which, in itself, gives this particular offense its true potential.

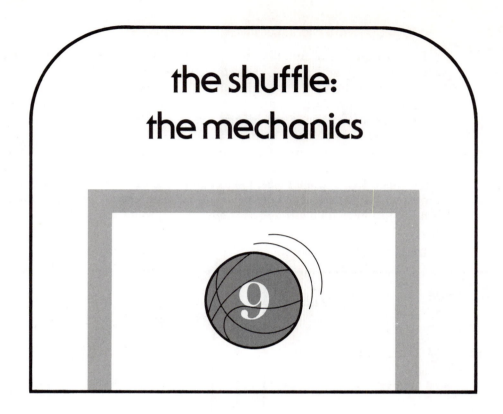

the shuffle: the mechanics

The primary objective of the Shuffle Offense is to score. This fact must be kept first and foremost in the minds of the players and the coach. Every time a player catches the ball, he is presented with several scoring options, the first being his individual move to the basket for a score. The defense must always be cognizant of each player's intent for a one-on-one move. Keeping the defense honest in this manner will open the door for many other scoring opportunities inherent to the Shuffle Offense.

As a coach, it becomes increasingly important to encourage your players to *look* to the basket each time they receive the ball. Whether they consider themselves in their spot, and ready for an individual scoring move, or whether they are perpetuating the offense's tempo, they will be adding a subtle but essential ingredient to the effectiveness of the Shuffle. Even when you are initially instructing the elementary patterns to your players in repetition, you must emphasize this point: Every position is a scoring position.

The place to begin discussing the Shuffle is with the court positions. These positions are an exaggerated overload on either side of the court. As play continuously flows from one side of the court to the other, these positions will be filled repetitiously by your players as they continue the offensive pattern. Bruce Drake called this motions his "change of sides." At the Air Force Academy, we ceased using the terminology of guards, forwards, and center, instead labeling each position on the court.

For the purposes of simplification in these diagrams, we will number each position and they will remain consistent throughout our discussion, i.e., #1 will always be the first cutter. Emphasis must be placed on your players knowing these positions and their names. They will soon click into mind each player's responsibilities in the offense, triggering his scoring options.

The heart of the Shuffle Offense is the Basic Cut. Even though this pattern is only one of many options in the finished Shuffle Offense package, it remains the key to its successful execution. As we define each position and its particular responsibility to the offense, I again emphasize the importance of visualizing the total picture of the offensive set-up, as illustrated in Diagram 9-1. Each definition to follow refers to the position's route in the Basic Cut.

Diagram 9-1   **Diagram 9-2**

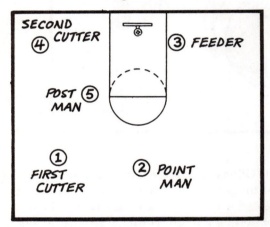
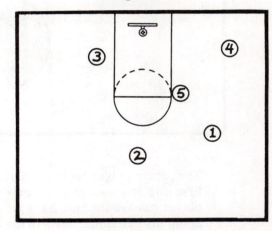

DIAGRAM 9-3: FIRST CUTTER TO POINT PASS

First Cutter: In terms of pure dimension, the first cutter sets up about six feet from the sideline and two feet higher than an extension from the top of the free-throw circle. The first cutter begins the Basic Cut by passing the ball to the point man. His intent then is to set up his defensive man to be screened by the post man as he makes a positive cut to the basket for a return pass and subsequent lay-up, as show in Diagram 9-4.

DIAGRAM 9-4: POINT TO FEEDER PASS

Point Man: The function of the point man is to swing the ball to the feeder, who is on the weak side of the court. The point man's position on the court is anywhere from the top of the free-throw circle to three or four feet higher. In order to insure an open passing lane from the first cutter, he may have to release higher. It is important to the offense to swing the ball quickly to the feeder. To execute this second pass, a two-handed overhead pass is the best technique.

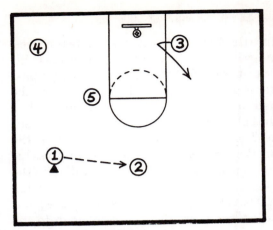

Diagram 9-3

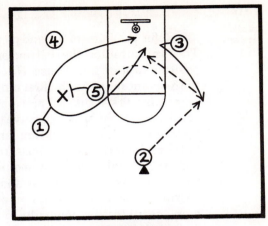

Diagram 9-4

Feeder: The feeder should line up *in-tight,* as deep as the white *bufferzone* mark on the free-throw lane. As the ball is passed from the first cutter to the point man, the feeder should fake inside with his body. He then should release (Diagram 9-3) to catch the pass from the point man, in a position on an angle from his starting point to a spot approximately six feet from the free-throw lane (Diagram 9-4). Once the feeder catches the ball, it is imperative he faces the basket, as now the true scoring opportunities of the offense begin. The timing of the play should be such that the feeder receives the ball with enough time to either make a quick individual drive to the basket, or shoot a high-percentage shot from this spot on the court. This means, the first cutter coordinates his cut to the basket with this in mind as in **Diagram 9-5**.

Before we continue with further definitions of player positions, let me tie together what the action in the offense is up to this point. Since timing is so important to this offense, you now must think about the action of these three players as happening simultaneously, and happening in such a manner as to provide the maximum opportunity for scoring.

Diagram 9-5

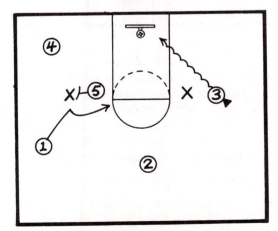

Refer to Diagram 9-1 and picture the five court positions and their names. The first cutter has the ball and brings it across half-court, maneuvering to his position to start the offense. He continues the dribble until he is ready to pass to the point man. As the first cutter is positioning himself on the dribble, the point man takes his defensive man to the top of the free-throw circle, then releases straight back to receive the ball from the first cutter. This move opens up that all-important passing lane. The feeder, who is set up down low on the bufferzone mark, sees the pass from the first cutter to the point man, gives his body fake inside, then moves quickly on an angle to receive the ball from the point man. The feeder turns and faces the basket, sizing up his own scoring possibility on an individual move. The first cutter, after passing to the point man, hesitates momentarily to allow the pass from the point man to the feeder, then sets up his defensive man for a pick by the post man. His full intent should be to rub his defender off on the post man, then cut to the basket and receive a pass from the feeder for a lay-up as illustrated in Diagram 9-6. If the first cutter's defender is expecting this screen and overplays, a backdoor cut by the first cutter is very effective as illustrated in Diagram 9-7.

Diagram 9-6	**Diagram 9-7**
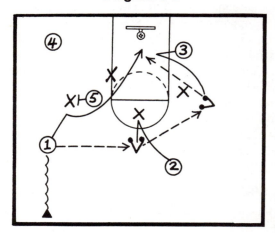	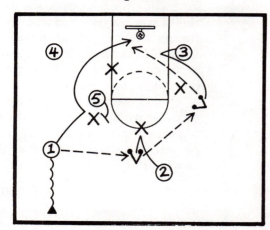

This play action just described is merely a part of the Basic Cut. As you can see, the offense already has provided several scoring opportunities. These opportunities are, of course, a jump shot by the feeder, a one-on-one drive by the feeder, and a pass from the feeder to the first cutter on his cut to the basket for a lay-up. Another important aspect to consider is that each of these possibilities provides a high-percentage shot.

Now let's include the definitions of the other two players.

DIAGRAMS 9-8 AND 9-9: POSITIONING AND SCORING OF SECOND CUTTER

Second Cutter: The second cutter initially lines up in a position in the corner about six feet from the sideline and at least three feet from the baseline. As the first cutter makes his move past the post man, the second cutter releases out to a spot even with the post man as in **Diagram 9-8**. His intent will be to utilize the post man as a screen. In the same manner as the first cutter, he will concentrate on rubbing off his defender on the post man so as to have a scoring opportunity coming over the top on a hard cut to the free-throw lane (Diagram 9-9).

Post Man: The post man initially sets up in a high-post position, just shy of the free-throw line. His purpose in the play of the Basic Cut is to provide an effective screen for both the first cutter and the second cutter. It is important to emphasize to your players the technique of *head-hunting*, which is where the post man seeks out the defensive man on the cutter and maneuvers himself to assure a proper and legal screen. Once the post man makes the screen for the first cutter, he should immediately think about making his next screen. These quick series of screens not only provide possible scores but also continue the rhythm and continuity of the Basic Cut.

Diagram 9-8

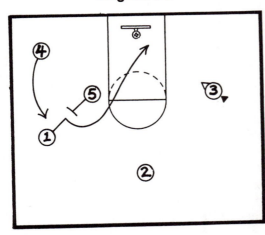

Diagram 9-9

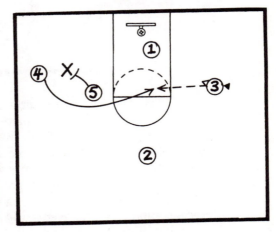

DIAGRAM 9-10: POINT SCREEN FOR POST

After the second cutter makes his cut, the post man will be alert for a screen by the point man and a subsequent scoring opportunity for his shot from the top half of the free-throw circle.

We have now run the Basic Cut. Before we begin our discussion about the continuity of the offense and how it fills in on the other side of the court, let's review the scoring options one more time. I cannot emphasize enough the importance of having your players realize when and where they can score, so they can be concentrating on their route to effect that objective.

The first time through the offense, the feeder is the first player with scoring options. He can make an individual move to the basket or shoot a jump shot from the spot where he receives the ball from the point man. His next option is the pass to the first cutter, who is breaking down the free-throw lane for a possible lay-up. If the first cutter is not open, he then looks for the second cutter coming over the top for a jump shot in the free-throw lane. His final option is to the post man coming off the point man's screen for a jumper at the top half of the free-throw circle. All told, there are four options for the feeder, any one of which will provide a high-percentage scoring opportunity.

Diagram 9-10

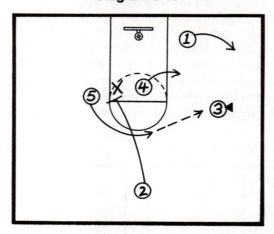

The continuity feature of the Basic Cut is inherent to every play-option of the Shuffle Offense and can be termed the primary threat of the offense. By constantly moving the offense from one overload to a corresponding overload on the other side of the court, and by always interchanging players through all positions, the defense will have serious problems stopping its many scoring threats. Another very important point to remember is: Even if the defense successfully shuts off the scoring opportunities the first time through, or the second time through, eventually a defensive man will be moved out of position, enabling one of your players a good shot to the basket. To defend the Basic Cut, each defensive player will be required to defend his man in each of the five positions, thus putting more pressure on his defensive skills.

DIAGRAM 9-11: PATTERN—CONTINUITY AND RESET

Illustrated here are the routes and new positions assumed by each player after The Basic Cut is executed once. To simplify, consider the following:

- First Cutter-to-*Second Cutter*
- Second Cutter-to-*Post Man*
- Post Man-to-*Point Man*
- Point Man-to-*Feeder*
- Feeder-to-*First Cutter*

Diagram 9-11

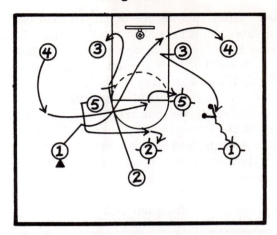

Let us take each man and explain how he reaches his next position.

DIAGRAM 9-12: FIRST CUTTER TO SECOND CUTTER

First Cutter: As the first cutter comes off the post man's screen, he should be ready to do one of three things. His first role is as a rebounder, in case the feeder takes a shot from his position outside. His second role is as a scorer. If he sees the feeder has not made an individual move, he should fully expect to receive the ball for the lay-up. This means he should be prepared to catch, then shoot. His third role is as a perpetuator of the offense. If he does not receive the feed pass from the feeder, he continues on through to the corner position and becomes the second cutter.

Diagram 9-12

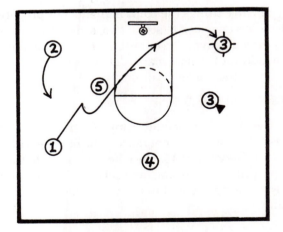

DIAGRAM 9-13: SECOND CUTTER TO POST

Second Cutter: After rubbing his defensive man off on the post man, the second cutter must be prepared to catch the pass for an open shot at the free-throw line. If he does not receive the ball, he then sets up to become the new post man. One of the little techniques which applies to the second cutter is where he sets up his new position as post man. When the second cutter does not receive the ball, he first should set up slightly lower and in good rebound position along the free-throw lane so as to open up the middle for the post man, who is coming off the screen by the point man. Once he perceives that the post man will not receive the feed pass, he then can adjust his position higher, or to where he is in the best position to set a screen for the first cutter as the offense comes back in another Basic Cut.

Diagram 9-13

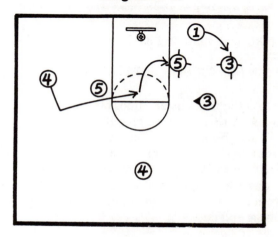

DIAGRAM 9-14: POINT TO FEEDER

Point Man: The five things the point man must be prepared to do, as shown in Diagram 9-14, are one, look to score; two, swing the ball quickly to the feeder; three, decoy his defensive man as best he can to keep him out of the free-throw lane; four, headhunt the post man's defender to set a proper screen; and five, set himself up in the feeder position.

DIAGRAM 9-15: POST MAN TO POINT

Post Man: The post man should come off the point man's screen ready to shoot. If he is not open or does not receive the ball, he will then become the new Point Man as in Diagram 9-15. Once he releases into the point man position, he must prepare an open passing lane between himself and the new first cutter and be ready to swing the ball to the other side of the court as the Basic Cut begins again.

Diagram 9-14

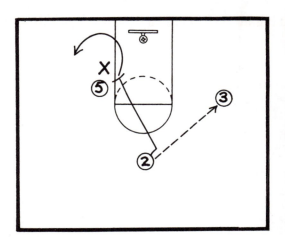

Diagram 9-15

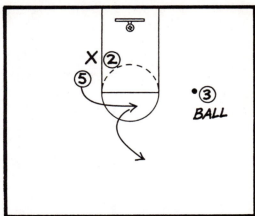

DIAGRAM 9-16: FEEDER TO POINT

Feeder: We've already discussed the feeder's responsibilities as both a scoring threat and a passer making the assist to the first cutter, the second cutter, or the post man as they make their cuts in the offense. If the feeder determines all of these options closed, he backs out and becomes the new first cutter. Notice, too, how the Basic Cut starts all over again with his pass back to the point man. The feeder should incorporate several subtleties to this position for better maintenance and efficiency of the offense. As he catches the ball initially from the point man, he must turn and face the basket to make his defensive man think he is a scoring threat. A good one-on-one stance is most appropriate here. The ball is to be held in front of him, knees slightly bent, feet shoulder-width apart, and eyes on the basket. A fake for the shot or a drive will keep the defensive man off balance. Then, as the cutters make their moves over the screens from the other side of the court, the feeder should look to them, even if he considers them out of position to score. A most important point to impart to your players, which applies to all positions, is the value of not using the dribble unwisely. If the feeder catches the pass, then immediately puts the ball on the floor, he does several negative things. He loses half of his individual potential to score; he makes his defensive man's job easier; and he makes the feed pass to any of his cutters more difficult because he must pick up his dribble before passing the ball. The feeder also needs the dribble to adjust his position to become the new first cutter as in Diagram 9-16.

By following the Shuffle through five Basic Cuts, you will see the flow of the offense and how each of your players will occupy every position. When you first teach the routing of the Shuffle, it may be advantageous to turn over the Basic Cut so your players will know the responsibilities of each position and how the offense flows. If your players work hard at understanding the Shuffle, and if they run through the Basic Cut repeatedly in the learning phase, the routing will become second nature to them. Once they have acquired this state of the art, they will cease thinking about "Where do I go next?" and start looking for the shots which will come at any time and in any position.

Diagram 9-16

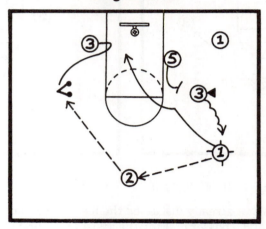

At this point in time, I think it would be best for you as coach to sit down with pencil and paper and become familiar with the routing of the Basic Cut. Take each position and use the diagrams shown thus far to become well acquainted with the Basic Cut's mechanics. Your knowledge of the Basic Cut will give you an idea of the flow and organization of the Shuffle's movement from one side of the court to the other and will facilitate the following discussions about the other play-options available in this total offensive concept.

THE STRONG SIDE OFFENSE (THE SPLIT)

I consider the Split as fundamental to the Shuffle as the Basic Cut. Combined with the Basic Cut, the Split offers a complete offense, and through the repetition and mixing of both, the Shuffle can be a complete offense within itself. The other play-options can be fed into your offense dependent on the progress of your players' understanding of the Basic Cut and the Split and their ability to use these two basketball patterns to their maximum potential.

DIAGRAMS 9-17 AND 9-18: SPLIT—INITIAL PASS AND FIVE-PLAYER ACTION

Consistent with the Shuffle alignment, the Split materializes from the Basic Cut line-up. Instead of passing to the point man, the first cutter hits the post man (Diagram 9-17). After the pass, the first cutter head-hunts the second cutter's defender for a legal screen. It is important for the second cutter to set up his defensive man for the screen by taking him inside toward the basket, then rubbing him off on the first cutter as he maneuvers to receive the ball from the post man for the shot, as in Diagram 9-18. On the weak side of the court, action is taking place for two reasons. The point man and the feeder in Diagram 9-18, are exchanging to keep the overall tempo of the offense intact, and more importantly, to take the point man's defender away from the scoring play of the Split.

The Split provides many positive aspects to the offense. Primarily, it offers another high-percentage shot. Secondly, it keeps the offense in a position to enhance the continuity feature.

Diagram 9-17

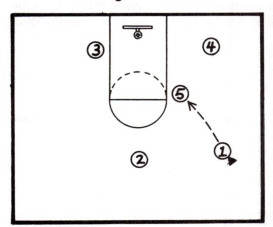

Diagram 9-18

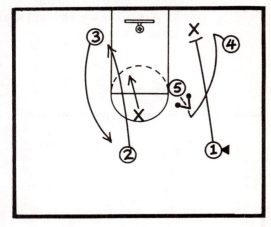

DIAGRAM 9-19: SPLIT TO BASIC CUT

The second cutter, if he does not have a shot, becomes the first cutter and can initiate the Basic Cut by passing the ball to the point man and making his cut to the basket. The first cutter, who set the screen in the corner, then becomes the second cutter and fills right into the Basic Cut.

Diagram 9-19

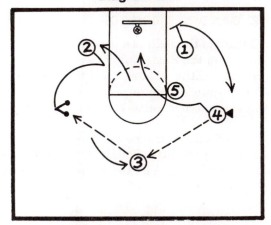

Against an aggressive defense, the Split also gives the Shuffle the option of remaining on the strong side of the court. This helps to alleviate the pressure of forcing the ball constantly to the point man for the swing pass to the weak side (Diagram 9-20). Most defenses will allow the pass to the post man by defending behind the post. Thus, the post man should always be an outlet. Also, as a result of the action of the Split, the Basic Cut will be easier to get into following this strong side play.

If a team tries to front the post man, the basic line-up of the Shuffle will allow for the lob pass to the post man releasing to the basket, especially if the feeder clears the area by making a hard cut to the free-throw line, as shown in Diagram 9-21.

Diagram 9-20

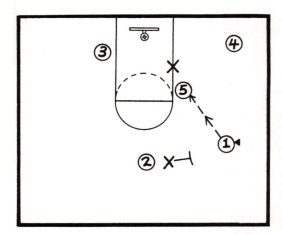

Diagram 9-21

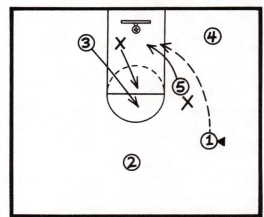

DIAGRAM 9-22: QUICK SWING INTO BASIC CUT

Another feature of the Split is a pass from the post man to the point man for a quick entry into the Basic Cut. The post man might elect to make this pass for two reasons. Either the second cutter coming off the screen has been well-defensed, or he quickly can reverse the play into a Basic Cut and open the first cutter (previous second cutter) on his cut to the basket.

Diagram 9-23 The Split also can be executed from the back side, or the second cutter position. If the first cutter finds both the outlet to the point man and the outlet to the post man closed, he executes a dribble exchange with the second cutter.

Diagram 9-22

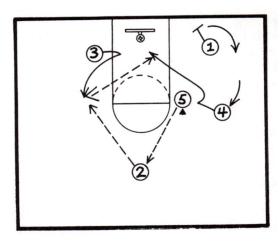

Diagram 9-23

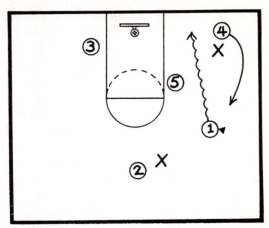

Diagram 9-24 Now he is the second cutter but has the ball in the corner. He makes the pass to the post man, then sets the screen on the defensive man of the first cutter (previous second cutter whom he exchanged with), and the first cutter uses the screen to get the open shot in the corner as in Diagram 9-24. The post man could also make a scoring move after receiving the pass.

Diagram 9-24

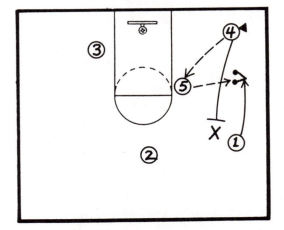

Now you have the meat of the Shuffle offense. By combining the Basic Cut with the Split you will give the defense nightmares and your offense many scoring opportunities. The smoother this offense is run by fluidly executing, for example, a Basic Cut, then a Split, then two Basic Cuts, followed by a Split, then corner exchange and a back door Split, the more bewildered the defense becomes. Right before your eyes, one of the opponents will tire of playing defense and one of your players will be open for a ten-foot jump shot or a driving lay-up, much to everyone's delight.

The beauty of the Shuffle lays also in the fact that whichever play-option is run depends on the defensive alignment. If the point man is being pressured, then you run a Split. If the defense tries to harass both the point man and the second cutter as outlets, the first cutter can pass to the post man, set a screen on the second cutter's defender, then roll to the basket on an easy pick and roll. Nothing precludes individual moves outside the pattern. And once your players have this offense down, and by instinct know where to go, they will be creating scoring opportunities for themselves by changing their movement by a step, or by going wide instead of tight. It gives them a foundation from which to work and, by constantly using it, they will frequently improvise new avenues to the basket.

If any individual scoring maneuver occurs due to an overplay or mismatch, the player must be ready to take advantage of it. It is no sin to break the pattern, providing it is a move to score. This opportunity will frequently take place in the feeder spot as his defensive man tries to overplay the pass from the point man. A fake and a reverse will generate an easy backdoor lay-up (the reason for two-hand overhead pass technique).

To reset the offense once the pattern has been broken is a relatively easy matter. It can be done by returning the ball to the backcourt either on a dribble or by a pass. The closest man to the post position fills it and then yells, "I have the post." All other players adjust accordingly.

the play-options

The following play-options are offered in less detail than the preceding discussion of the Basic Cut and the Split, but each gives the total picture more dimension. If you reach the stage in your Shuffle Offense where you are employing all of them, you will find yourself with the complete offensive repertoire. Then, depending on what the defense does to you, your offense will have a counterattack.

THE ROTATION—(MORE STRONG-SIDE ACTION)

The Rotation is used to loosen up the defense and to counter the overplay defense on the point man by keeping the ball on the strong side of the court. This play-option is an effective way to invert the defense by making the defensive forwards and center move outside while taking the guards inside.

DIAGRAM 9-25, 9-26, 9-27: ROTATION OPTIONS

The Rotation begins with the pass from the first cutter to the second cutter. As with all play-options, this pass identifies the play. Once the pass is made, the post man will screen the first cutter's defender as the first cutter makes the cut to the basket for a possible lay-up. As in the Basic Cut, the first

Diagram 9-25

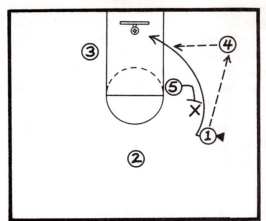

Diagram 9-26

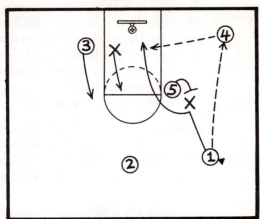

Diagram 9-27

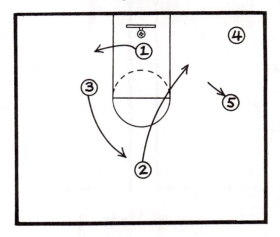

cutter can either make his cut straight line (Diagram 9-25) or a backdoor cut as in Diagram 9-26. It is imperative for the post man to release to the first cutter position as soon as he has fulfilled his screening responsibility, thus opening the middle for the point man to break down into the post man position. In Diagram 9-27, the feeder then *rotates* out to the point man spot and the previous first cutter will go on through and fill in as the feeder. A good play-option to follow the rotation, if the first cutter is not open on his cut, is a backdoor Split, as illustrated in Diagram 9-24.

DIAGRAMS 9-28, 9-29, 9-30: THE DIAGONAL OPTIONS

This particular play-option has gone by many names, most commonly the *blind pig* or backdoor. We call it the Diagonal because the word accurately describes the action of the feeder in this very effective maneuver. Again, this play-option will counter aggressive defense on the point man. When the feeder recognizes the closed passing lane between the first cutter and the point man, he quickly breaks to the free-throw line; this move should be coordinated with the point man taking his man higher and wider than normal as in Diagram 9-28. As the feeder arrives in the open key area, he receives the ball from the first cutter. The point man times his cut past the feeder to be open for the feed and inside shot or lay-up shown in Diagram 9-29. After the point man makes his cut past the feeder, the feeder may keep the ball; he then turns and faces the basket for a possible shot or drive.

Diagram 9-30 While this action, in Diagram 9-29, is developing, the first cutter head-hunts the second cutter's defensive man for a screen. The second cutter maneuvers as he would in a Split for a possible shot behind the post man, as he receives the ball from the feeder as in Diagram 9-30.

Diagram 9-28

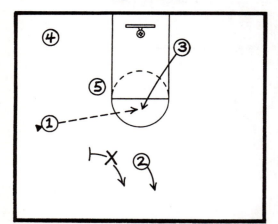

Diagram 9-29

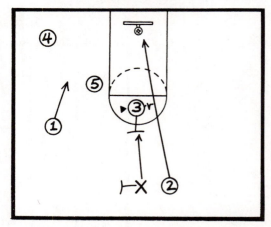

Diagram 9-30

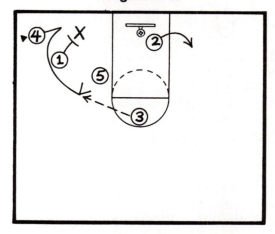

Diagrams 9-31 and 9-32 A variation of this strong-side play illustrated in Diagram 9-31, would be a double screen by both the first cutter and the post man. This opens the middle for the second cutter coming around and the post man rolling toward the basket. If all of these many scoring opportunities are defended, the feeder backs out and becomes the point man and the point man flares out after his cut and becomes the feeder. For a quick Basic Cut, a pass from the point man to the feeder and a strong cut by the first cutter (previous second cutter) should result in a lay-up as shown in Diagram 9-32.

Diagram 9-31

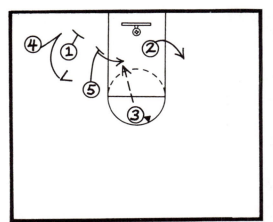

Diagram 9-32

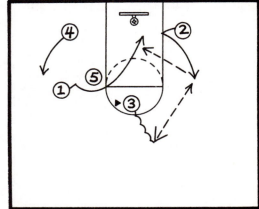

DIAGRAMS 9-33, 9-34, 9-35: THE KICKBACK OPTIONS

Throughout a game, the defense will attempt many adjustments to stop the Shuffle Offense, usually by applying *pinpoints* of pressure on certain positions. We've already discussed three counters to heavy pressure on the point man (the Split, the Rotation, and the Diagonal). The Kickback is an excellent change of pattern to offset aggressive overplay on the feeder.

In the previously discussed play-options, the first cutter keyed a particular play by his first pass. In the Kickback, the point man determines the counter. If the feeder is being overplayed, or if the second cutter's defender is sloughing off to the point where he is clogging the lane, this play-option will produce a score, and effectively keep the defense honest.

After receiving the pass from the first cutter as if to go on with the Basic Cut, the point man *fakes* to the feeder, as in Diagram 9-33, keying the first cutter to continue his cut to the basket. After the first cutter has gone off the post man, the second cutter will make his move as if he is going to come over the top as usual, but will stop short to align himself so that the post man is between him and the basket. The point man then makes the pass to the second cutter for the shot, shown in Diagram 9-33. If the second cutter elects not to take this good percentage shot, he and the post man have a natural isolated two-on-two scoring situation in which the post man can roll to the basket for a close-in muscle shot as in Diagram 9-34. Diagram 9-35 shows the reset in which the post man swings to the corner to become the second cutter, the feeder comes across the free-throw lane and sets up as the new post man, the first cutter becomes the feeder after his cut to the basket, the second cutter backs out to the first cutter position, and the point man remains in his spot. The Shuffle is ready to go again.

Diagram 9-33

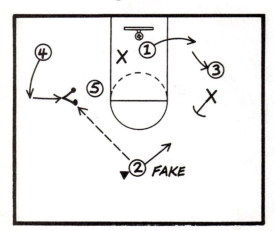

Diagram 9-34

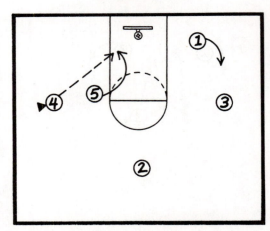

Diagram 9-35

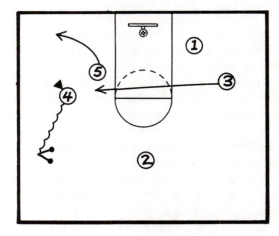

DIAGRAMS 9-36, 9-37, 9-38, 9-39: THE EXCHANGES

Several specific play-options have been offered to counter an aggressive, overplaying defense. Exchanges, on the other hand, merely interchange two players once an overplay is recognized. An exchange is an effective way to prevent the offense from bogging down. In most instances, an exchange will take place by using the dribble instead of a pass to get the ball to an intended position. The other player involved then will *exchange* positions and fill into the offense. For example, in Diagram 9-36, the first cutter realizes an overplay on the point man. Instead of forcing the pass, he simple dribbles over to the top of the free-throw circle and assumes the new position of point man and makes the pass himself to the feeder. The point man exchanges with the first cutter and makes the cut to the basket. Again, keep in mind the importance of maintaining the dribble; it should not be used unnecessarily.

Another point about the first-cutter–point-man exchange is that the first cutter should dribble to the outside of the point man, and the point man should pretend he is only changing places with the first cutter. These actions may lull the defense into a false sense of security. When the point man changes his pace with a hard cut to the basket, he in all probability will get one or two steps on his defender, setting up the lay-up.

Another exchange can be perfected between the first cutter and the second cutter. In this instance, as illustrated in Diagram 9-37, the first cutter dribbles toward the second cutter and the second cutter is handed the ball, freeing himself by using the first cutter as a screen. Notice, too, a corresponding exchange on the weak side of the court between the point man and the feeder. By action and exchanges, your players can open clogged passing lanes and the offense will keep its tempo. These exchanges, as depicted in Diagrams 9-38 and 9-39, can take place between any two players, with or without the ball; certainly two exchanges can be conducted simultaneously.

Diagram 9-36

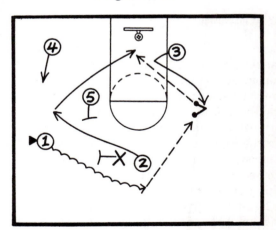

Diagram 9-37

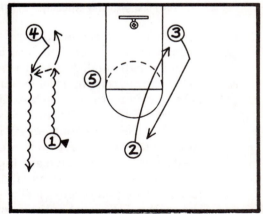

Diagram 9-38   **Diagram 9-39**

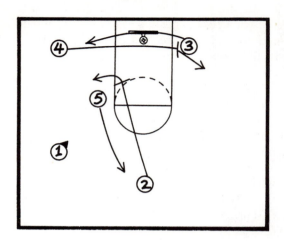

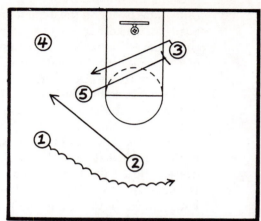

THE STRAIGHT-IN ENTRY

To make the Shuffle Offense complete, we found we could extend it to a full-court pattern to facilitate the generation of tempo as we brought the ball upcourt. This entry was formulated for two basic reasons. First, if the defense was slow in getting back into position, we could beat them down the court and score an easy basket or, at least, keep the pressure on them enough so they would have to think defense even while they were playing offense. Secondly, with a full-court entry, we would be better prepared to combat a full-court defensive press or any combination of an aggressive, pressure defense. Of course, in a full-court situation, the guards, or ball handlers, would handle the ball and the forwards and center would be positioned downcourt.

DIAGRAM 9-40: THE STRAIGHT-IN ENTRY TO A FORWARD

After an opponent score or turnover, #2 quickly takes the ball out of bounds as in Diagram 9-40, and makes a *controlled* pass to #1. The #1 guard (primary ball handler) sets up in an outlet position near the sideline, facing in so that he has complete vision of the court and can effectively move to get open. After receiving the ball on the out-of-bounds pass, he drives up the court with a speed dribble. The forward (#3 or #4) will make his button-hook maneuver so as to meet the pass from #1 in the high backcourt. In this diagram, #3 receives the pass to set the offense strong-side right in an extended first cutter position. #1 runs through and becomes the second cutter, in a position higher than normal. As this action is taking place, #2 sprints downcourt to fill the feeder spot on an extension of the free-throw line as #4 shifts his position to the center of the court as the point man. As the first cutter passes to the point man, #5 head-hunts the first cutter's defender as a quick, more open Basic Cut is accomplished. If the defense is overly pressing #1 as he brings the ball upcourt, he either can reverse his direction and bring it up the other side of the

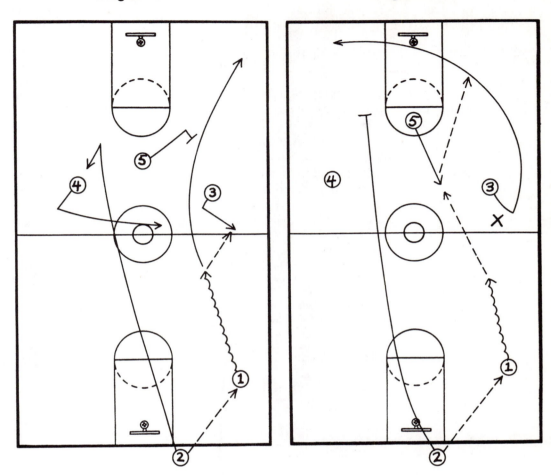

Diagram 9-40   **Diagram 9-41**

court, or he can pass to #2 and let him initiate the play from his side. In the latter case, Diagram 9-40 would be mirrored to the left side of the court.

DIAGRAM 9-41: THE STRAIGHT-IN ENTRY TO THE CENTER

The center must always be alert to help out in a pressure defense situation. If he sees the forwards are having trouble getting open, he should not hesitate to break hard for the middle of the court. He then becomes an outlet and if he receives the ball from #1, a backdoor cut by #3 should be open. If #3 does not receive the ball on backdoor cut, he continues on to the opposite corner where he sets up as the second cutter. #4 holds his position and will begin as the first cutter (without the ball) and #2 will set up as the post man. After #1 delivered the ball to the center originally, he continued on through to assume the feeder position and now should be ready to receive a quick pass back from the point man (#5). This entry again leads to an expanded Basic Cut. As in the straight-in entry to a forward, this entry can be mirrored to the other side of the court and either guard can initiate the play. It should be emphasized that whichever side of the court the ball is brought up determines the strong side responsibilities of the players and how they fill the positions for the Basic Cut.

rebounding patterns in shuffle offense

Now you have the complete Shuffle Offense. But before we leave the mechanics of this system, I think it is pertinent to discuss the rebounding responsibilities and opportunities found in this offense. A team has little chance of winning if it only has one shot at the basket per trip down the floor. Especially in the game today, offensive rebounding is a necessary ingredient of victory. In the following diagrams, we will look at a few of the rebounding positions to establish as several different scoring plays materialize. This will give you an idea of the natural rebounding patterns inherent to the Shuffle.

Some constants to remember when teaching rebounding in the Shuffle:

1. The post man is always a rebounder. If a player has already established himself in this position, he should always be ready to go to the board when a shot is taken; also, if he is enroute to the post man position, he should be equally ready to rebound.

2. The shooter is always the *half-man back*. This means, the shooter's first responsibility is to make the shot and he should have the luxury of full concentration on accomplishing that feat. We have found it unwise to make defense a shooter's assignment because his shooting concentration may be impaired. But after the shot is complete, the shooter then should fall back and help out defensively.

Here are some plays with resulting rebounding assignments.

DIAGRAM 9-42: THE SPLIT

- Second cutter (#4) shoots.
- Rebound Triangle: the first cutter off his screen; the post man; the point man on the exchange.
- Defense: feeder on the exchange is back for deep defense; second cutter after taking the shot becomes half-man back at free-throw line.

DIAGRAM 9-43: FEEDER SHOT

- Feeder (#3) shoots.
- Rebound Triangle: first cutter off his cut; post man; second cutter.
- Defense: point man back for deep defense; feeder after taking the shot; half-man back.

DIAGRAM 9-44: KICKBACK

- Second cutter shoots.
- Rebound Triangle: first cutter off his cut; post man, after the shot; feeder.
- Defense: point man back for deep defense; second cutter after taking the shot.

Diagram 9-42

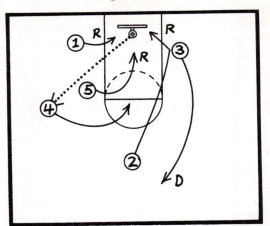

Diagram 9-43

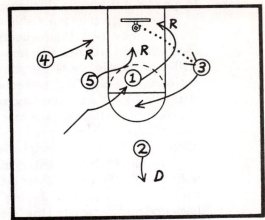

Diagram 9-44

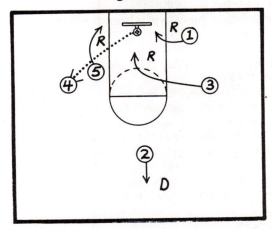

These diagrams give you a random sampling of how the rebound triangle develops and the importance of emphasizing rebound responsibility to your players.

attacking the zone defense

The Shuffle Offense is designed to counter a man-to-man defense. Many times, therefore, our opponents would play a zone so they would not have to prepare for the Shuffle. This admission was a feather in our cap, so to speak. But the strangest occurrence usually happened to those teams whose normal defense was man-to-man. At some point in the game, after playing an unfamiliar zone against our attack (which incorporated so much of the Shuffle movement), they would return to their preferred man-to-man defense. This would allow us to operate our Shuffle Offense against the defense we desired.

Of course, a zone is a viable alternative to man-to-man defense and many coaches advocate it. Consequently, a zone offense is essential. The particular zone offense I will describe here is separate unto itself from the Shuffle but still manages many of the same moves, shot selection, and certainly the patience, ball handling, and rebounding found in the Shuffle. For those reasons, we like it and were successful with it. Coach Smith will offer other approaches to attacking the zone in this text, and perhaps you already have a zone offense with which you are happy and confident. My point is any zone offense can be used to complement the Shuffle.

No matter what we anticipated the opposition's defense to be, we started with the Shuffle to test their defensive configuration. The straight-in entry was very effective in gathering this intelligence. If the defense was pulled back and huddled around the free-throw lane and looked like a zone, we would run a Basic Cut to see if the first cutter was defended by one player all the way through to the corner. Naturally, any surprise element or confusion on our part was eliminated immediately.

Our zone offense has always been predicated on a few relatively simple principles.

1. Begin your attack by filling the open areas of the zone and establishing *triangles* (**Diagram 9-45**).
2. Move the ball quickly with four or five passes to force the zone to match up in a pseudo man-to-man (Diagram 9-45).
3. When your defender is playing you one-on-one, swing the ball and go to an open area on the opposite side of the court (**Diagram 9-46**).
4. Keep your best rebounder in a low post and moving, but not so he positions himself too far under the basket and out of good rebounding position.
5. Maintain a scoring threat in the high post at all times. If he vacates the area, someone else should fill it immediately.

Diagram 9-45	**Diagram 9-46**

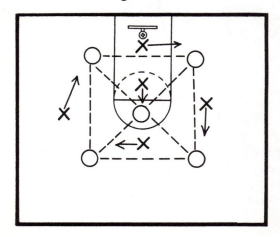
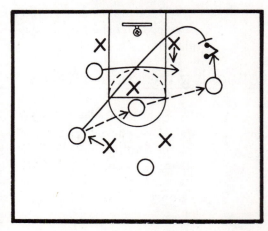

Diagram 9-47

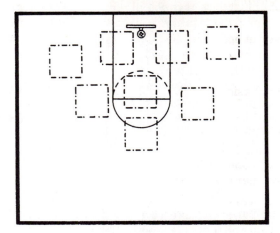

6. Work for the same shooting spots found in the Shuffle (**Diagram 9-47**).

7. Every player should attempt to make the defense think he is a scoring threat.

8. If the zone does not match up but prefers to play the passing lanes, penetrate to force a defender to pick up, then pass off.

the game strategy of the shuffle offense

In the preceding discussion, I have attempted to present a fairly complete description of the Shuffle Offense. As a coach, you can study the mechanics, and transform the diagrams and associated explanations into live action on the court. But we must be realistic. In a book representation, a few liberties have to be taken. For simplification and better understanding by the reader, the material is presented in the context of the ideal situation. The X's and O's are perfectly routed; the defense does what we want it to; and often, the total picture and much of the action is sidelined for purposes of focusing on particulars.

I make no excuses for these realities because I feel each segment of the Shuffle must be understood before it can be joined into the finished, utilitarian product. Once you, as the coach, know the patterns of the offense and how they all interact, you will discover that the whole is indeed more than the sum of its parts. This attribute is the underlying beauty of the Shuffle Offense.

Many variables combine to determine the finesse of your Shuffle's execution. Player quality, their knowledge of what the Shuffle is and what it can do for them, and of course, the tenacity of the opposition are just a few of the major inputs in a game situation. The fundamental purpose of the Shuffle, or any offense, is to capitalize on the strengths of your players by implementing them into an organized attack which will exploit the weaknesses of the opponent, or at least, neutralize their power. With good performance, the Shuffle will certainly do its part in this respect.

At the Air Force Academy, the Shuffle was but one-third of our basketball scheme. Combined with this potent offense, a very aggressive three-quarters court man-to-man defense and an organized fast break kept constant pressure on the opponent and worked to maintain our desired tempo throughout the game. We did not feel we could keep a high level of concentration on the offensive end of the court without a corresponding intensity on defense. We also wanted the opposition to sweat on both ends of the court; we knew the Shuffle would put their defense to task. A pressing and switching defense by our team would require their offense to operate under strained conditions. With our emphasis on the quick outlet pass either from rebound or turnover into an organized fast break (ball handler in the middle, the outside lanes filled for a three-on-two attack) our opponents were forced to always think defense, even when playing offense.

This total concept is successful in the game of basketball. Though mistakes and sub-par performances by your own players will occur, the emphasis on organization and team play (both offensively and defensively) compensates for these recurring problems. Every schedule will have opponents who are "powerhouses," and others who are "push-overs," but the majority of your opponents will have relative equality to your team. And unless you are one of those coaches who is blessed with outstanding players year after year, you are well ahead of the game if you inject organization and team play into your basketball program. Believe me, even the winning coaches with the big superstars have organization in their game—the difference is that they just have more freedom to exert their players' power.

Through scouting reports, most teams are aware of another team's playing style and the abilities of their individuals. In major college basketball, scouting is very important to coaches; it is a security factor. But then again, these universities have the financial budget to send their people far and wide to watch their opponents in action against other teams. In high school, lack of personnel and money often disallow this advantage by a team, and they have to go into games unprepared. This reality in itself should be incentive for a coach to have sound organization and a consistent game plan.

Since we knew a great deal about all our opponents, we were confident in our game plan and used the scouting reports for general information, i.e., defensive match-ups and insight into their offense and defense. You do not change a game plan after practicing it and molding it into an effective weapon. You may alter little things; it is smart basketball to change defenses to match up with the opposition. But the Shuffle, because of its many counters, needs no changes. It is a totally flexible offense.

As I have said before, every game has its own personality. But let's speak generally about how we approached the real game situation.

Defensively, we would begin with the pressure defense *picking up* at three-quarters court. Whether we pulled back into a half-court defense or extended out into a full-court press depended on how the flow of the game was progressing. Throughout the contest, we tried to mix up our defensive *points of contact* in hopes of keeping the other team off-balance.

Offensively, we liked to use the first five minutes of each half to probe the defense. We were subject to scouting too, and every team which played us had some gimmick they thought would stop the Shuffle. Basically, we expected to see one of four different defenses: 1) fundamental man-to-man, with each player maintaining good defensive position but making no overt attempt to prevent passes or Shuffle movement; 2) aggressive man-to-man, with heavy pressure on the ball and outlets, especially the pass from the first cutter to the point man; 3) a deep, sagging man-to-man, or a collapse, into the free-throw circle to jam all cuts in hopes of preventing the lay-up; or 4) a zone.

We emphasized to our players the importance of being patient in these opening minutes of the game; to use the offense to discover how this particular team would combat the Shuffle and how their individual defensive man was playing them. This technique would allow the players time to adjust to the defense and find the options which were open for the good scoring opportunities. Once we found out the defense's weaknesses, we would attempt to take advantage of them as much as possible, while at the same time giving the green light to one-on-one moves. In turn, because the defense had to adjust to those productive options in the Shuffle, we would find their initial pressure points softened and thus, could utilize the play-options which they tried to stop originally. Consequently, the middle thirty minutes of a game were wide-open, yet still organized to the degree where we tried to make the other team play at our tempo.

Except in those cases where you are coasting to a victory, or where you are pursuing a hopeless catch-up game, the last five minutes of a contest are vital and, more often than not, decide the final outcome as either a win or a loss. At the Academy, we felt it essential to seize control of the tempo during these waning minutes. If the small difference in the score favored us, we chose to turn the offense over for several reasons. One, it made the defense nervous to be behind without the ball and they were prone to mistakes, resulting in either a lay-up for us or a foul committed by them. Two, the clock was working for us; as long as we had the ball, the opponent could not generate a comeback. Three, by turning the offense over again and again, a sense of rhythm and control was instilled in our players and relieved some of the tension common to a close finish. Four, we felt we would eventually get the opportunity for a high-percentage shot, one which the players would be confident in making, thus reducing the probability of a forced shot or a low-percentage shot.

If we were behind by a short margin, we would place considerably more effort in our defense and try to capitalize on turn-overs. This is not to say we were in a desperate, crazy press; we maintained our defensive integrity with more pressure on the ball, overplayed any man one pass away, and frequently gambled to set up a blind steal on the pass. We would never shut off the fast break, as we might if we were ahead, and we would use the Shuffle to get those good, percentage shots. Even when we were behind with time running out, we often turned the offense over. Through experience, we found that less time is wasted by working for the familiar shot than throwing up a poor shot and then having to play defense before getting another chance.

Naturally, if these tactics were not closing the gap, we would gamble in every way possible to win—but you don't need a book to tell you how to go crazy in the last minute of a game.

I could tell you some thrilling stories about many of our games but this is not the time or the place. My point in this dissertation is the need to stress organization in your game and practice planning. If you truly have it, you will have better odds at victory and enjoy a successful season. I am not a magician and I certainly do not possess the coveted formula for winning every game. Such a formula does not exist. But upsets do, and winning seasons do, and coaches and players with smiles on their faces do, and title trophies do. And those stories are true about giant killers who somehow take the Big Apple, even though no one knows the names of the players. I think the Shuffle Offense, especially when combined with an aggressive defense, is an avenue you can take to reach your goal of success. It is only one, but a worthy avenue indeed.

I have always believed in the basic coaching formula: Drawing Board + Teaching Methods = Execution and Victory. Many coaches become very skilled and innovative with X's and O's scribbled on blackboards and napkins and reverse sides of bar tabs, or any other available scrap of paper. But, the true mettle of coaching comes when these paper philosophies are transferred onto the court. How well a coach uses his practice time and relates to players— which means how well he incorporates his drills into a comprehensive program—determines the success of his communicative process. If the coach can inject rhyme, and reason, and reality, *and* consistency into his drills, and if these drills serve the common purpose of offering to the players a well-developed scheme, the coach maximizes the time allotted through organization. This organization reduces chaos in the minds of coach and player alike. Thus, when game time rolls around, the team with the best organization, which has been instilled in *practice*, will, in all probability, execute its game plan with finesse and, consequently, have a better chance of winning.

teaching the shuffle offense

Although many coaches are very interested in the Shuffle's philosophy and concepts, they become discouraged with its early implementation and reluctantly abandon it. This reluctance is due to several reasons, the main one being a lack of understanding of how to teach its patterns and the practice techniques necessary to embody the Shuffle into a daily routine. This chapter is designed to alleviate your anxieties about practicing the Shuffle and getting your players *into* it.

Before I talk about specifics, I want to expound on the other reasons why coaches shy away from the Shuffle. I think it is important to dissolve these conflicts now so you can enter into a Shuffle program not only with confidence, but also with a knowledge of what you are up against when embracing this complete offensive system.

The Shuffle is an offense to be used against a man-to-man defense. It can be frustrating to invest a great deal of time and energy to hone the Shuffle, only to be confronted by a series of opponents who utilize a zone defense. On the surface perspective, it may seem to be a waste of time and self-defeating. However, this is not true. The basic principles of the Shuffle can be applied to any zone offense and, by practicing the Shuffle daily, the players will find their scoring spots, all of which will be the same as those found against zone. If you elect to use the zone offense I have already described, you will find an easy transition between the Shuffle and the zone offense. This is certainly a plus factor in a game situation where probability says your opponent likely will switch back and forth between a man-to-man and a zone defense. The quick passing, the side-to-side movement, and the patience of the Shuffle are very effective against a zone.

The time factor has been offered as another reason why the Shuffle has been scrapped. When you only have three or four weeks to get ready for your first game of the season, many facets of the game must be taught in preparation. Hopefully, the drills outlined in this chapter will give you methods of consolidating both teaching the Shuffle and improving fundamental skills. These drills have been designed specifically for this purpose. Many coaches have separate drills for passing, dribbling, running, shooting, for the offense, and for the defense. Since they are separate, more time is necessary to run them all. We tried to incorporate the Shuffle, in one phase or another, in every drill in practice. Our players lived in the Shuffle from the very beginning.

If you are teaching the Shuffle for the first time, or if your players are not familiar with its design, I suggest you keep it simple by teaching the Basic Cut and the Split initially. The other options can come later or can be fed into the system once your players pick up these two fundamental patterns.

Primarily, the efficiency of teaching the Shuffle depends on you, as the coach, to study it, and know it, and display your confidence in it to your players. If, on the first day of practice, you are still hazy on what the Shuffle is designed to do and how to accomplish that design, you are far behind the power curve. Chapter 9's description of the Shuffle can provide you with the expertise necessary to pass on to your players an in-depth knowledge of the Shuffle's nuances. You can then orchestrate your team's progress, and the implementation will be much easier on everybody.

To begin your instruction, I think it is important to communicate to your players what the Shuffle is all about. Describing to them the Basic Cut and the Split in a blackboard session of at least an hour will be helpful. Perhaps an hour a day for the first week of practice will be necessary for this introduction. Their knowledge can also be enhanced by issuing to them playbooks showing as simply as possible these fundamental parts of the Shuffle Offense. This head-start will make the drills come easier and also give them an objective and a mental awareness of what the drills are designed to do. Anything you can do as coach to prepare your players for the Shuffle is to your great advantage.

the basic cut drill

The Basic cut drill is the first exercise to use. This drill emphasizes the first cutter's break to the basket and the movement of the other players *after* the play to fill their positions in the offense. It is simplified by eliminating the second cutter, instead using this position for a rebounder and filler to keep the drill moving smoothly. But still it is consistent with the actual Shuffle pattern; as **Diagram 10-1** illustrates, the rebounder (eliminated second cutter) fills the post man position after the shot, just as the continuity of the basic cut demands of the second cutter. Also, the first cutter will become the filler, or second cutter just as he would in the Basic Cut, except that he does not go all the way to the corner. The other positions should perform in this drill exactly as they would if the Shuffle was being run in its entirety.

As, coach, you should focus on several things as your players run this drill. 1.) The timing of the first cutter. He must not enter the scoring area before the feeder has a chance to handle the ball; neither can he delay too long to bog down the tempo of the offense. 2.) The action of the feeder after he catches. Now is the time to ingrain in your players that all-important *look* to the basket and the one-on-one stance. 3.) The proper movements by all players as they perform the continuity of the offense. Teach them the correct way to make their moves into the next position the first time, so they know what is expected of them. 4.) Encourage your players to acquire a variety of inside shots as they receive the pass from the feeder. In a real situation with defense, the first cutter will not always get a pure lay-up. 5.) The ball-handling. Emphasize to your players the necessity for accurate, fundamental-style passes. We insist on two-handed chest passes and two-handed overhead passes. Wild, one-handed passes will hurt you in the long run. Now is also the time to point out the importance of judicious use of the dribble. Absolutely forbid your players to bounce the ball once and pick it up. Once the dribble has been initiated, emphasize the importance of keeping the dribble alive until ready for the pass.

DIAGRAMS 10-1 AND 10-2: THE BASIC DRILL

- #1—FIRST CUTTER: Passes the ball to the point man and makes the cut to the basket for the lay-up or inside shot. Becomes the filler (second cutter).
- #2—POINT MAN: Swings the ball to the feeder (good technique: two-handed overhead pass.) After the cut by the first cutter, he should go through the motion of

Diagram 10-1

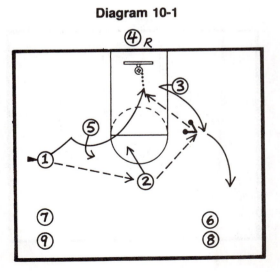

Diagram 10-2

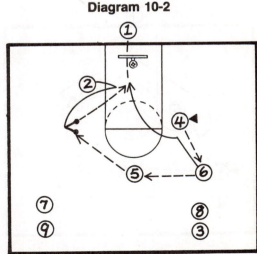

setting the screen for the post man. Becomes next feeder.

- **#3—FEEDER:** Receives the ball from the point man and looks for individual move. He makes the scoring pass to the first cutter, then fills in at the back of the line in the backcourt.

- **#5—POST MAN:** Sets the screen for the first cutter, waits for the screen by the POINT MAN, then goes to the top of the free-throw circle as the point man. Should practice making a scoring move from around the point man's screen.

- **#4—(SECOND CUTTER) FILLER:** Retrieves the rebound then takes the post man position to the opposite side of the free throw lane than the last play. Passes the ball to the new first cutter to continue the drill.

DIAGRAMS 10-3 AND 10-4: THE BASIC CUT PRACTICE DRILL WITH DEFENSE

The basic cut practice drill is an excellent pre-practice and pre-game warm-up. I suggest it be conducted at least ten minutes daily. As the players become more and more familiar with the drill, defense can be added on any position you deem necessary.

During our practice sessions, we placed a defensive man on both first cutter lines and on the feeder. At first, the defender on the first cutter would allow himself to get screened and the feeder's defender would allow the catch. As the skills and execution became more proficient, the defense became more aggressive as in Diagram 10-3.

The opponent's defense will usually resort to harassing and physically denying the first cutter from his normal path. Diagram 10−4 illustrates how we practiced against this defensive tactic. The defender on the first cutter should hold, block, or in some way impede the first cutter's cut to the basket. This action does two things: One, the first cutter will be forced to better set up his man for the screen; and two, the post man will have to head-hunt the defensive man in order to help free the first cutter.

Diagram 10-3

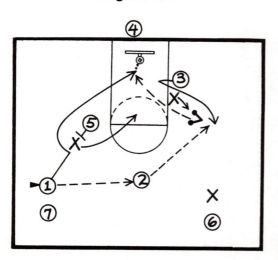

Diagram 10-4

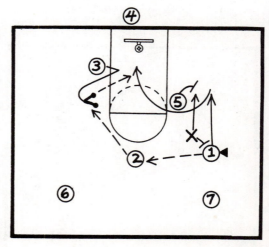

The high-percentage shots which must be practiced repeatedly are those to be expected in the Split, from the feeder position, from inside the top of the free-throw circle (post man coming off the screen by the point man), and the second cutter's shot at the free-throw line. As you will see, these drills isolate these shots for purposes of quick repetition, but the action involved imitates that to be found in the full Shuffle. Again, pay attention to the location of these shots. You will see they are those shots most common to a zone offense.

DIAGRAM 10-5: THE SPLIT DRILL

- #1—FIRST CUTTER: Should be on the dribble as if he has dribbled up-court or has backed out of the feeder position. He makes the pass to the post man, then sets the screen for the second cutter. After the shot, he rebounds, then becomes the filler.
- #5—POST MAN: Receives the ball from the first cutter and looks for an individual move (good technique: catch, then glance over his shoulder towards the basket). He will protect the ball then feed the second cutter. After the rebound, he fills to the back of the second cutter line.
- #2—SECOND CUTTER: As the pass is made from the first cutter to the post man, the second cutter should make his move down the baseline, then come around the screen to receive the ball from the post man. After he shoots, he fills into the first cutter line.
- F—FILLER: This man has a ball in his hand and, after the play, becomes the new post man on the same side of the court. He is a function of the drill only. Once the filler becomes the new post man, he passes the ball to the new first cutter who initiates the play again. NOTE: Whoever rebounds the ball on the shot should pass it to the previous first cutter because he is the new filler.
- Variation: Begin the ball in the SECOND CUTTER position for practice on a back door split and corner shot.

Diagram 10-5

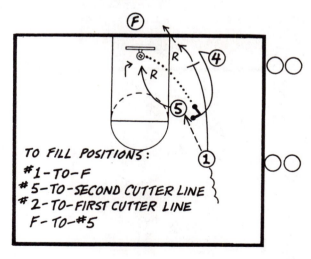

TO FILL POSITIONS:
#1-TO-F
#5-TO-SECOND CUTTER LINE
#2-TO-FIRST CUTTER LINE
F-TO-#5

Diagram 10-6

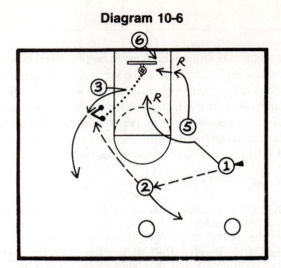

DIAGRAM 10-6: FEEDER DRILL

- **#1—FIRST CUTTER:** Starts on the dribble and passes to the point man. He makes a normal cut, timing it to give the feeder the opportunity to shoot, and positions himself for the rebound. Becomes the filler.
- **#2—POINT MAN:** Swings the ball to the feeder and fills to the back of the first cutter line.
- **#5—POST MAN:** Sets the screen for the first cutter, rebounds, then becomes the new feeder.
- **#3—FEEDER:** Fakes inside with his body then cuts hard on an angle to catch the pass from the point man. Makes a driving fake without dribbling then shoots the jump shot. Goes to the back of the point man line.
- **#6—FILLER:** Has an extra basketball in his hand and becomes the new post man after the play. Passes to the first cutter to begin the drill again.
- Variation: Either pretend defense on the feeder or actually place a defender on him to prevent the pass. Practice feeder reverse, as depicted in *Diagram 10-7*.

Diagram 10-7

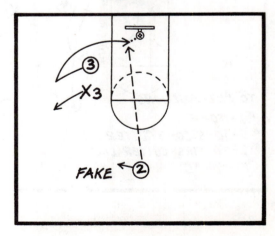

- #3—FEEDER: Starts with the ball. He passes to the second cutter on his cut to the free-throw line. After the second cutter shoots, he rebounds, then becomes the filler.

- #5—POST MAN: Sets screen for the second cutter and rebounds the shot. Fills to the back of the second cutter line.

- #4—SECOND CUTTER: Makes the hard cut to the free-throw line area as he would in the Shuffle. Receives the pass from the feeder and takes the jump shot. (Coaching tip: As the second cutter approaches the shooting spot, he has his hands up ready to receive the ball. He catches, gets set by putting full weight on inside foot as he pivots to face the basket. He relaxes, then shoots. This can be done in one rapid, coordinated move.)After he shoots, the second cutter fills at the back of the feeder line.

- F—FILLER: Replaces the post man, same side.

- NOTE: 1) Whoever rebounds practices a quick outlet pass to the new feeder and the drill begins again. 2) For half the time spent on this drill, run it as described. For the rest of the time, move the post man to the other side of the free-throw lane and execute the drill in the opposite direction as shown in **Diagram 10-9.** This will give your players practice cutting from both directions. 3) Add defense as you deem necessary (suggest defensive man on the second cutter).

Diagram 10-8

Diagram 10-9

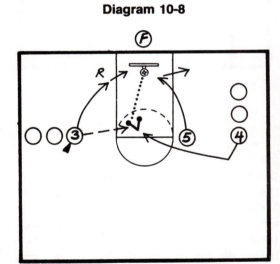
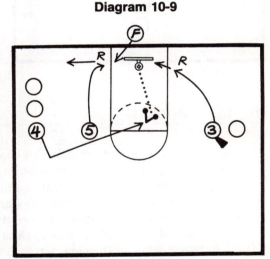

DIAGRAM 10-10 AND 10-11: THE POST MAN DRILL

- #2—POINT MAN: Starts the drill by passing to the feeder. He then sets the screen for the post man, waits for the post man's shot, then rebounds. Fills to the back of the feeder line.

- #3—FEEDER: Receives the ball from the point man, and feeds the post man for the shot. Rebounds, then fills into the post man line.

- #5—POST MAN: Waits for the screen by the point man, then makes a quick cut to his shooting position to receive the pass from the feeder. Sets, then shoots. He fills to the back of the point man line.

- NOTE   1) To practice the quick outlet pass after the rebound, have the rebounder pass to the first man in the line on his side, who then will relay the ball to the new point man. Once the point man receives the ball, he should hold it and allow the next set of players to get properly positioned before beginning the drill again.   2) For variation, (as in the second cutter drill) exchange the responsibilities of the feeder line and the post man line, so the players will have the practice of shooting this jump shot from a starting point on either side of the free-throw lane.   3) Add defense as you deem necessary. (Suggest defensive man on the post man.)

Diagram 10-10   **Diagram 10-11**

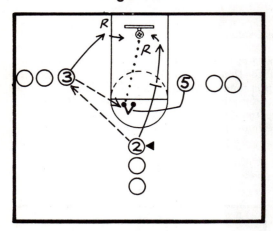   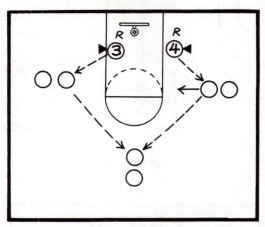

the fast break

I include the fast break in this chapter because of the importance it had in our game plan. The drill we used in practice is an excellent exercise for many reasons, the most important being its authenticity. In a game, we wanted our fast break to be organized; we wanted a three-pronged attack with a good ball handler in the middle and the outside lanes filled. To begin the fast break, we wanted a sure rebound as the first priority, then a controlled pass to one of the two guards on the side court, no further downcourt than the free-throw line extended. As a guard received the pass from the rebounder, the other guard would time a cut to the middle of the court (about the top of the free-throw circle), where the outlet would feed him. The guard would then command the fast break on the dribble down the middle of the court. If the outlet guard feels that the middle of the court is too congested, he should sprint dribble down the sideline to the mid-court line. If there is still no opening in the middle, he should continue his dribble, still unbroken, to the top of the key. The outside lanes are filled by any player motivated to get an easy lay-up as illustrated in *Diagram 10-12*.

The primary player who makes this fast break click is the guard in the middle. It is his timing and finesse which will get the easy score at the other end of the court. After he receives the ball, he uses ninety-percent speed as far as the half-court line. Since he is in the middle of the court, he must be careful to prevent the steal by a defender coming up from behind. Once he reaches half-court, he must slow his charge to allow the lane men to catch up with him and to permit them to make their cut to the basket. This timing should be precise enough to coordinate the middle guard reaching the top half of the free-throw circle as he delivers a feed pass to one of his lane men. This pass, in perfect execution, should arrive to the lane man so he need not dribble before the lay-up as in *Diagram 10-13*. To accomplish this timing, the guard might even be walking by the time he gets to the circle. The guard stops at the free-throw line, is completely under control, in order to make his pass with the timing and accuracy necessary. The guard also should be looking for his own jump shot at the free-throw line. The reasons we felt it important for the guard to stop at the free-throw line were: One, he would not jam the free-throw lane by his own presence, thus keeping the lay-up shot clear for the cutting lane men; two, he would be a scoring threat for a jump shot, thus, one defender would be committed to stopping him and, in a three-on-two situation, only one defender would be left to guard the two lane men; three, by planning on stopping at the free-throw line, he would have the tendency to be in control further back upcourt and the transition from the dribble to the pass, or shot, would be much easier for him; four, the defenders did not know he would be stopping at the free-throw line, but he did, which gave him a plan of attack and a distinct advantage over the defense; and five, since he was in control when he reached the free-throw line, he would not have a tendency to force the play and consequently, if his scoring options did not materialize out of the break, he could just back out into the point man position, let the other players quickly fill into the Shuffle positions to either side of the court and, once he hit the feeder with a pass, we were running into a quick Basic Cut. Many times, we would not get the lay-up or the shot at the free-throw line on the fast break, but because we set up into the Shuffle so quickly, we would score off the lay-up by the first cutter on the first cut. By carrying the fast break right into the Shuffle in this manner, the defense could not let up or else we would capitalize.

The fast-break drill also provides practice on many fundamental skills essential to sound basketball. Passing, catching, running, and shooting, and timing them all at different speeds, makes this drill a practice session on fundamentals. It gives the players incentive to perform these skills well and as they are designed to be performed because they will be performing an exact replica of the drill in a game situation. It is also an excellent conditioning exercise.

Diagram 10-12   **Diagram 10-13**

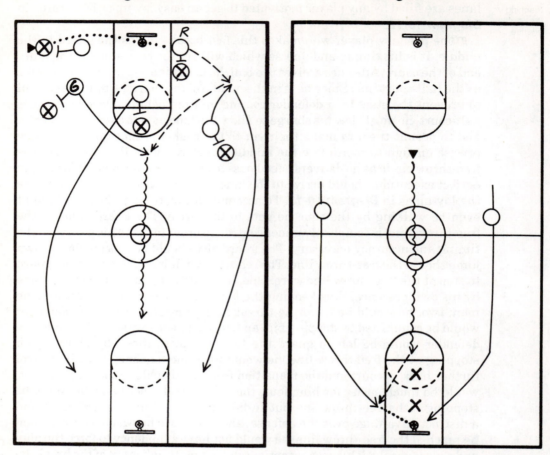

the dummy offense

When using time to concentrate fully on the Shuffle Offense, it becomes extremely important for your players to run the Basic Cut in repetition so they will come to know the tempo required in the offense as they fill the positions in the pattern flow. We accomplished this feat by using a drill called the *dummy offense*. In the pure sense of the word, it was not a drill where players were rotated in and out of play in an isolated action sequence as in Diagram 10-1 and 10-2. This drill utilized five players on each end of the court (with one or two substitutions for each set) and a coach to instruct the proper techniques of the Shuffle.

I think it is important for your players to know how each position is played and the routing to the next spot. Consequently, when you are first teaching your players the Shuffle, it may be advantageous to run five Basic Cuts so every player acquires a feel for every position. After five Basic Cuts, the feeder can make a decision as to which scoring option to use to end the play.

Especially during this early learning phase, it will be your responsibility as coach to closely monitor each player's actions as the offense is perpetuated, to make certain he is making the proper movements. If your players from the beginning understand their responsibilities throughout the offense, they will more easily progress in their knowledge and execution.

To initially set up the offense, I suggest you use your ball-handling guard as the first cutter, as if he has brought the ball upcourt from the defensive end. The point man will be your other guard, and your best rebounder can set up as post man. Actually, the feeder, the second cutter, and the post man can set up the first time downcourt on offense any way you think advantageous according to their skills. For convenience and simplification, it helps to assign a position to each of your men the first time downcourt, or when you first put the offense on the court to practice the dummy offense. In later stages of development, these hard assignments to begin the offense will not apply since your players will be reacting to the defense instead of thinking the Shuffle routes.

The dummy offense uses no defense, hence its name, and focuses strictly on the repetition of routing in the Shuffle. By spending at least ten minutes a day on this drill, the tempo will quickly gather momentum and you will see your players increase their awareness of what the Shuffle is supposed to do. Once your players achieve a certain dexterity in the offense, you can alter your structure of the dummy offense.

When you see your players are fluidly running the Basic Cut through five times, you can then instruct your players in the ways of the Split. At first, run the Split without any other play, and make sure the weakside exchange is being performed. Interchange your players so each of them is involved in the activity of the nonshooting Split and knows what to expect. When they get the feel of the timing of the Split, then combine it with a Basic Cut. Run a Basic Cut, then a Split, then a Basic Cut, then a Split for a shot. Mix the two plays up any way you want, or give the freedom to your players to determine how they want to interchange the two patterns. But emphasize repetition.

DIAGRAMS 10-14 AND 10-15: NO SHOT—KEEPING THE OFFENSE CONTINUITY

The next step in the process is to allow the players to run these two play-options in any manner they desire, and to make any feed pass they desire. But instead of allowing them to end the play with a shot, make them carry the play through and reset. An alternative is, after the feed pass to one of the scoring outlets, then make the first cutter dribble the ball to his next position and go into an immediate Basic Cut, or Split. For example, Diagram 10-14, the feeder passes to the second cutter as he comes into the lane over the top. Instead of shooting, the second cutter takes the ball to the post man spot (his next position in the continuity). A split is automatically performed when the first cutter (previous feeder) sets the screen for the second cutter, who comes around the screen for the feed by the post man. But instead of shooting, he initiates the Basic Cut by passing to the point man and makes his cut as in Diagram 10-15.

Diagram 10-14   Diagram 10-15

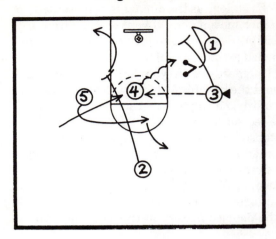
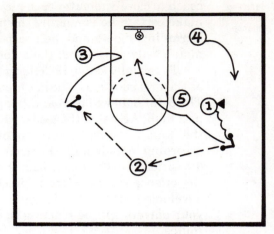

Diagram 10-16   Instead of passing to the second cutter, the post man may elect to make the pass himself to the point man, and the first cutter (previous second cutter) reacts by making his cut off the post man.

Diagram 10-17   illustrates a feed to the first cutter, who takes the ball to the corner, then initiates a back door split.

By mixing up these two patterns and trying to cover all possible options, and emphasizing the reset and/or an immediate entry into another play-option (the Basic or the Split), your players will become well acquainted with the tempo and know how the mixing of these two patterns can be accomplished with rhythm and absence of confusion. The Shuffle is designed for the players without the ball to know what is expected of them as the action unfolds. Depending on what happens to the ball, they should immediately react properly within the offense.

As you can see, the dummy offense is a tool to sharpen the Shuffle and provide your players with a feeling of flexibility within its network. This particular drill also lays the groundwork for putting the offense up against a defense. At any time in the process of instructing your players about the Shuffle, you can add defense. At first, you may only utilize one or two defenders on selected positions and slowly work up until you have what amounts to a half-court scrimmage. But I must advise you to be patient; do not put defensive pressure on your players too soon. Let them at least reach the point where they have a good feeling about what the Shuffle can do for them, and how it will provide the scoring opportunities and the continuity.

I suggest you also incorporate into the dummy offense the *exchanges.* Because these maneuvers are relatively simple, they can be quickly picked up by your players after they know the continuity of the Shuffle. Once the players have a strong understanding of the Basic and the Split and the *exchanges,* you will be ready for a full-fledged scrimmage and soon, your first opponent.

The dummy offense can be a negative experience. Your players may think the offense mechanical, and may feel they are nothing more than robots spinning dizzily through an endless pattern. The purpose of the drill, of course, is not designed to foster these feelings. It is used strictly to teach the rhythm and continuity and give your players the knowledge of how they fill their positions as the offense swings from one overload to another. Think of the repetition as a learning process knowing that the one thousandth time through the Basic Cut, a player's cut will be a reflex action providing the player full concentration on scoring. Though there is no defense present, passes must be made sharply and crisply as if the defense were present. As a coach, do not accept any sloppy passes. Try to command their attention to these desired outcomes, and keep your players aware of why they are performing this drill. You, as coach, can manipulate the drill in any manner you wish to keep the interest of your players, just try and give all your players knowledge of all the positions in the entire continuity system. Executing this drill immediately after the Basic Cut drill and the shooting drills earlier described, your players should know the scoring opportunities will come, especially at the development stage where they are fulfilling the obligations of the Shuffle's continuity requirements.

Diagram 10-16

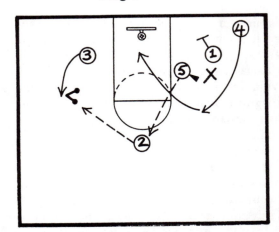

Diagram 10-17

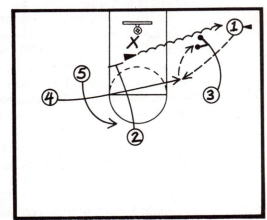

The dummy offense is used to incorporate the additional play-options when you feel your players are ready for their introduction. Like I have said before, the injection of these play-options into your offense will depend entirely on you as coach and upon your feelings towards your players' execution of the Basic Cut and the Split and the exchanges. Or, if you think all the play-options are necessary from the very beginning, they can best be introduced in the dummy offense.

Before these advanced play-options are implemented, you as coach should instruct the optimum times in the Shuffle when these play-options will materialize. By giving your players this insight, they will begin looking for them when confronted with the situation you have described, instead of trying to make one of the play-options go when the action dictates something else. The play-options are designed to counter certain defensive overplays. If the players understand this point, they will associate a particular defensive move with the counter play-option. Consequently, the learning phase for these play-options will pass expeditiously. For example, the rotation, and the diagonal as well as the Split, are most effective against heavy pressure on the point man. The kickback and the Split are best used against heavy pressure on the feeder, or a sagging defense. By letting your players know the *whys* of the play-options, they not only will pick them up quicker, but the execution in the games will be as prescribed.

scrimmage

After several practice sessions spent on the drills already outlined, your players will be anxious to put the Shuffle to the test against a defense motivated to stop them. Once you feel your players are ready, organize a half-court scrimmage.

By the time your players are ready for this phase of practice, you as the coach may have a good idea of which players are the first five. If you do, you might allow them to run the offense full-time against *the second five* on defense, especially those first few times the half-court scrimmage is utilized. Or, if you feel your top ten players are equally proficient in running the Shuffle, place them into teams according to *first five* and *second five*, or mix the players for balance. Then, allow one team to keep the ball as long as they run the offense without a turnover, and as long as they keep scoring. After each score, the team which made the basket again will have the ball and will begin action again from a static position with the defense in place. If the shot is missed, the defense should immediately react to the fast-break opportunity or quickly go to the other end of the court to reset the drill. This technique will eliminate wasted time and create incentive for the teams to run the Shuffle as it was designed to be run, and to take the shots which they think they can make.

At this point it is imperitive to thoroughly explain the rebounding responsibilities as discussed in Chapter 9 (Diagrams 9-42 through 9-44) and the importance of maintaining defensive balance.

In the half-court scrimmage, do not hesitate to interrupt the play if you see a player improperly executing the continuity, or forcing a shot. It is a matter of tact how you handle individual moves. Of course, you do not want to discourage a player for making a one-on-one move, because it is extremely important to your offense. But if you are trying to practice the continuity of the Shuffle, these individual moves may be detrimental to those desired outcomes. To begin, you might not say anything about individual moves and see what happens. If there are few of them, and your players seem to be interested in staying in the Shuffle, then you have no problem. But if individual moves get out of hand (i.e., one strong player has no one who can contain him), explain what you want from the scrimmage while praising him for his ability. I mention this particular *problem* only to warn you in advance.

When you begin using the half-court scrimmage for realism and proficiency, I suggest you have some rules to make this practice time efficient and to reduce frustration. Those players on defense will anticipate what is going to happen before it actually does happen because it's their offense, too. This occurrence is good in that your players will be forced to mix up the play-options more and will vary tempo in hopes of fooling the defense. In fact, the toughest defense against the Shuffle will be your own players. Permit the defense to play aggressively, but at first do not cut off swing passes. This will give the players the feeling of having ten men on the court, and will not restrict their play action to just one side of the court. The term *forced shot* is the only term used to discourage a player's attempt to score when under extreme pressure. Of course, a forced shot will differ for each player in accordance with his abilities to alleviate the pressure. By spending considerable time in this half-court–full-court drill, your players will enjoy the realities of a true game situation.

But before we end this discussion on this valuable learning device, I want to mention the importance of stressing *rebounding* to your players. As you watch the action in the half-court scrimmage, pay particular attention to how your offensive players are approaching the basket for a rebound. Are they getting too far under the basket? Are they trying to establish position on their defensive men, and blocking out? Are the players who should be rebounding from their Shuffle positions actually doing their jobs? These questions will be answered as the half-court scrimmage unfolds and I cannot emphasize enough the importance of rebounding. Watch your defensive players, too. By right of position, they have the inside track to the boards, and if they properly block out, they should get a rebound. For both sides, the half-court scrimmage is valuable for practicing this all-important facet of the game.

The full-court scrimmage is an embodiment of what it's all about. It is the practice session for combining all parts of your game and to give your players experience in a game situation. Don't allow this scrimmage action to get ragged; otherwise little accomplishment results. Then again, don't break the action too many times. In a full-court scrimmage, your players will have a tendency to want to be in control and their imaginations will put them into the game situation where you won't be allowed to halt the action. As in the half-court scrimmage, start with a lot of coach control in your first full-court scrimmage, and as your players and their basketball skills improve with ongoing practice, and as they learn your game plan, you can loosen the reins on their play proportionately.

So there you have it. In two short chapters, you have a very succinct composite of years of labor—some blood, some sweat, and tears, but mostly joy. I look back on those years of coaching the Shuffle and I see peaks and valleys. I can still remember a few humiliating defeats, but I see more upsets and exciting victories, accomplishments which left some people in wonderment. Of course, I cannot say I ever coached a powerhouse to a national championship, but I can say I was involved with a basketball program which yielded much happiness and which molded teams which battled a good number of those nationally ranked teams to the finish. Over the years, we came away with our share of stunning victories.

Let's face it, there are so many little corners of the basketball universe which never receive the acclaim given the superstars and the super teams. Only a small minority of teams reach the pinnacle, but there are thousands of teams who love the competition of basketball, who find their success in struggle. Success is relative—victory is relative.

In conclusion, our philosophy at the Air Force Academy was to play a well-balanced schedule, one which included teams we should beat, others which could be considered of equal talent, and then others which were nationally recognized for their prowess. By implementing our system of both offense and defense, we could keep equal footing with teams which otherwise would have outmanned us individually. Consequently, our players developed a great sense of accomplishment when they found themselves to be competitive on every basketball level. We generally won all those games we were favored to win, won most of the evenly matched games, and pulled off three or four upsets every year from those teams which clearly outmatched us. The "Marquettes" and "Notre Dames," the "WACs," "Big-8s," and "PAC-10s" came to respect us because, for one, they knew we would not be intimidated, and two, our system of basketball would make them work hard for a victory. When any of these teams came unprepared, we would stun them by pulling off one of those unexpected upsets. Over the years no particular game stands out, because there were so many great ones. But I think a good example of the Shuffle's potential, especially when combined with a pressing man-to-man defense, was our victory at Berkeley in 1970 over the University of California. That year, U of C placed four players on the court who would be drafted by the NBA. We had a group of unsung players, the tallest of whom was 6'6". We were able to neutralize their great individual talent while maximizing our advantages of organization and strategy. We won, 56-55, and it was a very memorable experience. Down through the seasons, all our players remember vividly upsets such as these; surely they remember also those very close games which we lost to teams which, during that particular time of the season, were the dominant forces in the game. By participating in such exhilirating events, every participant in our basketball program enjoyed those sensations of the fun of competition, of the sadness and despair of coming *so close*, and of the pride in self and team when they played so well as to pull off upsets no one thought possible.

The Shuffle can do many positive things for your basketball program. The bottom line, though, is that it gives your players unity and it combines their talents in an organized, effective manner. Everyone knows what they're doing and everybody has a part. It is a *system*, and depending on how well it is taught and executed, the Shuffle Offense can be a vehicle to success.

defensive

basketball

3

philosophy of defense

Basketball defense is somewhat unique compared to our two other major sports in this country.

The football coach, for example, doesn't have to worry that his players may put more effort into offense than defense. The two-platoon system eliminates that possibility. The separate defensive unit has a single purpose. Its achievement is measured strictly on the basis of how well it shuts off the opposing team's offense.

The game of baseball draws a less dramatic comparison to basketball in this respect, but the differences are still significant. The pitcher represents the nucleus of the team's defense. His position is prestigious and no one expects much of an offensive contribution from him. The defensive value of a great infielder is also easily recognized. A skilled glove between second and third base rarely goes unnoticed, and often compensates for a weak bat. Other players in baseball are expected to make both offensive and defensive contributions, but the circumstances still are different from basketball.

Offense and defense in baseball are separated by half innings. The team on defense stays in the field until the third man is out. Defensive concentration cannot be distracted by the anticipation of a fast break into offense. Each man knows that he can exert himself fully on defense and still be well-rested by the time his turn comes to bat.

Football and baseball defense differ from that of basketball in another major respect. The defensive goal is clear cut. The object is simply to minimize the number of points (or runs) scored by the opponent. A great effort could result in keeping the opposition scoreless. This is not a realistic possibility in basketball. Furthermore, many coaches, myself included, do not feel that merely holding the opponent's score down necessarily constitutes good basketball defense.

The comparisons between basketball defense and that of football and baseball were used to illustrate the need for two elements which we feel are essential to a good defensive basketball system.

First, we feel that players must be sold on the need to work as hard, if not harder, on defense as they do on offense. Secondly, we believe that a team should have clearly defined defensive objectives that are compatible to its overall goals.

personnel

The value of each player's awareness of the importance of team defense cannot be overestimated. The quick transitions between offense and defense in basketball sometimes obscure the value of concentrated defensive effort. Scoring occurs rapidly and more easily than in other sports. Because of this, players are more susceptible to believing that a letdown on defense can always be quickly compensated for on the subsequent possession. Perhaps it's more convenient in basketball to rationalize inadequate defense with the old cliche about the best defense being a strong offense. Unfortunately, the offense-oriented statistics we have made popular in our sport do little to offset this accent.

Human nature, in general, is such that we instinctively feel more aggressive and exuberant when we take the offensive, as opposed to finding ourselves on the defensive. At North Carolina, we have tried to alter that accustomed role. We believe in *taking the offensive on defense*.

It does take a good deal of dedication and commitment on the part of players to constantly exert initiative on defense. We have been fortunate to have had such players at North Carolina through the years. However, it is still important for the coaching staff to constantly sell defense and stimulate individual pride in defensive performance.

Basketball's offensive skills are easily recognized by the press and spectators. Unfortunately, as we implied earlier, defensive dedication often goes unnoticed. We try to offset this by constantly praising (both publicly and privately) good defensive play. I rarely find it necessary to mention our leading scorer during a post-game interview. Instead, I make it a point to highlight players whose defensive performances helped our team. Our players also are rewarded tangibly for their defensive efforts with playing time.

We attempt to instill team pride in defense. A *team* effort must be required in order to get the job done. The pressing, pressure defense which is our primary attack requires five defensive players working together against four offensive men. We are usually off someone, overplaying, always helping, and always looking for help. Of course, we do assign individual match-ups prior to a game. However, we seldom tell a player that he has the sole responsibility of keeping his man down. His job is to contribute his efforts in an overall manner that will help our team keep our opponent down.

Some coaches try to build individual pride by assigning a strict match-up to one man. If his man scores, it is that defensive man's fault. If a coach is having trouble building team morale, this may be a good defense, since pride becomes a factor. In fact, in All-Star games, I often suggest a substitution for the defender who allows his opponent to score two field-goals. I usually can depend on individual defensive dedication. I cannot say this system is ineffective, if it brings results. However, since basketball is a team game, we would like to have the same pride and motivation as a team, not just individually.

Personnel on hand is obviously a factor that could influence the type of defense used. A very small team with much quickness could compensate for their lack of size by pressing extensively and looking for the steal. This would limit the number of shots, and subsequent rebounds, by the taller team.

In this respect, our dedication to aggressive defense probably stems from my own playing days at the University of Kansas during the early 1950s. Our teams were relatively small then and needed a means of overcoming this handicap. It was during this period that Assistant Coach Dick Harp, along with Head Coach Dr. Phog Allen, innovated the concept of pressure defense, which directs the defensive men to play the passing lanes between their men and the ball. Prior to that time, defensive players were taught to play between their man and the basket.

Our team won the NCAA championship in 1952. We came within one point of repeating in the 1953 NCAA Finals despite the fact that our lack of size had us picked for fifth place in the Big Eight conference before the start of the season.

This same style of defense was used effectively at the Air Force Academy, where our teams were very small and unfortunately, also slow. Coach Bob Spear, whom I assisted, did an excellent job of putting the pressure concept to great advantage despite the lack of good quickness.

What type of defense might a tall team look to play? If a team *had* to use several big men with minimal speed and quickness, they might logically look to greater use of zone defenses.

Coach Frank McGuire, whom I assisted at North Carolina was an excellent zone coach. His 1957 NCAA championship team was primarily a two-three and two-one-two zone team, unless they were playing a relatively weak team. Coach McGuire wisely would play the weak team man-to-man.

However, since our defensive philosophy is based on initiating the action on defense, we have avoided extensive use of zones. They do have excellent value for us when we use them sporadically to change our look. The zone can also be used to alter tempo, and we will go to them at certain strategic points in the game. We made better use of the zone during the 1974–75 season than at any other time. Generally, however, it is used late in the game.

Rebounding is certainly an important part of defense. However, I do not feel as some coaches do, that the zone provides for better rebounding coverage.

I think it is much easier to box out for position when playing man-to-man.

The best way to limit an opposing team to one shot is with a sagging man-to-man defense, having the defense stay between their men and the basket. This gives the defense inside position when a shot is taken. Pressure man-to-man is better than a zone for rebounding, however, in my opinion.

We also feel that much can be done to teach and greatly enhance most players defensive skills, regardless of their physical limitations. We have had some tall players at North Carolina who were not blessed with great quickness or speed. Many, such as Rusty Clark and Mitch Kupchak, became outstanding pressing specialists, because they used their intelligence and put forth the necessary effort to improve their defensive abilities. Bobby Jones, who was big and had great quickness as well, was one of the finest defensive players we ever coached.

Knowing how strongly we feel about defense, some coaches have asked me if we devote more practice time to defense than offense. We do not. However, if I were coaching at either the high school or especially the junior high school level, I would be very much inclined in that direction. I would even go as far as to say that at the junior high level most games probably could be won exclusively on defense, especially a good pressing defense.

Ball-handling skills are far from fully developed at this age. Most youngsters at this level still dribble the ball with their eyes towards the floor. Defensive ability, on the other hand, is not as much a natural skill as a *practiced* one. Consequently, a well-coached, aggressive defense should have a decided edge over an equally well-coached offense. This same principle would apply to a proportionately lesser extent at the high school level.

We do feel, therefore, that most of the defensive concepts covered in this chapter can be used to very good advantage at the secondary level. Unfortunately, coaches at these levels rarely get the help or the credit they deserve. These men and women are often instrumental in shaping the futures of potentially outstanding players. Youngsters who aspire to higher levels of attainment on the basketball court could be at a considerable advantage if they are exposed to a defensive-oriented coach at an early age.

determining defensive goals

At coaching clinics, I'm sometimes asked my opinion of the NCAA statistic which attempts to rate defensive leaders by averaging the total points scored against its member teams. I have to admit this is a pet peeve of mine. As I indicated earlier, I do not believe the quality of a team's defensive ability can be gauged this way. Obviously, any team can do much to limit their opponent's total points merely by exercising ball control on offense. This is not to say that there aren't many fine ball-control teams which in fact do play fine defense. However, as a better basis of understanding our defensive philosophy we should refer back to our discussion of *possession evaluation*.

Possession evaluation serves as the basic statistical criteria we use to determine our major offensive and defensive objectives. Our goals are to exceed .85 points per possession on offense and keep our opponents below .75 points per possession through our defensive efforts. The extent to which we minimize our opponent's points per possession (as opposed to total points) is the criteria we use to determine how well we are playing defensively.

There are several ways a team could go about decreasing the opponent's points per possession. One would be to place all emphasis on lowering the other team's field-goal percentage. This could be done by attempting to limit the opponent to the low-percentage shot. Although this is one of our aims, we probably allow our opponent a slightly higher field-goal percentage as a result of our pressure defense, which is designed to maximize the opponent's loss of ball.

We feel the slight percentage we give away here comes back to us in dividends. When we are successful at forcing the turnover, we not only lower our opponent's points per possession, which is our ultimate defensive goal, we frequently increase our own points per possession at the same time. As we stated in Chapter 1, *Philosophy of Offense*, our high field-goal percentage over the years is largely a factor of our pressure defense resulting in many easy baskets provided through the fast break.

Consequently, our defensive philosophy compliments the type of overall tempo we usually like to establish, and is designed to help us achieve our *total* objectives. As is the case with good offense, there are many ways good defense can be employed. We never want to convey the impression that we feel our methods are necessarily best. Hopefully, however, our approaches to the game are in the best interests of our overall objectives. This, we believe, is what every coach individually should strive to accomplish.

ACTION VERSUS ACTION VERSUS REACTION

The principle upon which we pursue our defensive goals is best illustrated through the action vs. reaction theory. You can demonstrate this theory, as I sometimes do at clinics, with the old dollar bill trick.

If you hold a bill between your thumb and forefinger and challenge your opponent to catch it the moment you drop it, you will win most of the time. Your opponent may put his hand half-way up on the bill which, seemingly, gives him time to catch it. However, unless he guesses, he very seldom would catch the dollar bill before it drops through his fingers. Your opponent will be reacting to your acting and the actor usually has the edge over the reactor.

Many defenses are predicated on reacting to the action initiated by the offense. Our aim, as we indicated earlier, is to initiate the action on *defense*, and force the offense to react to us. By keeping our opponents busy trying to work their way out of our defensive attack, we hope to prevent them from doing what they want to do and generally do best.

We believe that defense dictates the game and is certainly a big part of our offense. Obviously, coaches cannot say before a certain game, "Tonight we will play a zone offense," when, in fact, the defense may be man-to-man. However, the defense can take the initiative and say, "Tonight we will play a man-to-man defense, or a zone, or a pressing defense." It may be good to point this out to the team and say that what we do defensively will affect our offense greatly.

MULTIPLE SYSTEM

Since change necessitates more reaction than a constant, we find that one of the best ways to keep the offense reacting is through multiple defense.

Let's go back to the example of baseball. The pitcher must keep the batter guessing. If he has nothing but his fast ball working for him on a particular day, he'll find himself in trouble as soon as the batters adjust their timing to his speed. The manager may then bring in a junk-ball pitcher who will use his slow stuff to catch the batters ahead on their swing. Once they get accustomed to his delivery, another fast ball pitcher exits the bullpen and the batters must adjust again.

We feel the same principle of *change for change sake* applies to basketball defense. Our 20 defense (pressure man-to-man) is our basic defense. We use it most of the time and we do work towards executing it well. Our other defenses are thrown in strictly for their change of pace value. We do not devote much practice time to them. Consequently, their execution often leaves something to be desired. Yet we frequently get amazing results with these *junk* defenses strictly because the offense is unaccustomed to the look and caught off-balance.

In 1972 Coach Eddie Sutton (then with Creighton, more recently with Arkansas) and Coach Bobby Knight of Indiana visited our campus to discuss basketball. After looking at our films, each suggested that we might lose some of our execution with our 20 defense by adding our *30* (run-and-jump) and *40* (Combination man-to-man and zone) defenses. I agreed with them that we might not be as sharp with our 20 by adding the 30 and 40, but we felt the change far outweighed that disadvantage. In recent years, both Coach Sutton and Coach Knight have given their players the prerogative to *jump the dribbler* within their basic man-to-man pressure defense.

Actually, many teams are already somewhat multiple in their defense. Changing zone defenses, for example, have been commonplace for many years. A team would start out in a one-three-one zone, but if the offense begins hitting shots from the corners the coach may switch to a two-three alignment.

All teams are usually prepared to switch defenses if the opponent begins hurting them badly. We would rather not wait for this to happen. Therefore we carry the concept of multiple defense one step further by alternating defenses throughout the game. This way our opponents seldom get accustomed to any one look.

The multiple system also has a side benefit of helping our offensive preparation. By working several defenses in practice, we simultaneously expose our offense to a number of defensive looks we may see in an opponent. As a result we rarely have to devote valuable practice time to simulating a defense in preparation for a particular team.

North Carolina defenses and the numbering system we use to differentiate between them are charted in **Diagram 11-1.**

Diagram 11-1

NORTH CAROLINA DEFENSES AND NUMBERING SYSTEM

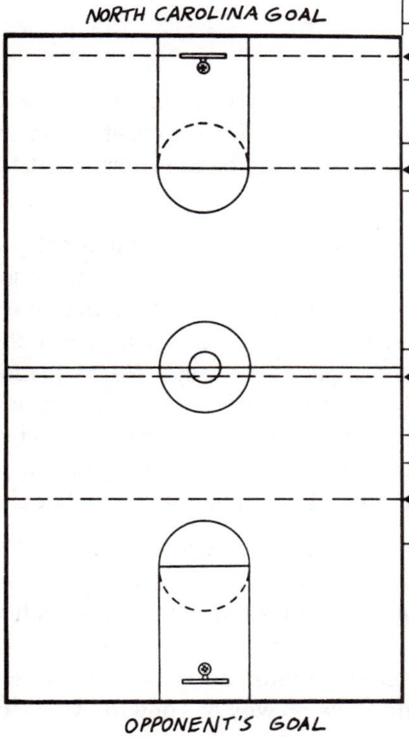

NORTH CAROLINA GOAL

OPPONENT'S GOAL

	DEFENSIVE POINT OF ATTACK INDICATED BY ARROWS BELOW	INDIVIDUAL DEFENSES			
		20 DEFENSE	30 DEFENSE	40 DEFENSE	50 DEFENSE
		LINE UP MAN TO MAN			
		STRAIGHT MAN TO MAN PRESSURE	RUN AND JUMP	COMBINATION MAN AND ZONE	PURE ZONE
←		24	34	44	54
←		23	33	43	53
←		22 FAST BREAK DEFENSE	32	42	52
←		21 SAGGING MAN-TO-MAN			51 PURE ZONE BACK

At first glance it may look as though we have as many as fourteen different defenses. The system, however, is not nearly as complex as it initially appears. Our freshmen have little difficulty picking it up within the first six weeks of pre-season practice. Bob McAdoo, the only junior college transfer we ever recruited at North Carolina, didn't have much difficulty picking up the defense during our pre-season practice. Bob, of course, was an outstanding player and has achieved enormous success in the NBA.

There are basically only four defenses in our multiple system. Each of these is identified by the first digit of every number on the chart. The second digit refers only to the point on the court at which we will use that particular defense to pick up the offense. The zones (*50* defense) will vary more than the 20, 30, or 40 with the second digit.

When *4* is used as a second digit it signals *total pressure—prevent the in-bounds pass*. Using *3* as the second digit number would key our defense to pick up the offense at three-quarters court. Using *2* would have us initiating the defense at half-court, and "*1*" would key us to apply the defense as the opponent begins to set up in its frontcourt. For example, if number 23 were called, our players would look to initiate our straight man-to-man pressure (identified by the number 2) at three-quarters court (3). We would remain in 20 defense until the opponent lost possession of the basketball or the clock was stopped.

INDIVIDUAL DEFENSES

The basic defenses used in our system are identified by the numbers 20, 30, 40, and 50. We have devoted a separate chapter to each of these defenses in this section of the book. However, a brief description may be appropriate at this point.

20 Defense   The 20 defense is our straight man-to-man pressure defense. It is the heart of our defense and the attack we use predominately. The defense is designated to prevent the opponent from running its intended offense. We do this by overplaying the offensive players in an effort to direct them where they do not wish to go. We act, and try to force the opponent to react. We try to move the ball handler to the sideline, and attempt to cut off the perimeter pass, thereby preventing the pass to the player who is one pass away from the ball. At the same time, we want to be ready to support on any dribble penetration by the opponent. Most of our defensive practice time is spent on 20 defense.

30 Defense   We refer to our 30 defense as *run-and-jump*. It is a rotating man-to-man defense. It also might be described as an attack which encompasses some principles of a zone press while remaining man-to-man, which we believe is a safer defense.

The 30 defense starts out straight man-to-man as do the 20 and 40 defenses. Consequently, the offense should have no way of knowing if we will depart from our straight man-to-man defense. In 30 defense, the change takes place if and when the dribble occurs. The dribbler is initially covered by his usual *match-up* defender. However, as the dribbler moves in the direction of the next defensive man, the change occurs. The defender toward whom he dribbles suddenly leaves his man and *jumps* the dribbler in an effort to surprise him. The dribbler's original defender will leave immediately and look to pick up an open man downcourt. If the element of surprise has its effect, the dribbler may either throw the ball away, charge the defender, walk with the ball, or pick up his dribble. If he does pick up his dribble, we then would attempt to press him and cut off his outlets. Again, there is no difference between the 20, 30, and 40 defenses if a dribble does not take place.

40 Defense   The 40 defense, often referred to as The Scramble, is designed to exploit the double-team concept. The defense might be described as an extension of the run and jump. Again, we start out straight man-to-man and jump the dribbler in the same manner described in 30 defense. In 40 defense, however, the dribbler's original defender does not leave to look for the open man. He remains to form part of the double-team. By starting out man-to-man originally, we are attempting to accomplish two objectives. The first is to disguise our eventual switch to a zone press. The second is to encourage the man with the ball to put it on the floor, since a double-team is much more effective once the ball handler has used up his dribble. Once a double-team occurs, we are no longer in a man-to-man. The defense takes the form of a two-two-one zone press. The first two men form the double-team. The next two men back must move to fill the holes as *interceptors*. The last defender back serves as *goaltender*. If the man double-teamed gets off a perimeter pass, we move to double-team the receiver and continue in our zone press. However, if the offense succeeds in getting the ball to the middle with what we refer to as a *gut* pass, we immediately sprint back to regroup our defense in order to stop the penetration. Note: 40 and 30 defenses are activated only if the ball handler puts the ball on the floor. If no dribble occurs, we stay straight man-to-man (20 defense) even if 30 or 40 defense was called.

50 Defense   Our 50 Defense is a pure zone which, if run in the full-court, takes us into man-to-man when we get downcourt (as though we were defending a fast break). The difference between 43 and 44 versus 53 and 54 is that in the 50 defense, we show our opponents a zone initially and in 40 defense we show them man-to-man until the dribble occurs. It is important that 53 and 54 go back to the same defense at the other end of the court, as do 43 and 44. That could be *either* zone or man-to-man. However it would be difficult to have the 50 defense go back to a zone while the 40 went back man-to-man. Both defenses are identical once the double-team occurs, and having them go back the same way cuts down on the amount of defense our players have to learn.

The reason we start out man-to-man in the 40 and zone in the 50 is to give the offense another look. During one season, we decided to have both go back to zone. At the time, we were thinking ahead to the day when the thirty-second clock could become the rule. Since it does take time to break a good zone, the combination of a press in the backcourt and zone in the frontcourt could work well together against the clock.

Our 54 defense puts pressure on the offense to get the ball into play. We normally use it after a successful foul shot when the defense can set up more quickly. It is very similar to our 53 defense which picks up the offense after the ball has been in-bounded. 54 and 53 generate the same type of two-two-one zone press alignment described in the 40 defense.

The 52 defense is a straight zone picked up at half-court. It is a one-three-one alignment. It remains in this same one-three-one alignment.

The 51 defense is what we refer to as a $1-2-2$ zone. 51 also begins in a one-two-two alignment, but bends itself to form more of a match-up zone. It is the only passive defense in our repetoire.

CONDITIONS DICTATING THE USE OF SPECIFIC DEFENSES

Our quarterback has the responsibility of calling all defenses. The only exceptions occur when there is enough time for the coach to signal or confer with the quarterback. We always discuss the opponent with our quarterbacks prior to game time. The coach will usually take that opportunity to suggest appropriate defensive ratios based upon his knowledge of the opposition.

There are however certain conditions which dictate specific defenses. Our players are thoroughly familiar with these rules and respond to them automatically.

MISSED FIELD-GOAL ATTEMPT

After any missed field-goal attempt on our part, we always sprint back to the 22 defense and stay man-to-man for the duration of the play. This represents our defense against the fast break. We do not believe in *jumping* the rebounder or *pinching* the outlet pass. Our quarterback is always back on defense unless he is driving for a lay-up, in which case the #2 guard would take his defensive responsibility. Our #2 guard is usually in a position to pick up a long rebound but can come back quickly. Our three frontcourt men are designated rebounders. However, once the rebound is taken by the opponent, they too must come back at top speed.

The ability to make this swift transition from offense to defense is an absolute prerequisite to successful defense. Most players are prone to make the change from defense to offense much more quickly than from offense to defense. The potential two points serve as the motivator. We constantly stress the importance of the quick offense to defense transition and exercise our substitute rule when a player is no longer able to sprint back at full speed. We also encourage our players to take *themselves* out of the game when they recognize, before we do, that they have reached this point of fatigue. The clenched fist pointed at the bench brings the player a rest and with it, the prerogative to put himself back in the game when he's rested. When a team is back on defense at full speed, the fast break will rarely hurt them.

JUMP-BALL SITUATIONS

If the opponent gains possession off a jump ball, we treat the situation as if it were a missed shot. We are quickly back into 22 defense to offset the possibility of the fast break. The same holds true for any situation (such as an interception by our opponents) in which the opponent does not have to take the ball out of bounds.

BASELINE OUT-OF-BOUNDS SITUATIONS

When our opponent has the ball under its own basket, we generally call one of our zones, either 51 or 52. We do this to encourage the outside pass. The offense is in a good position and we don't want them to score a quick basket inside. When the opponent takes the ball out of bounds under our basket the defense is called by the quarterback.

SIDELINE OUT-OF-BOUNDS SITUATIONS

Sideline out-of-bounds situations are also called by the quarterback. If the ball is taken out of bounds in the opponent's half-court, our choices are 22, 32, 42, or 52. If the ball is taken out of bounds in our half-court, we can go to 23, 33, 43, or 53. In these situations, our team has a choice. We can put a defender on the man in-bounding the ball or use that defender in another capacity. We vary these two, but generally we play off the in-bounds passer. Theoretically, the offensive player making the in-bounds pass has used up his dribble and can't move onto the court. Therefore, we elect not to guard him. Instead, we use the extra defensive man to free-lance or play goaltender.

Of course, it is impossible to accurately determine how often this alignment is more effective than one which has a defender harassing the in-bounds passer. Our approach, however, has proved extremely valuable to us on more than a few occasions.

One of the more dramatic examples occurred during the 1973—74 season in a game against Duke University on their home court. Duke had the ball out of bounds on the side in their backcourt. The score was tied and only seconds remained on the clock. Bobby Jones, who was extremely quick for his 6' 9" size, was playing the free-lance role for us. He managed to intercept the in-bounds pass, drove to the basket, and scored at the buzzer to give us a 73—71 victory. Bobby, incidentally, was one of the most outstanding defensive players we've ever had at the University of North Carolina.

AFTER SUCCESSFUL FOUL SHOTS

When we are fouled, and go to the line we are in excellent position to change defenses. Our huddle at the free-throw circle, which we began many years ago, is used for this purpose. Some of our players started this *huddling* during a scrimmage one day to prevent their teammates on the opposing team from hearing the signal. We have used it in game situations ever since. Our choices for the call in the huddle are 54, 53, 44, 43, 34, 33, 24, or 23.

AFTER MADE FIELD-GOALS

The quarterback is responsible for calling the defense after each of our successful field-goal attempts. When a shot is taken by our team, the quarterback usually is running back to mid-court for defensive balance. After we score, he generally can be seen by our other players as they turn and move back to defense. The quarterback's hand signals key our players to the specific defense we will use for that play. For example, if the quarterback raises two hands our players are keyed to 20 defense. One hand raised indicates 30 defense, and two hands lowered signals 40 defense.

In all honesty, we have had difficulty in trying to run four defensive signals after a made field-goal. We did do this successfully for two years, although, I will admit that sometimes, not all of the players had the correct signal. We now run three defensive signals. I would suggest that secondary schools never run more than three. It would be easier for secondary schools to use only two signals after made field-goals.

Although it is difficult for the opposing quarterback to spot and identify these signals, we do try to change them each season. At one time, we thought we could change defenses by the position of our player who scored the field-goal. For example, if a guard scored, we would go into our 20 defense. If the basket was made by a forward we would automatically be in 30 defense, etc. We also considered changing defenses by the opponents score on the basis of *odd or even*. After trying all these methods in practice, we found the hand signals to be best for us.

Now, how do we inform our players as to the *point* on the court we will initiate the particular defense signaled by the quarterback? Although crowd noise after a field-goal would be a problem, conceivably, the quarterback could attempt to call a two digit number signal such as 22. This would indicate both the defense as well as the pick-up point. However, we prefer not to do this after our field-goals. Instead, a consistent pick-up point is determined prior to the game by the coach, based upon the coach's knowledge of the opponent. This predetermined pick-up point remains in effect until game conditions warrant a change.

Each of the four possible pick-up points (indicated by the dotted lines in *Diagram 11-2*) are specified by a color code. The four possible defenses that can be used at that pick-up point form the *series*. The series are illustrated in Diagram 11-2.

If, for example, we tell our players before game time that we will be in the blue series, they know that we will *automatically* pick up the defense at mid-court each time we score a field-goal. The defensive choices then become 22, 32, or 42. If the quarterback raises one arm after a particular field-goal, the players are keyed to run-and-jump the opponent at mid-court (32). Two hands raised will signal our man-to-man pressure at that *same* mid-court point (22), etc.

The names you choose for these series are obviously unimportant. The green series is rarely used. Most teams playing against us have learned to jump out of bounds and throw the ball in quickly to avoid this kind of pressure. We use the red series late in the game when we are in our delay offense. This discourages the opponent from driving on us in an attempt to draw the foul. The white series, which for all practical purposes represents full-court pressure, is used when we wish to speed up the tempo. Conversely, the blue series slows the tempo more than the white series. We'll go to it when we are up against an extremely quick guard who has repeatedly demonstrated the ability to beat the press.

Diagram 11-2

DEFENSIVE DETERMINATION AFTER NORTH CAROLINA FIELD GOALS

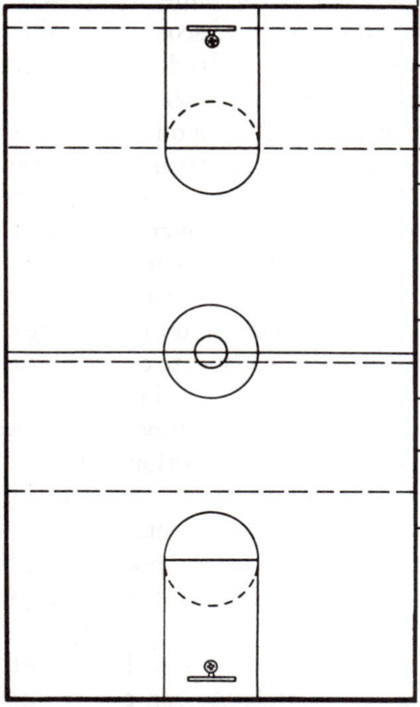

NORTH CAROLINA GOAL

OPPONENT'S GOAL

AFTER N.C. FIELD GOALS	SPECIFIC DEFENSE DETERMINED BY Q-BACK THRU HAND SIGNALS			
DEFENSIVE POINT OF ATTACK DETERMINED BY COACH BEFORE GAME BY DESIGNATING ONE OF THE FOUR SERIES BELOW	20 DEFENSE	30 DEFENSE	40 DEFENSE	50 DEFENSE
GREEN SERIES	24	34	44	54
WHITE SERIES	23	33	43	53
BLUE SERIES	22	32	42	52*
RED SERIES	21			51

*52 ALSO USED AS PART OF RED SERIES

OPPONENT IN BONUS SITUATION

Game conditions will obviously have a bearing on defensive strategy. The bonus situation is a good example. From the point of view of possession evaluation, the one-and-one bonus imposes a strong penalty after the sixth foul. Considering the fact that most college players will average about seventy percent from the free-throw line, a little mathematics will point out that the one-and-one will average out to little over one point per possession for the bonus team. That is awfully hard to beat.

Consequently, after our sixth foul, we sometimes go to some defense that will minimize our fouling. It is usually the red series described earlier. Even in the red series, composed of 21, 51, and 52 it will only be called after our made field-goal. On a missed shot, regardless of the circumstances, we're always back on 22 defense. Therefore, we are never in a zone defense one hundred percent of the time.

BEHIND LATE IN THE GAME

If we are very much behind late in the game, we do have a catch-up defense we use. It is a gambling, double-teaming type of defense, and we don't use it unless the situation is desperate. Under these conditions, we will be in the green series if possible, but we encourage 40 and 30 defensive calls by the quarterback.

On the other hand, if our opponent is desperately behind late in the game, we will go to the red series to offset the opponent's usual strategy. A desperation offense will normally attempt to get the ball to its best driver in an effort to pick up the possible three-point play and stop the clock. The zone does take time to offense properly and tends to inhibit this type of strategy.

Summarizing our defensive philosophy, we do believe that defense makes the difference between a good team and a great team. Good defense, unlike shooting for example, does not require fine skill. Good defense requires learning and effort. Once learned and applied regularly, it tends to become a habit. Consequently, a well-coached team defensively should be relatively consistent in its play. The team that depends too much on its offense, however, may suffer badly when its better shooters have an off-night. Our defense has pulled us through many games when we had more than our share of problems putting the ball through the basket.

We have also found that it is extremely hard to overcoach defense. The more effort you put into this aspect of the game, the more you get out of it. On the other hand, many coaches, myself included, have occasionally been guilty of overcoaching the offense with an excessive number of play options.

One final point, which is most important: We would rather not approach defense with a view toward *forcing* our players into something they will not like doing. Quite the contrary, once our players absorb the fundamentals of our multiple defense, they become quite enthusiastic. They know that our defense helps our offense. It is hard to play aggressive defense without being a fast- breaking team, and most players thoroughly enjoy that overall style of play.

20 defense:
pressure man-to-man

The 20 defense is our predominate defensive attack. We use the term attack for our pressure man-to-man defense since our objective is to initiate the action on defense, disconcert our opponents, and force them out of their intended offense. When we are successful in this effort, we usually decrease the opponent's points per possession and often increase our own at the same time, which is our major goal. To obtain these results with the 20 defense we look to accomplish three key objectives simultaneously.

First, we try to pressure the opponent to put the ball on the floor and force him to the sideline with it. It is always easier to attack a dribbling type offense than one which moves the ball rapidly with quick, sharp passes. The reason it is easier to defend against a dribbling type offense is that players guarding men without the ball have the opportunity to see both the ball and their men much more easily. If the opponents were moving themselves and the ball, it would be hard to keep our objective if seeing both man and ball. Our purpose in forcing sidelines is to create, and ideally maintain, a weak side from which to draw our support.

Secondly, we try to play the ball and the immediate outlets very aggressively. We overplay each offensive man one perimeter pass from the ball, and we try to block every passing lane. By taking the action on defense this way we are attempting to make the opponent react to us by forcing them where they would rather not go and making them do what they may not do best.

Finally, we try to constantly support this aggressiveness with help from the weak side, as referred to earlier. Since defense will usually be beaten in a one-on-one situation on a high skill level, we feel we can best attack the offense through a team concept of man-to-man defense as opposed to the more orthodox total dependence on individual match-ups. We do assign individual match-ups, but ideally we would like to have five defensive players working together against four offensive players, four-against-three, three-against-two, and two-against-one.

Ours then is very much a helping or support-type defense, and there are some rules for our players to learn. Our principles, however, remain constant regardless of the type offense we are facing. Most of the principles are taught to our players through four relatively simple drills. We eventually will focus this chapter around these drills as a means of explaining the 20 defense to the reader just as they are introduced to our players.

To begin with, however, let's start our explanation of the defense by covering the responsibilities of the man guarding the ball handler.

guarding the man with the ball

There are three circumstances under which a defensive player may find himself guarding the man with the ball. The offensive player may have his dribble *alive*. He may have used his dribble, or he may be dribbling. We will cover the dribble-alive situation first.

DRIBBLE ALIVE

Stance　When playing the man with the ball (on the perimeter) whose dribble is alive, we want the defender to have his tail low, be on-balance, and have a hand up over the ball. We do want one foot forward, but we do not specify the particular foot. We prefer that the player make that choice himself based upon what comes most naturally to him. Certainly, in forcing a dribbler to the sideline it would make sense to have the right foot forward on the defensive right side of the court as you look at the basket, and the left foot forward on the left side of the court as you face the basket. Above all, we want him to be comfortable so that he can react quickly to any offensive maneuver. We also like the defensive man to feel more weight on the front foot since any movement the offensive player makes in starting his dribble requires the defensive player to push off that front foot. If the weight were on the back foot, the defensive player would have to shift it to the front foot and then push off. We want the defender to concentrate on the ball handler's stomach. When the stomach moves, the defender should be prepared to retreat accordingly. We believe in a step-slide and prefer that our man not cross his feet when he moves with the ball handler. Sometimes, however, if the defender is being beaten, he must cross his feet to run and catch up. We use a special drill daily during the pre-season to build the step-slide habit.

Creating pressure Since we are initiating the action on defense, the defender guarding the man with the ball has the responsibility of creating pressure regardless of the area on the court the ball handler is being covered. Whether four feet or forty feet from the basket, the defensive player creates pressure by being active. He plays close to his man, ideally about two to three feet from the ball handler. He has a hand up in his face. He is dodging and faking at the man, and doing what he can to bother the ball handler without fouling him.

If the opponent gets the ball within fifteen feet of the basket, (we say *if* because we don't want him to get it there) the defender is then all the way up on the ball handler, standing more upright than he does in guarding the perimeter man. He gives no ground and must make the ball handler drive when he is that close to the basket.

We want the man inside to put the ball on the floor since, if the ball is inside, the defense is jammed back. This provides us with an excellent opportunity to steal the ball, particularly from a big man who is usually the one to get the ball inside. If the offensive man has his back to the basket ten to fifteen feet from the basket, we are then off the man about three feet to allow teammates to slide through.

Forcing the dribble As we indicated in our introduction, we want the offense to put the ball on the floor and we also want to influence the direction taken by the dribbler. We call this *forcing the dribble.*

When we speak of forcing to our players, it is another way of telling them that we want them to take the action on defense as opposed to reacting to the ball handler. For example, if a defensive player crowds the ball handler on his right, he forces the opponent to go left. If he crowds left, the ball handler is usually forced to go right. If the defender lays off the ball handler, he's inviting him to shoot. If he's playing him extremely tight (within a foot or so of the ball handler), he's telling him to drive one way or the other.

Diagram 12-1 We want the man guarding the ball handler to force the dribble at a forty-five degree angle. It is important to note that we do not want to overforce the dribble, since doing so could lead to a direct drive down the middle, which is what we want to avoid completely. Forcing the dribble wide takes precedent over forcing in a particular direction. Ideally, we want to do both.

As we indicated earlier, our purpose in forcing sidelines is to create a weak side from which we may draw our support. To maintain this weak side we must prevent the guard-to-guard pass. This is extremely important to us. Let's see why with the aid of **Diagrams 12-2** and **12-3**.

In these diagrams, the offense has progressed into its frontcourt. X1 is on the ball handler trying to force him sidelines, which we roughly define by the shaded area on the right and left sides of the court. If #1 were out of the shaded area we would then play between the man and the basket (straight up), forcing the dribbler to go wide in either direction. If #2 had the ball, X2 would attempt to force him toward the right side of the court. The defense now must stop that pass from #1 to #2.

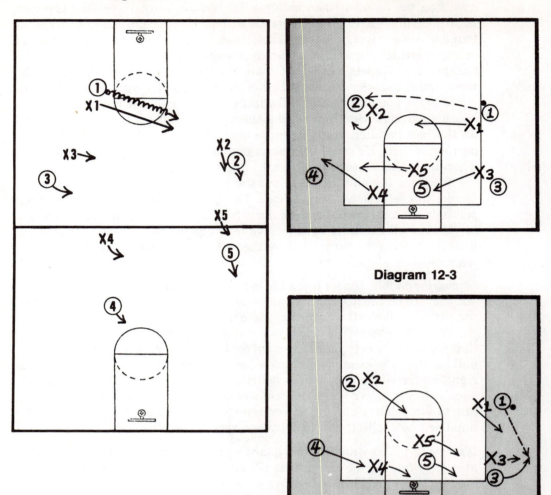

Diagram 12-1

Diagram 12-2

Diagram 12-3

Later in the chapter, when we detail the rules for guarding the man without the ball, you will learn that the position of a defender one perimeter pass away from the ball is between his man and the ball. The position of a defender two perimeter passes away is in the lane. He is the support man. The pivot defender is told to front his opponent on the side of the ball.

Without elaborating on these rules, let's examine the defensive adjustments required for X3, X4, and X5 when the offense manages to complete the guard-to-guard pass in Diagram 12-2. Compare those adjustments to the same in Diagram 12-3, when the pass is attempted on the right side of the court instead. The reasons we try to prevent the swing pass shown in Diagram 12-2 (which many teams *give* the offense in pressure defense) should be evident with this comparison.

Our thinking is that far too much adjustment is required and consequently the defense is frequently broken down when this pass is allowed to go. This weakening of the defense, by frequently changing sides of the court, is precisely what we try to do ourselves on offense. Therefore, if we were able to keep the action between #1 and #3 on the right side of the court as in Diagram 12-3, we will have done a great defensive job by our own standards.

You will note, however, that X3 is also trying to block the #1 to #3 pass in Diagram 12-3. As we indicated in our introduction we are ideally trying to accomplish two objectives simultaneously here. If we felt we could not do both, we would definitely give priority to preventing the guard-to-guard pass so that we could keep the ball on one side of the court.

Dribble Used Should the ball handler use his dribble, the defender must move up very close with both hands up. In the *dribble used* situation, we want our players to set the goal of not allowing their man to immediately catch the ball unless he has reversed to the basket. With all outlets aggressively covered this way, we minimize the chances of the ball handler finding an open teammate and the chances of an intercepted pass, a pass thrown out of bounds, or a five second violation are increased. We will diagram a dribble used situation during one of our drills later on in the chapter.

Ball handler begins to dribble and/or is dribbling When the offensive player begins to dribble, we want the defender to maintain the relatively same position he was maintaining before the dribble began. The defensive man's head should ideally be over the elbow of the dribbling hand, thereby forcing the dribble at a forty-five degree angle.

Initially, we do not want our players reaching or swiping at the ball for two reasons. First, we do not believe that this will often result in stealing the ball from a good player at the college level. Secondly, the moment a defensive man reaches, his feet tend to stop moving. It is very difficult to keep reaching and keep your feet moving at the same time. We hope that the pressure on the ball without gambling defensively will cause the offensive player to miscue.

However, after about two weeks of practice we do give some players who have exceptionally quick hands the freedom to *reach* and try to steal the ball. These two or three selected players are told that they may bother the ball handler whenever they wish with one exception. This exception is when the opponent is in the bonus foul situation at which point we stop reaching and gambling. We do not want to give the opponent a one-and-one foul-shot opportunity.

My recommendation to junior high coaches would be to allow all defensive players at that level to reach until the bonus situation. The limited ball handling skills at that level makes reaching a definite asset for the defense.

Designated *reachers* at North Carolina during the mid-1960s through the 1970s have been Dick Grubar (1967−69), Charles Scott (1967−70), Steve Previs (1970−72), Walter Davis and John Kuester (1973−77) and Dudley Bradley (1976−79). Each of these players had an excellent attitude towards defense and played defense with great dedication. Each had excellent hands and the savvy to know when to reach.

guarding the man without the ball

Obviously, much more time is spent guarding the man without the ball than guarding the ball handler. In team pressure man-to-man defense, the defender guarding the man without the ball assumes a great deal of responsibility. His position in relation to the ball and his man is extremely important.

GUARDING THE PLAYER ONE PASS AWAY FROM THE BALL

When guarding a man who is one pass away from the ball, we want the defender to be in overplay position (between his man and the ball) denying that immediate pass. His body should be facing his man, but his head is turned so that he can see both the ball and his man. His stance is not quite as low as it is when he is guarding the ball handler, but he is still down and ready to move. His nearest arm to the ball is extended out into the passing lane along with part of the torso denying the direct pass from the ball handler. Positioning himself this way, the defender is now hopeful of forcing his man to reverse to the basket without the ball.

The further away the offensive man is from the ball handler, the further off the defensive man should be. As the distance between the ball handler and the outlet decreases, the distance between the defender and his man decreases as well.

We can return to Diagram 12-1 to observe this in the full-court. Diagram 12-1 illustrates a typical formation in 23 defense. We would use 23, for example, when we are in our white series and the quarterback signals our pressure man-to-man defense after one of our field-goals. We would then be attacking the offense at three-quarter court with our 20 defense.

Note that #2 and #3 are both one perimeter pass away from the ball handler. X3, however, is much farther off his man than X2. The greater distance between #3 and the ball allows X3 to be further away from his man, without jeopardizing his ability to recover if #1 threw long to #3. X2, on the other hand, shortens the distance between himself and #2 as the distance between #2 and the dribbler decreases.

Most of the rules of 20 defense come into play when the offense succeeds at getting the ball into the half-court. Considering this, and the fact that most of our teaching efforts are accomplished through the four part-method drills referred to earlier, we thought we might take a slightly different approach in this chapter. Rather than place these drills at the conclusion of the chapter, we will use them at this point to explain and illustrate our 20 defense principles the same way we cover them with our players. There are essentially three reasons we do so much of our 20 defense teaching through four-on-four drills. First, we believe that when players initially learn their responsibilities four-on-four in a helping-type defense, it becomes much easier to play five-on-five ultimately. Secondly, it helps our post men. They may not always be playing their men inside. The four-on-four work helps them learn to play out on the court. We will elaborate on this when we cover pivot defense. Thirdly, and most important, we are giving confidence to the defender guarding the man with the ball to put pressure on his man. He *knows* he has help. If we began teaching one-on-one or two-on-two defense, I believe the defenders would not put pressure on the ball because they would be afraid to be beaten to the basket.

four part-method drills used to teach the 20 defense

Before detailing our four part-method drills, note that players are inverted in all our drills. #1 and #2 will assume the #3 and #4 positions and #3 and #4 will assume the #1 and #2 positions after going through a drill once.

DIAGRAM 12-4: SWING DRILL

The swing illustrated in Diagram 12-4 is the first drill we use to introduce our players to the 20 defense. The offensive men remain stationary since the primary purpose of the drill is to teach the defensive players their positions relative to the ball. #1, #2, #3, and #4 do get the opportunity to practice their passing as they swing the ball around the horn.

#1 has the ball at the start of the drill. X1 is on him applying pressure and trying to force him to the sideline.

Diagram 12-4

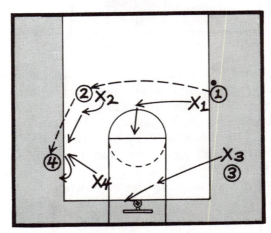

Note the positions of X2 and X3. They are in overplay position between their men and the ball, maintaining the previousll discussed rule for defenders whose men are one perimeter pass away. They face their opponents, but turn their heads to continue seeing #1 with the ball at the same time. X2 has his right arm extended on the line between #1 and #2. X3 uses his left arm in a similar manner to discourage the #1 to #3 pass.

Earlier, we detailed the reason we work so hard to stop the guard-to-guard pass. But what about the #1 to #3 pass here? Why try to block this one also? Why, in fact, do we try to block every pass? We indicated that the reason for this is to make the opponent dribble, or to take the opponent out of its intended offense. Let's elaborate on this now with the aid of Diagram 12-5.

In Diagram 12-5, we have split the half-court to illustrate the basic difference between overplay pressure and the more traditional man-to-man defense, which has the defense playing between his man and the basket. In both instances, we will assume that the offensive objective is to get the ball to #5 in the middle, which is always a good place to have the ball.

Diagram 12-5

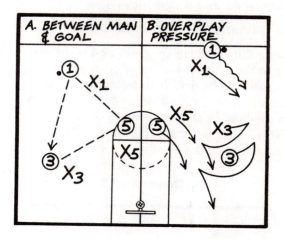

In *Diagram 12-5A*, the offense has no difficulty accomplishing its objective. #1 can get the ball to the middle directly or through a pass to the wing who, in turn, pitches to the high post.

In *Diagram 12-5B*, the immediate pass is contested. Even if #1 succeeds in getting the ball to #3 despite X3's efforts, we hope that X5's overplay position will inhibit the #3 to #5 pass. In Diagram 12-5B, the offense is prevented from getting the ball to the high post. X1 plays a key role in this effort by forcing #1 sidelines rather than allowing him to penetrate into the middle. This is what we mean when we speak about taking the opponent out of its offense.

There is nothing necessarily wrong with the defensive strategy illustrated in Diagram 12-5A. X3 and X5 could make it very difficult for their respective men to get off the high-percentage shot. However, since our ultimate goal is to increase our points per possession while decreasing the same for our opponents, we think we have a better chance of accomplishing this by overplaying the immediate pass. The chances for a turnover are much greater in diagram 12-5B than they are in Diagram 12-5A. At the same time, we hope that our aggressiveness, backed by our support, will serve to minimize the opponent's chances for the high-percentage shot as well.

At clinics I'm often asked by coaches about the defensive rebound situation if #1 shoots and X5 is around on #5, or X3 is overplaying #3, as in Diagram 12-5B. Obviously, if we have good pressure on the ball, the man with the ball will not be looking to shoot. However, if X5 and X3 read that #1 is about to shoot, each must move inside for defensive position.

I agree that the best possible *rebounding* defense is one that has the players playing between their men and the basket as illustrated in Diagram 12-5A. However, we feel that overplay defense gives us many more advantages which make it a superior overall defense.

GUARDING THE PLAYER TWO OR MORE PASSES FROM THE BALL

Principle: The position of a defensive player guarding a man two or more perimeter passes from the ball is in the free-throw lane.

This principle is demonstrated in Diagram 12-4 by the position of X4, the weak side forward, who is initially two perimeter passes away from #1 with the ball. X4 is therefore in the free-throw lane. He positions himself somewhere off that line between his man and the ball, pointing to both at an approximate forty-five degree angle. The better the defender's peripheral vision, the closer that angle between man and ball may approximate one hundred eighty degrees. X4 constantly adjusts this completely opened position in the lane in an effort to continue seeing his man and the ball at all times. He keeps his head steady, but moves his feet. As important as this is, it is also very difficult to do all the time. Sometimes it is impossible, and we will cover that contingency later on in the chapter.

Why do we put the two-passes-away man in the lane? What does he do there? And why, if we are applying pressure, isn't he playing closer to his own man?

To begin with, when X4 is in the lane he should be able to beat #4 to the ball should #4 decide to move closer to #1. If #1 gets the pass off to #2, X4 then should have enough time to get back into overplay position between #4 and #2.

Ideally then, if we don't need X4 on top of his man when he is two passes away, we can certainly use him more advantageously in that vitally important help position in the lane. There, X4 will be ready to aid any teammate who may need his support. His presence alone in that *clean up* spot should allow the man guarding the ball handler and the one-pass-away defenders to play their men more aggressively. Look back to Diagram 12-5B. If you can picture X4 in the lane supporting his teammates, it is easier to see how X3 and X5 can play in front of their men with more confidence.

The help man's position in the lane should enable him to accomplish the following important functions when necessary: one, support on any backdoor move made by an offensive player one pass away; two, cross the lane to stop a baseline penetration dribble; and three, protect against the lob pass when the offense has a pivot man in the center. We will cover each of these situations in detail shortly.

As the swing drill begins in Diagram 12-4, #1 passes to #2. In a game situation, both X1 and X2 obviously would work very hard to prevent this pass. In this drill, however, all the perimeter passes are allowed to go. The defensive players merely wave at the ball.

This first pass from #1 to #2 keys a change in the position of each defensive player, as indicated by the initial movement arrows in the diagram. It underscores a very basic defensive premise we try to instill in each player very early in their training. The good defensive player must learn to move when the ball moves *regardless of whether or not his man moves.*

Principle: When the defender's man passes the ball, the defender retreats in the direction of the pass.

When #1 passes to #2, X1 retreats in the direction of the pass immediately, regardless of where his opponent chooses to move. You might wonder at this point whether the *retreat* rule is in conflict with the one-pass-away rule? We did, in fact, say that one pass away was played tough. Suppose #1 passed to #2 and stood. #1 would then be wide open for the return pass when X1 retreated. The retreat rule is an exception to the one-pass-away rule, but it serves a very valuable purpose. By retreating in the direction of the pass, the defender is preparing to beat his man to the ball on a possible offensive move to the basket. If, for example, #1 decided to cut to the basket after passing to #2, X1 would easily have an advantage on him as Diagram 12-4 illustrates.

On the #1 to #2 pass, X2 now has the responsibility of playing the man with the ball. He therefore readjusts his position on #2 and plays him very aggressively. To re-emphasize, X2 will play him straight up if #2 is out of the shaded area (nonsidelines). However X2 will force him to his right (sideline) if #2 has the ball in the shaded area.

X4 is no longer two passes away. The #1 to #2 pass now puts #4 one perimeter pass away from the ball. Consequently, X4 must rush back into position between his man and the ball.

X4's quick move back into overplay position here should illustrate why the defender two passes away must always try to see both ball and man at the same time. There are two ways #4's position can change from two passes to one pass away. #4 can move in the direction of the ball becoming one pass away or, as in Diagram 12-4, the ball can move toward #4, such as in the #1 to #2 pass. Consequently, X4 must keep *both* man and ball in his field of vision simultaneously in order to know when either of these situations is occurring.

Although X4 sprints out of the lane to get back quickly, his last few steps must be made under control. Otherwise, he would run the risk of #4 going back-door easily. X4 consequently runs the first few steps and then step-slides the rest of the way.

When #2 has the ball, #3 becomes two perimeter passes away. Therefore, following the rule, X3 becomes the help man, and moves into the lane keeping his man in focus with the ball.

As the drill continues, in Diagram 12-4, #2 passes to #4. The second movement arrows in the diagram trace the defensive changes on this pass. X2 retreats in the direction of the pass. X4, now guarding the man with the ball, must readjust his position accordingly.

Contrary to orthodox defensive teaching, X4 does not place himself between #4 and the basket. Instead, X4's back is parallel to the baseline, or to put it another way, he is facing in the direction of the sideline, as he guards #4 with the ball. In this position X4 is, in a sense, inviting #4 to go baseline, but *not* on a straight line to the basket.

Many coaches, including my own college coach, Dr. Phog Allen, have felt strongly about *not* allowing the offense to go baseline. Actually, we feel that the baseline is an excellent area for trapping the ball handler. We will attempt to illustrate this theory when we detail the support drill later in the chapter.

X3 is already in the lane prior to the #2 to #4 pass. On this pass, he moves a little farther off, readjusting his position to see both #3 and the man with the ball, who is now #4. X1 retreated on the pass from #1 to #2. He now comes back even farther into the lane since his man, #1, has become two perimeter passes from the ball. Therefore, X1 can really *cheat* as long as he continues to see both his man and the ball.

The swing drill teaches and reinforces what we consider to be the most fundamental and important defensive concept: When the ball moves, either through a pass or dribble, we expect each player to move and readjust his position accordingly. The defense which fails to respond to the movement of the ball becomes vulnerable. This, as we indicated in our introduction, is why a passing-type offense is more effective than one which depends on a lot of dribbling. It is why we, for example, require a minimum of three passes before dribbling or shooting is permitted in our own free-lance passing game unless we have a lay-up possibility. A twelve-to-fifteen-foot pass requires the defense to make a considerable adjustment in the short time it takes for the ball to move through the air. On the other hand, the dribble allows for gradual adjustment on each bounce of the ball which is obviously easier for the defense.

PIVOT DEFENSE

Before we move on to our next drill, we should introduce the pivot defender into our description.

As we indicated earlier, one of the reasons we do not use five-on-five to teach the 20 defense is because our post men will not always find themselves inside the perimeter in a game situation. When they are playing outside on the court, they have the same responsibilities as any other defender. Consequently, our four-on-four drills, which bring the post men outside, as well as inside the perimeter, benefit them as they do our other players.

In a game situation, when the pivot defender is guarding a man at a high or medium post, he does not leave his man to help. If he did, the offensive center would be too easy a target for a high pass and a score. When playing his man on the low post, however, the defensive center is automatically *on* the perimeter, as opposed to being inside it. For all practical purposes, he is not guarding a center at that point and does help out when necessary.

Any good offensive player receiving the ball in the low post should almost always score or be fouled. Because of this, we always have the low post completely fronted. The high post will be side-fronted on the ball side. The medium post can either be side- or completely fronted. Therefore, unless his man is out on the court, the defensive center always plays in *front* of his man. On the court, the pivot defense will still have his arm and part of his torso between the ball and his man. To do so confidently, however, the defensive center must know that he has help behind him, since the lob pass is constantly used to feed the pivot man who is fronted.

Diagram 12-6 Here we pick up the action where we left it in the previous diagram. The only change we have made is to add #5 and his defender. X5, in keeping with the rule, is fronting #5 on the ball side. The situation gives us the opportunity to show how the help man provides us with valuable assistance against the lob pass.

#4 has the ball and X3, the weak side forward, is in the lane. As soon as X3 sees the lob pass coming, he crosses the lane in an effort to draw the charge or steal the pass. On the pass, X1 and X2 jam in.

It is important to note that X4 has a very important responsibility here. The more pressure he can put on #4 making the pass, the less likely it is that a good pass will be completed. An effective method for stopping the lob pass is to place considerable pressure on the ball.

Diagram 12-6

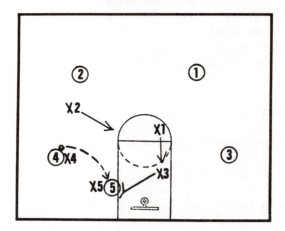

DIAGRAM 12-7: SUPPORT DRILL

Principle: When a dribble penetration occurs, the defender closest to the man guarding the dribbler must support on the drive.

The support drill illustrated in Diagram 12-7 teaches many things, but it is designed mainly to teach each player how to help stop dribble penetrations to the basket. The defender one perimeter pass away from the ball must move his feet quickly to help his teammate stop the penetration, and then move back to his own man. In moving to help when a penetrating dribbler comes into the heart of the defense, the helper must keep his own man in his field of vision.

The offensive players in the drill are told to simply dribble, penetrate, and pitch. The drill, incidentally, provides the offensive players with some good zone offense work. #1 has the ball again at the start of the drill. X1 is on him. #1 dribbles hard into the hole between X1 and X2. X2 must now switch from his overplay position on #2 and support X1 in the effort to stop the dribble. X2 keeps his own man, #2, in clear sight and moves back to him after stopping #1's penetration.

Diagram 12-7

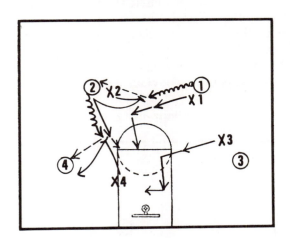

The defender one pass away has a great many responsibilities. Admittedly, it is a tough position. His first job is to keep his man from getting the ball. At the same time, however, he must support on the dribble. "Help and get back" is a key phrase in our defensive work, and one that we constantly use with our players to remind them of their dual responsibility. The help rule, however, works both ways. The helper knows that he himself will have assistance when he needs it.

After X2 stops #1's penetration, #1 pitches to #2. X2 recovers and gets help from X4 as #2 begins his dribble penetration.

If #2 gets by X2 and X4 on the penetration dribble, X3 should be in the lane and ready to help out as the back-up man. If X3 commits himself to stop #2, X1, the weak side guard, must move in on #3. We call this *helping the helper*.

Perhaps this possible, although unusual, occurrence illustrates what we mean when we refer to the 20 as a helping-type defense. Getting back to concept, a coach might ask why we bother with all of this? Why not keep X4, X3, and X1 tight on their own men and let X2 try to hold his own against #2. The answer again is that all players have become stronger offensive threats through the years. Left to themselves, #2 would have the edge over X2 most of the time.

Principle: The defensive player in the lane must cross the lane to help stop baseline drives. When this occurs, the weak side guard moves in to help the helper.

Diagram 12-8 is a continuation of Diagram 12-7. The ball is now with #4 in the corner. When guarding the man with the ball on the sideline we want the defender to make him go wide on the dribble. X3, in the lane, is prepared to stop a baseline driver from getting into the lane. Therefore, at this point in the drill we want #4 driving baseline to teach X3 to cross the lane with his hands up. X1 must move in deeper to help the helper and protect the weak side. X2 jams back as well.

Earlier in the chapter we mentioned that, contrary to some defensive philosophies, we feel that the baseline is a good place to trap the ball handler. Perhaps the introduction of this principle and its example in Diagram 12-8 will illustrate this point. X4 obviously has a lot of help as #4 drives baseline.

Diagram 12-8

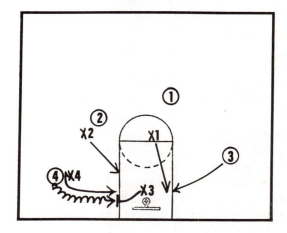

Another factor worth noting is that there are very few passing angles available to #4 at the point he is stopped by X3. On the other hand, if we encouraged #4 to drive into the middle, he could subsequently pass in either direction.

I'm asked often at clinics what we do once we stop the dribbler on this baseline drive. There are basically two possibilities. Some years we had the initial man guarding the dribbler (X4 in Diagram 12-8) go right on through once he gets help from X3 as we still do on a #2 to #4 backdoor pass. X4 would then pick up #3 if the play continues. The play rarely gets that far, however. We will frequently draw the charge on a baseline drive such as this. Sometimes *we* are called for the foul. Other times a #4 pass to #3 will be intercepted by X1, or #3 may get the pass and score if X1 doesn't react to the baseline dribble. If #4 picks up his dribble after #3 stops him, #4 pivots out looking to pass to #2. X2 should be there to prevent the outlet.

The other option on this play the coach may wish to consider is a temporary double team which we have been doing for some years. Therefore, rather than have X4 continue across the lane to pick up #3, we have him stay with X3, temporarily double-teaming the dribbler, #4. If #4 is successful in finding an outlet, the double-team obviously will be broken and each defensive man must return to his original man. When this double-team is used, it marks our only exception to the help and get back rule. You would help and *stay* if you have the opponent trapped on the baseline, outside the lane.

How is our baseline drive principle affected when the fifth offensive and defensive men enter into the situation? If #5 played a high or medium post, there would be no change. X5 in keeping with the rule for the pivot defender, would continue to front #5. He would not leave his man to help out on the baseline drive. However, if #5 was on a low post, X5 would automatically be fronting him *on the perimeter* as #4 drove baseline. X5 would therefore be the next logical help. Under these circumstances, he would assume the responsibility of crossing the lane and stopping the drive.

Principle—Line of Ball: In almost every instance we want the defensive player to stay within the line of ball.

Diagram 12-9 Before we leave the support drill we should cover the line of ball principle.

Diagram 12-9

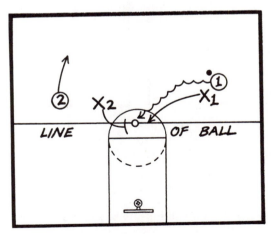

In this diagram, #1 has the ball and begins a penetration dribble in the direction of X2, the one-pass-away man. In the meantime, #2 moves way up in the direction of the mid-court line. However, he is still one perimeter pass away from #1. What does X2 do? He knows he must support X1 on #1's penetration dribble. However, he has also been taught to get back to his man one pass away and prevent that pass. #2's move into a high position now makes it impossible for X2 to simultaneously accomplish both objectives. The *line of ball principle* resolves the conflict. To determine the line of ball we simply visualize a straight line drawn through the ball from sideline to sideline. X2 will not move far from that imaginary line in pursuit of #2. He waits and helps on the penetration instead. If #1 wishes to pitch back to #2 beyond the line of ball, we let the pass go and rebuild our pressure at that point.

In a dribble-used situation, the line of ball principle does not apply, however. If #1, in Diagram 12-9, picked up his dribble, X2 would forget the line of ball in an effort to clamp his man and make him reverse.

DIAGRAMS 12-10 AND 12-11: TRANSITION DRILL

Our third drill has the offense making prescribed moves. We refer to it as the transition drill because emphasis is placed on the defensive transitions from two passes to one pass away and visa versa.

Diagram 12-10   **Diagram 12-11**

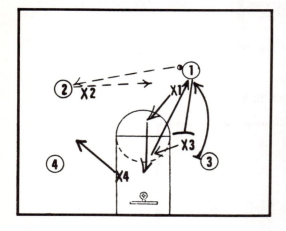   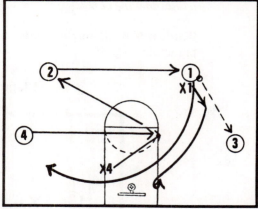

On the #1 to #2, pass in Diagram 12-10, X4 must return from the lane to his one-pass-away position between #2 and #4. After passing to #2, #1 either sets a screen or exchanges with #3. #2 then throws to #3, who has come up into the position just vacated by #1. After passing to #3, #2 exchanges or screens for #4.

One of our major efforts here is to teach X3 to quickly get off #3 on the initial #1 to #2 pass. Even though it is a drill situation, X3 must presume he does not know what #3 is going to do. All X3 knows is that he must move with the pass. The next thing he sees is #1 setting a screen at him away from the ball and #3 moving up to #1's former spot. X3 must now get back into overplay position and prevent the #2 to #3 pass. There is no reason why X3 can not beat his man to the ball despite the screen, presuming it is a legal screen. X3 can sprint at top speed without being overly concerned about a possible reverse on the part of #3. If #3 started up and then reversed, X1 would be there to help. X3, therefore, should have no difficulty slipping around #1's screen *in the direction of the ball* and beating #3 to the pass. This is the way we play the screen away from the ball. Periodically, as a surprise, X1 could switch to X3 coming out in an effort to steal the #2 to #3 pass. The decision on switching is up to X1, the man guarding the screener.

guarding against the back door

The good basketball player who is being overplayed will go backdoor looking for an easy lay-up. Let's suppose #3, in Diagram 12-10, cuts to the basket when #1 has the ball initially. How do we want X3 guarding against the reverse?

X3 is overplaying #3 one pass away. He faces #3 with his back to the ball and extends his left arm to deny the pass. Although facing his man with his body, X3 positions his head toward a point past his left hand (in this case), which is extended, allowing him to see his man *and* the ball. If #3 fakes one step to go to the basket, X3 should not take that fake. However, if #3 suddenly goes hard to the basket, X3 goes with him. In doing so, X3 turns, so that his *right* hand is now extended, and when glancing back at the ball, he does so over his *right* shoulder. We want X3 to play the reverse this way instead of turning his back on his man and facing the ball. When X3 reaches the lane, however, he will stop, open up, and see what is coming.

There are times when it is impossible to see both your man and the ball. When in doubt, meaning, when the defender cannot see *both* his man and the ball, we choose the *man*. We make this choice because we feel we can better accomplish our overall defensive goal this way. If we were playing strictly a support-, sagging man-to-man- type defense, we would choose ball over man. However, our type of pressure defense is predicated on keeping the ball away from the man in order to move him from his preferred position on the court. We therefore feel we can best accomplish this objective by choosing man over ball when we can't possibly see both at the same time. This principle is particularly applicable in a situation such as the backdoor cut described above. If X3 opened to the ball and lost his man, there would be simply too much territory involved to enable X3 to recover.

In Diagram 12-11, we add the guard-to-forward pass to the transition drill as the offense rotates in a clockwise direction. #1 passes to #3. #4 is instructed to sprint to the ball in the high-post area. If #3 can hit #4 there, X4 has not done his job. #4 then goes back up to replace #2 who has moved to #1's former position if he (#4) doesn't get the pass from #3.

Principle: When the offense attempts to clear a side to create a one-on-one situation for the dribbler, the defender does not follow the man clearing. Instead, he stops at the lane and opens up to see what is coming.

X1's job in our transition drill is the one we concentrate on heavily. When #1 throws to #3, X1 retreats in the direction of the pass. X1 stays between the ball and his man all the way to the lane, at which point #1 begins to approach that two-passes-away position. Therefore, when X1 hits the lane, he is taught to *open up* to see what is coming. By this we mean he stops and positions himself so that he can see both the ball and #1. When X1 crosses the lane and moves around to the other side, he is actually moving into a position *three* perimeter passes away. Consequently, there is no need for X1 to chase him around the other side of the court. Instead X1 is ready to help in the event #3 decides to drive to the basket.

If, in a game situation, #1 came all the way around into one-pass-away position, X1 could just come up the middle to beat him to the ball. Opening up at the lane to see what is coming should make it virtually impossible for the offense to get a full clearout on this type of defense.

DIAGRAM 12-12: ALL PURPOSE DRILL

Our final drill, which we use each day, permits the offense to incorporate all of the moves described in the first three drills. They may pass the ball around the horn as they do in the swing drill. They may penetrate, dribble, and pitch as in the support drill. They may pass guard-to-guard and go screen away, or pass to the forward and cut through, as in the transition drill.

As such, this all-purpose drill provides the defensive players with practice at putting many of our 20 defense principles to work. The offense, incidentally, is instructed not to shoot the ball until some time has elapsed in the drill.

Since the offense is given considerable latitude in our all-purpose drill, it is impossible to diagram the exact order of offensive patterns used. However, we might take this opportunity to illustrate a dribble-used situation which could easily come about during this drill.

Diagram 12-12

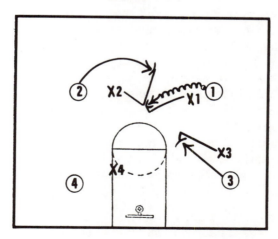

#1 begins the all-purpose drill in Diagram 12-12 with a penetration dribble. X2 comes down to support. X1, with X2's help, makes #1 pick up the dribble, which causes a free-lance offense if #1 doesn't throw to #2 immediately.

X1 now moves in tight on the ball-handler. X2 ignores the line of ball principle as he rushes up to close in on #2. X3 similarly attempts to clamp his man. Whenever the dribble is used by an offensive player, our weak-side deep man plays any one who reverses to the basket. X4, in this case, would be back to stop a possible backdoor cut by #3. X4, however, still has the primary responsibility of beating his own man to the ball. If #4 moved toward the ball, X4's immediate concern would be to get there first.

If the defense recovers fast enough to close the outlets, it could intercept a pass, force a pass out of bounds, or come up with a five-second count for a jump ball. The best we have done to date in this latter category was to force five jump balls against Ohio State in the 1968 NCAA Semifinals.

After affectively learning these four-on-four drills, we will on occasion (about three times a week) let the offense do anything it wishes in an effort to score, wich helps the Passing Game. Otherwise we simply scrimmage four-on-four. We do keep score for the defense on the five possessions allowed the offense. If the defense keeps the offense from getting off a shot, the defense gets two points. If the defense gains possession from a missed shot they get one point. If the offense scores or is fouled, the defense receives no points. The maximum number of points on five possessions would be ten for the defense if the offense never gets a shot off. The defensive teams for the day compete with each other to determine who has the highest defensive score. The losing team will run a sprint at the end of practice.

BREAKDOWN DRILLS

The preceding four major drills are used to impart our principles and facilitate most of our 20 defense teaching needs. We do, however, break these drills down even further to teach the basic individual skills which are required to ultimately execute the defense properly.

Diagram 12-13 is an example of this breakdown. The zig-zag drill illustrated on both the left and right side of the lower half-court is designed to teach the defender how to guard the dribbler. The defensive man's head should be in line with the elbow of the dribbling hand at a forty-five degree angle.

The most important premise to teach in pressure defense is to avoid fouling. Sometimes we use this drill in a specific way during the early weeks of practice to reinforce this point. When used for this purpose, the defensive men in the drill are required to grip their own shirts, or hold a towel with each hand, as they guard the dribbler up the court.

X1 and X2, in Diagram 12-13, reverse positions when they get to the mid-court stripe and rework the zig-zag back to the endline.

Diagram 12-13

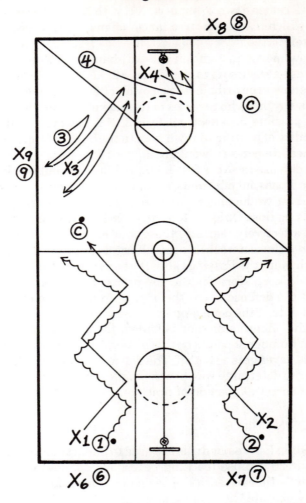

In the upper left half-court, X3 is learning how to keep the ball away from his man. When #3 is very close to the coach initially, X3 must be closer to his man in his overplay position. X3 learns, however, that when there is distance between his man and the ball-handler, the best way to keep #3 from the ball is to stay *away* from him. Therefore, as the distance between #3 and the coach widens, X3 allows the distance between himself and #3 to widen proportionately. #3 realizes that the best way to get free for the pass is to get extremely close to X3 and then break away. X3 must prevent this from happening by moving *away* from his man when he approaches. X3 also works to keep his head steady, and tries to see both man and ball.

Meanwhile, another drill is shown. In the upper right half-court X4 is learning how to beat his man to the ball when he must come from two passes to one pass away. As X4 comes toward the coach, his left arm is extended in an effort to deflect a possible pass to #4. When #4 sees that he's being beaten, he reverses to the basket. X4 must turn and extend his right arm onto the new line between the ball and the man as he pursues #4 low.

We do allow X4 to turn and face the ball on this reverse cut of #4 if he feels more comfortable doing so. Since there is very little distance for #4 to travel on the reverse, we give the defense this option. We believe this situation is somewhat different than the situation of beating the opponent to the ball farther out on the court because of the distance involved.

Beginning in 1976, we actually preferred the defense to face the ball and front the man as he approached the ball in low. The reason for this preference is that officials tend to call the foul on our X4 even though #4 might be pushing off. We discovered that X4 could actually hold or *box out* #4 moving to the ball without the official calling a foul.

The Zig-Zag drill (guarding the man with the ball) is done in practice at one end of the court, while *one* of the other two drills (guarding the man away from the ball) is done at the other end. We then rotate the groups.

SCREENS INVOLVING THE BALL

We do not use any of our four major drills to incorporate our defense against the screen at the point of the ball. There are basically three types of screens which can be used this way. Although we will cover them in order at this point, I do not think they should be taught to players this way. I recall having once confused a team on the first day of practice by introducing all three at the same time along with our defensive reaction to each. We would suggest, therefore, that they be covered individually over a long period of time.

The three different type of screens at the point of the ball are: one, the weave-type screen, in which the screener has the ball; two, the dribbler coming toward a stationary screen; and three, a screener coming to the man without the ball who has not dribbled.

The Weave   The screen at the point of the ball in the *weave* is illustrated at the top of **Diagram 12-14**.

#1 dribbles in the direction of #2. X1, with his head in line with the elbow of the dribbling hand, is guarding #1. X2 is moving to support on the dribbler while keeping an eye on his man, #2. In this situation, the screener #1 has the ball as #2 comes off #1 to take a handoff.

We defense the weave by jump-switching it. When X1 sees #2 coming to take the handoff, we want him to jump out into #2's path, ideally drawing the charge. X2, of course, is responsible for stopping #1's dribble, which follows our support theory. This, then is the way we attempt to defense the weave and guard the screener who has the ball.

Offensive Man One Pass Away Screens for Dribbler   Another common type of screen used is one which has the ball-handler dribbling *toward* the screen as illustrated on the left side of Diagram 12-14. X2 has a difficult job here, since his responsibility is keeping the pass away from #2. How does X2 know when

#2 becomes a screener instead of a logical receiver? This is one of the most difficult things for any player to learn in our pressure defense. It requires a great deal of practice before players can begin to recognize when that change takes place.

Diagram 12-14

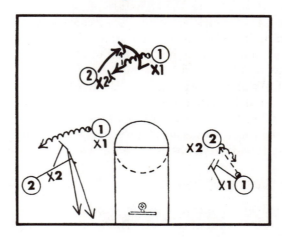

When X2 realizes that his man is setting a screen, he must yell "*pick*" and then "*get high on the screen.*" (By definition the *high side* of the screen is the side to which the dribbler is attempting to dribble.) Therefore, X2 must leave his overplay position, and come to a position on the outside shoulder of #2. He may go either in front of or behind #2 to get to that position. By X2 getting in the path of the screen this way we hope to accomplish one of the following objectives: one, if X2 surprises the dribbler, #1 might pick up his dribble; two, #1 might charge X2; or three, #1 might be forced to veer wide, as illustrated in the diagram. This would widen the path between #1 and #2 and allow X1 to get through over the top of the screen.

X2's defensive maneuver here is called *fake switching*. We want him to stay on the high side of the screen for a second or two, and then back off to his original man. He does continue to touch his man when he is on the high side of the screener. If the screener leaves early, he will go with him since he is guarding the screener.

Switching is permitted. However, we want to vary this throughout the game. We do not want a team preparing for us to know whether or not we will switch on each screen at the point of the ball. When screens involve players of the same relative size, switching is not excessively detrimental to the defense. A switch which would have a center or tall forward screening for a small guard would hurt us more. If such a switch is to occur, the man guarding the screener is the one who makes this decision and yells "switch."

Many coaches feel that you can get hurt on a *screen-and-roll* offense. This can be true if the screen-and-roll is done well. If X1 jumps in #2's path and yells "switch," it will be difficult for X2 to pick up #1 rolling to the basket if the screen-and-roll is properly executed.

In order to avoid getting hurt in this type of situation, it is important that each of the three defenders not involved with the screen get off their men and move into the lane to help. They should be able to give much ground here, since the man dribbling off the screen invariably will be looking to shoot or hit the screener going to the basket. I can't recall ever having seen a dribbler come off a screen and look across the court for an outlet. Therefore, one of our principles is that when a screen occurs at the point of the ball, the three defensive players away from the screen attempt to move into the foul lane to help. They continue to see their own respective men, however, along with the basketball.

Fighting Over the Top   Before we move on to the third type of screen, we should detail the job of the man guarding the dribbler who is about to use a screen from a teammate. He must be aware that a screen could occur at any time and be alerted to a pick call from a teammate. As he approaches the screen, the defensive man must get as close as possible to the dribbler without fouling. This should enable him to step *between* the screener and the dribbler, particularly if his teammate makes the dribbler go wide with the fake switch. We call this *fighting over the top of the screen*. We fight over the top of all screens regardless of where the screen occurs in the defensive half-court. Basketball rules do allow for some negligible contact as the defensive players go over the top of the screen.

This method of defending against the screen should not be confused with the *sliding through* technique which has the defender sliding between the screener and the defensive man on the screener. We feel that sliding through provides the offense with too much of a scoring opportunity and too little pressure on the ball.

Some coaches have asked me why we don't permit sliding through when the screen occurs far from the basket. It is true that sliding through the screen thirty feet from the basket will not hurt the defense. However, we do want to build a good habit here. We also would prefer not to burden the defender with having to decide if a particular screen is occurring eighteen feet or twenty-three feet from the basket.

Screen for Man Holding Ball   The third type of screen in Diagram 12-14 illustrated on the right side is very similar to the *fighting over the top* screen.

#1 gets the pass off to #2 and comes to set the screen for him. #2 waits for the screen before starting his dribble. X1 again must recognize he now is guarding a screener and find that position on the high side of the screen. X1, in this case, will attempt to have #2 veer his dribble as he comes off the screen so that X2 may go over the top and stay with #2. It should be pointed out how important it is for X2 not to let his man dribble away from the screen. With X1 on the high side of the screen, X2 must force #2 in that direction. Should #2 drive past X2 away from X1, you can easily see where two defensive men would be out of the picture. In this case, I think you could gamble sometimes, and have X1 and X2 both jump the first dribble by #2, in a double-team situation.

We have been experimenting with this double-teaming on all screens at the point of the ball, as outlined. In this experimentation, we simply tell the two defensive men involved to double-team the man with the ball coming off the screen, whether it be a weave, a dribbler off the screen, or a man beginning his dribble off the screen. We think the double-team is an effective surprise to that man with the ball. The problem with this type of gambling defense is that if the offense is successful in making one pass the defense will have difficulty picking up a man. However, if you simply wanted to pick up tempo, you would be forcing the team to do something it really did not want to do.

If #2 veers as X1 jumps in his path on the fake switch, X2 should have plenty of room to fight over the top. We show this reaction in the diagram. We could just as well have shown X1 switching with X2 which is an alternative move.

_____THE 20 DEFENSE AGAINST THE ONE-FOUR OFFENSE

As we indicated in our chapter on the one-four offense, the reason we use this alignment against pressure defense is to remove defensive help.

In **Diagram 12-15**, each offensive player is tentatively one pass away when #1 has the ball in the middle. If we let #1 stay in the middle, there would be no help available. Consequently, the defense would be vulnerable to a quick score off a backdoor cut.

Our job on defense to is make the offensive quarterback go to one side and then keep him there in order to create and maintain a weak side. This, of course, is compatible to our overall 20 defense goals regardless of the offense we are facing. In Diagram 12-15, X1 forces #1 to the left. X3 moves off his man on the weak side to a position in front of #5. This allows X5 to move back as the help man. If #2 or #4 were to reverse to the basket, X5 should be then in position to cross the lane and stop the move to the basket.

_____TRANSITION FROM OFFENSE TO DEFENSE

Any time we miss a field-goal attempt, we automatically are back into our 22 defense in an effort to stop the fast break. As stated in our philosophy of defense chapter, we do not jump the rebounder, nor try to pinch the outlet pass. Although many teams attempt to stop the break *high*, we feel that doing so can create some problems. We prefer to stop the break by sprinting back downcourt.

Our #1 man is always back on defense (as in **Diagram 12-16**). #1's job during the transition is to come back *into the hole* and take the basket. Our #2 guard is usually in a position to pick up a long rebound. However, he also should be able to get back quickly as well. He plays the ball in the vicinity of the foul line, as illustrated in Diagram 12-16. When necessary, the guards switch these responsibilities.

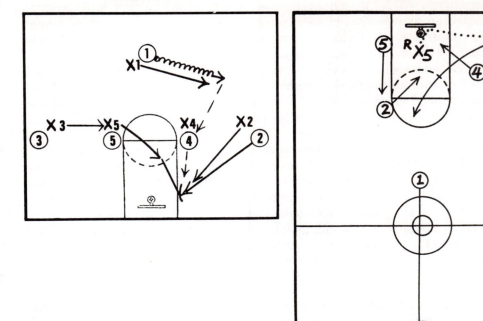

Diagram 12-15

Diagram 12-16

Our #3, #4, and #5 men have the rebounding responsibility. However, once the opponent has possession, our frontcourt men must race back quickly as well. If our guards have been able to stop the ball by making the offense pass at least once in this scoring area, our players should be able to begin picking up their respective men.

With a little practice, #2 should be able to recognize if #1 is through shooting a lay-up or a baseline jump shot. This recognition will allow #2 to be the first man back on defense. In addition, if our #3 man shoots an outside jump shot, #2 can go ahead and hit the offensive boards with #3 helping #1 back on defense. I think it is very difficult for an outside jump shooter to be an effective offensive rebounder. However, we do want him moving toward the middle of the court, and then back on defense after a shot.

We fully realize, however, that it is not always possible for each defender to pick up his own man during the transition. This is where *talking* comes into play, which is very important. For example, suppose our X2 must pick up the opponent's #3. X2 then has the job of calling out the number of his original match-up man so that he can be picked up by a teammate. As X3 comes downcourt, he looks for his own man, #3. When he spots X2 on #3, he listens to hear which man he now has to pick up.

Of course, whenever possible, we prefer that our players pick up their own men to minimize the defensive confusion that often results at the tail end of the break. We spoke about that situation at length prior to the introduction of our secondary break in chapter seven.

Two-on-One Situation The two-on-one situation is one we would obviously prefer not to be in defensively. However, when it does occur we do not want the defender to give up without some effort. If the offense puts the ball on the floor, the defender can attempt a guessing game with both men. For example, he might fake away from the dribbler initially and then jump back over in his path, hoping to draw the charge. The two-on-one is a tough situation, and the only way the defender stands a remote chance of beating it is to fake one move and then come up with an unexpected move. Of course, we don't want to give the opponent a three-point play.

Three-on-Two Situation We do not think it is possible to keep an offense coming down three-on-two from taking an outside jumper. Therefore, the job of the two defenders is to force the offense to make more than two passes before the ball goes up. This should give us enough time to get our help back.

If our guards are unsuccessful at delaying the shot, they look to box out the opponent's bigger players. Our own big men should have an excellent chance for the rebound, if our opponents miss the jump shot.

Most of the methods we use to teach the transition and the counterbreak are covered at the conclusion of our chapter on the fast break. In addition to the drills described in that chapter, we always stress the importance of defensive balance whenever we work the dummy offense in practice. To emphasize this point during the dummy offense, we have our quarterback, or the appropriate player, automatically sprinting back to mid-court whenever a shot goes up.

numbering system applicable to 20 defense

We have not spent much time discussing the numbering system of the 20 defense. The 22 defense is our basic half-court, man-to-man pressure which we have discussed throughout this chapter. The same principles apply to the 23 defense except that the pick-up point of the dribbler would be at three-quarters court instead of half-court. The 24 defense is run a few different ways which we will describe at this point.

This utilizes the 20 defensive principles. However, the pick-up is at full-court. In 24, we do not want the offense to make the in-bounds pass successfully. The man responsible for the player in-bounding the ball has the responsibility of preventing a long pass or a lay-up, and is back as illustrated in **Diagram 12-17**.

In this diagram, #3 is taking the ball out of bounds. Therefore, X3 is back. If #2 was taking the ball out of bounds, X2 would be back, etc.

If our opponent has one man back at their basket, X3, the free-lance man, could then come up to double-team #1 or #2. The free-lancer has the job of guessing with the throw-in, but at the same time he is responsible for preventing the lay-up on the first pass.

We use the same defensive philosophy on the sideline out-of-bounds play, rarely playing the man in-bounding the ball. If the throw-in was being made in our opponent's offensive end of the court, the 22 defense would have everyone playing his man tough with one free-lancer guessing with the throw-in.

Diagram 12-18 illustrates an alternate 24 defense which we refer to as *24 all-over*. We usually use 24 all-over when our scouting tells us the opponent will keep a man downcourt. We like to vary this call on made foul shots, alternating between 24 straight and 24 all-over. However, we are also more likely to use 24 all-over when the man out of bounds can not move and must maintain his designated spot. This would be true for sideline out-of-bounds situations. We also use it when we are behind late in the game. We dare our opponent to throw the long pass, and hope that it will not be successful.

Our 24 defense must almost always be called on a foul-shot situation, or as the referee is setting up the players to throw the ball in-bounds. Since most of the teams we play in-bound the ball quickly after we score, it is very difficult to set up 24 after a field goal. For terminology's sake, if the ball is taken out on the sideline at three-quarters court, we play the same defenses described above, calling them 23 or 23 all-over. The same would hold true, using 22 or 22 all-over, if the ball was in the opponent's half-court. In each of these situations, we play everyone one-pass-away tough. The difference is whether we play all over the man taking the ball out of bounds or have his defender as a free-lancer.

If 34 or 44 defense was called, it would look identical to Diagrams 12-17 and 12-18. The line-up is the same. However, once the ball is in-bounded, we would go with the principles of the defense being used.

When we are in our 23 defense we pick up the opponent at three-quarters court, as illustrated in Diagram 12-1. If you look back to Diagram 12-1 and then look ahead to Diagrams 13-1 and 14-1, you will note that our attacks are initiated identically in our 20, 30, and 40 defenses. This is intentional and designed to prevent the offense from knowing which defensive attack we plan to use.

Diagram 12-17

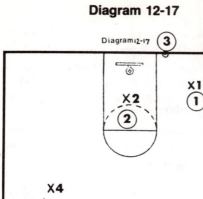

Diagram 12-18

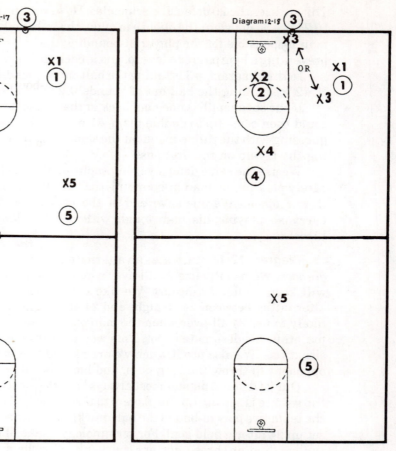

202

the run-and-jump defense

13

The *run-and-jump* is a rotating man-to-man defense which, while more conservative than a zone press, affords many of the same opportunities for interceptions. It is very much a man-to-man defense. However, there is no set assignment after the first run-and-jump occurs, and any one defensive man may be guarding another offensive man.

It all began, as far as I am concerned, back in the 1952-53 season at the University of Kansas. We were in true pressure defense, as outlined by Dr. Phog Allen, our head coach, and Dick Harp, his assistant. We had won the NCAA Championship in 1952 because of the excellent play by our center, Clyde Lovellette, and a pressure defense which placed the defensive man between the ball and his man rather than the man and the basket, which was typical in those days.

One of our players during those years was an extremely competitive athlete by the name of Al Kelley. Al did not play regularly as a sophomore in 1952, but I do remember that none of our players wanted Al guarding them during practice. Al was very aggressive. In fact, to the best of my knowledge, he led the nation in personal fouls as a junior in 1953.

It was in practice that I remember Al guarding a defensive man one pass away from the ball. A guard began dribbling in his direction. Instead of supporting to help out on the dribbler, Al left his man completely to take the ball away from the dribbler about ten feet away. Of course, the man guarding the dribbler automatically reacted by picking up Al's man, although he was probably upset with Al for not doing what he was supposed to do. However, Dick Harp, the assistant coach, actually congratulated Al for making things happen, even though he fouled the ball handler when he surprised him.

Many times, from that point on, Al would make the dribbler charge him, or the dribbler would pick up the ball and throw it out of bounds. Al was the only player who could do this, although several of us decided it would be fun to surprise the dribbler. It was all part of our basic man-to-man pressure, and was not used as a separate defense at that time. This is how the run-and-jump came into being, as far as I can remember.

If we had stopped to think about it back then, we would have labeled the play the *run and surprise*. That is probably an even more appropriate description of its intended effect.

Morgan Wootten, the highly successful basketball coach at DeMatha High School in Washington, D.C., liked our run-and-jump defense and instituted it at DeMatha. He called the defense "the blitz", which is perhaps better terminology.

We used the run-and-jump sparingly at the University of Kansas. However, in 1953, when most of the team was lost to graduation and we were very small, our coaches felt we might be able to make the defense our true offense. We would take the action defensively and make the offense react to us by doing so-called *stunting*, as football teams do. Keep in mind that this was during the early 1950's when teams either zone pressed or played a straight man-to-man press. Our relatively short team, with 6'2" and 6'1" forwards, managed to win the Big Eight Conference (after being picked to finish low in the Conference) and lost to Indiana by only one in the NCAA Finals.

Coach Bob Spear had seen the 1953 finals and was impressed with the Kansas pressure defense. He wanted to know more about it when I joined him as his assistant at the Air Force Academy. Our Air Force Academy team was extremely small and we needed to do things defensively instead of sitting back and letting the offense handle us. The man-to-man pressure defense, incorporating the run-and-jump, became one of our primary defenses at the Academy in the years that followed. It was during this period that we first used the run-and-jump as a full-court defense occasionally. Prior to that time at Kansas, it had been used strictly at half-court out of our basic pressure defense.

When I first assumed the head coaching position at the University of North Carolina, we again were very small, but did have three very quick guards in Larry Brown, Donnie Walsh, and Yogi Poteet. All three picked up the run-and-jump quickly and executed it well. Their success with it encouraged the forwards (who were sometimes really guards in size) to enter into it any time a dribbler approached them.

In fact our players enjoyed it so much during those early years at North Carolina, it eventually created a problem for us. Up to that point, the run-and-jump was not a separate defense, but part of our basic pressure defense. Our players were given the freedom to use it at any point on the court they felt they could surprise an approaching dribbler. However, since surprise is important to the run-and-jump, its effectiveness tends to diminish when it is used too often. When our players become too keyed up over the play, we finally had to do something to cut down on its frequency. We did this in 1965 by making it a separate signaled defense.

The only major change effected by this step was one of control. The 30 defense is still generated from our basic man-to-man alignment. However, we can now take advantage of the surprise element a little more effectively by preventing its overuse. Our players also can anticipate more easily the Rotation (picking up the open man) as a result of the defense being signaled.

uses and advantages of the run-and-jump

Although we now use the "Run and Jump" as a separate defense, we should point out that its main purpose (along with our 40 and 50 defense) is to show the offense a different look. As we indicated in our philosophy of defense chapter, these secondary defenses in our multiple system are used *primarily* to support our basic man-to-man pressure attack. When they work well for us, it is usually because our opponents are more disconcerted by the change than necessarily overcome by their quality or execution. However, the run and jump does offer some other advantages in addition to giving the offense another look.

To begin with, it is hardly a passive-type defense, but one that very definitely initiates the action on defense. Therefore, when successful, it tends to prevent opponents from organizing their planned attack. When a defensive player leaves his man completely to run and surprise the dribbler, it is going to result in *some* type of reaction on the part of the offense. If the move achieves maximum success at that point, the ball handler could either charge the defender, walk with the ball, or lose it on a steal. If we succeed in making the ball handler pick up his dribble , we then would try to press him and cut off his outlets. If we do not prevent the pass, we might still be able to offset offensive organization by forcing the ball handler into a pass he didn't intend to make originally. The run-and-jump usually gets things going and for this reason it can be used to advantage against ball-control teams or to speed up tempo. When this is our purpose, we will sometimes run-and-jump in the full-court even if we do not have the strong element of surprise going for us.

Another time we may run-and-jump without a complete surprise would be to make the other team's best ballplayer give up the ball. During the years we played against David Thompson, the great All-American from NC State, now with the Denver Nuggets, we would tell our players to leave their man if Thompson started dribbling toward them, even if we were in our straight man-to-man defense. By doing so, we would make Thompson give up the ball. We then attempted to keep him from getting it back. We realized that the man to whom he passed may have a good shot but, at least Thompson was not the one hurting us. He was their team's best shooter so, by using the run-and-jump, we perhaps could make someone else shoot the ball, instead of their star player.

The run-and-jump also can be an effective defense to use against a team that likes to set screens for the dribbler at the point of the ball. These screens often can be offset by having the screener's defender run-and-jump the approaching dribbler. Therefore, a screen never should be able to be set at the point of the ball unless the screen is set before the ball handler begins his dribble.

As a catch-up defense, the run-and-jump has a lot going for it as well. This, of course, would be true of any aggressive defense that is designed to maximize opponent turnover.

One final advantage of the defense is the fact that most players seem to enjoy it greatly. The run-and-jump is a fun type of defense. Consequently, the players usually go at it with much effort and enthusiasm.

weaknesses of the run-and-jump

The run-and-jump is very much a gambling-type defense. We sometimes like to characterize it as a defense that gives the thrill of a zone press while maintaining the advantages of the more sound man-to-man alignment. Hopefully, this is true most of the time. There are, however, those vulnerable few seconds when the defense is somewhat in limbo, when it is neither man-to-man nor zone by strict definition. This is the phase of the defense when the players must quickly rotate as their teammate jumps the dribbler. As we'll point out later, we have no set rules to determine who picks up the open man during the rotation. Sometimes confusion occurs, which can work to the advantage of the offense. When this happens, the defense can get hurt by an open fifteen-foot jumper. This should not occur frequently, however, if the man jumping the dribbler succeeds in surprising him and then works to block his view of possible outlets.

Defensive rebounding could pose some problems. True, we are defending man-to-man essentially, which gives each defender a man to box out. However, we can get caught behind an opponent while rotating. A possible mismatch resulting from a switch in assignments could also hurt us under the board. These possibilities, however, are countered somewhat by the likelihood that our opponents may not be as well prepared for offensive rebounding as they intended. Since the run-and-jump is designed to take the offense out of its usual game, the shot often comes up unexpectedly without the usual built-in offensive board protection.

Some college coaches, after implementing the run-and-jump, have indicated to me that it tends to make the players careless in their execution of the team's basic defense. I think there is merit to this criticism. As we said initially, the run-and-jump is strictly a gambling-type defense. Players are looking to leave their men and much of the emphasis is on stealing the ball. These can be bad habits for players to get into in terms of the kind of defense we look for with our own 20 defense (pressure man-to-man). Possibly, we could execute our 20 defense somewhat more consistently if our players had no exposure to the 30. However, I do think we gain much more from the change of look and the steal which often leads to a high-percentage shot for us than we lose through occasional carelessness on the 20. We do consider it important, however, to constantly stress 20 defense principles to keep any inclinations towards carelessness to a minimum.

run-and-jump at the secondary school level

Several years ago, we conducted an experiment with a group of thirteen-year-olds at our summer camp. We divided twelve youngsters into two groups placing the six most highly skilled boys on the same unit. Both groups were given identical attention and each worked similar drills for two days with one exception. The less-skilled youngsters were given 30 minutes of instruction and practice in the run-and-jump. The other group was not prepared accordingly. On the third day, we scrimmaged the groups against each other and the results were remarkable. By using the run-and-jump, the less-skilled youngsters were totally successful in defending the better players. In fact, the other group was not even able to get off more than a couple of shots during a full ten minutes of play.

Of course, even the more skilled youngster at this age is still not fully proficient at handling the ball. The same is sometimes true, but of course to a lesser extent, at the high school level. We do believe that the less matured the ball-handling skill, the more effective gambling-type defenses such as the run-and-jump will be. We have recommended the 30 defense to both junior high and high school coaches at clinics and have heard from many of them subsequently who were extremely pleased with the results.

One junior high coach who has come to our practices and has been to several clinics, decided to use the run-and-jump as a continuous defense. He made what I consider to be a fine move with a man guarding the ball. He told the man on the ball to force the dribbler to his weak hand (his left hand if the ball handler was right-handed). At the junior high level, few young men have developed the skill to dribble equally well, left- or right-handed. Therefore, by jumping a right-handed ball handler in a manner that forces him to go to his left hand, the dribbler could possibly be caught with his head down.

Another example of success with the run-and-jump could be found in Barberton, Ohio, where high school coach Jack Greynolds has been teaching defense for some time. Coach Greynolds has told me he would let the players run-and-jump as soon as the dribble occurred without even waiting for the surprise element. He had watched several of our practices and came upon this idea on his own. Of course, Coach Greynolds does a great job of teaching, as does Morgan Wootten, in running our defense. DeMatha has an outstanding record and, much to Coach Greynold's credit, Barberton won the 1976 Ohio State Championship with some very small but active players.

run-and-jump at the pro level

Judging from the above, one might think that the highly proficient ball handling seen in the pros would rule out the run-and-jump as an effective defense at that level. Surprisingly, the defense has made its way to the pros with some degree of success.

Larry Brown introduced our run-and-jump defense when he took over as head coach of the ABA Carolina Cougars in 1972. Larry had served as an excellent assistant coach to me during the 1966-67 seasons after playing the run-and-jump as a player in 1962 and 1963. He knows the defense as well as anyone and has great teaching ability, which he employs now at UCLA.

I have to admit I was doubtful initially that the run-and-jump would be successful against some of the outstanding ball handlers the Cougars would be up against. Larry believed it would work, and the defense was effective at that level. Its success may be due to the pride or *ego* on the part of some professional players who are reluctant to give up the ball, which offsets their super ball handling skills. Larry used the defense to make the super player give up the ball by running at him. In addition, he made tremendous use of the run-and-jump to speed up tempo and get the opponent to put up the shot more quickly. He taught me that the run-and-jump, at the pro level, should be used only at certain times and could not be used throughout the game.

run-and-jump in the full-court

To begin our diagraming of the run-and-jump, let us assume that we will be picking up the offense at three-quarters court. The quarterback signals the run-and-jump. We are now in 33 defense: run-and-jump at three-quarters court. Keep in mind, however, that the run-and-jump can be used at any point on the court, and at times other than following our field-goals.

If we call for 33 defense, we continue to use the run-and-jump throughout that particular possession of the opponent. Even if the opponent shoots and gets the rebound, we stay in our 30 defense. The same would hold true if we begin in 32 defense, which means that we would be picking up the offense at half-court.

A problem that might occur at this point is the possibility of the opposing quarterback stealing the defensive signal, thereby negating the surprise aspect of the run-and-jump. Certainly, it could happen, but it's really not a serious consideration for the defense. In the first place, the quarterback on offense is usually preoccupied with becoming an outlet for the in-bounds pass. As such, he usually has his back to the defensive quarterback. Secondly, most coaches, myself included, would not want to burden their quarterbacks with the additional pressure of spotting and interpreting defensive signals.

Diagram 13-1 picks up the action after the in-bounds pass has been made to #1. At this point, our players are in the same position on defense as they would be if the quarterback had signaled either our 20 or 40 defense. This helps us disguise our defensive attack. *In fact, if no dribble occurs and the ball stays in the air, we remain in 20 defense (straight man-to-man).*

Diagram 13-1

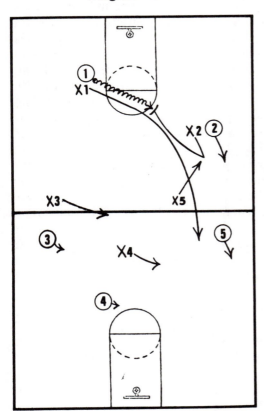

Diagram 13-2

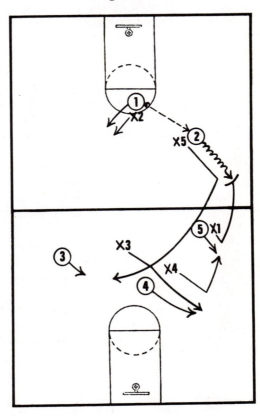

Except for X1, we want our players staying as far from their offensive men downcourt as possible without jeopardizing their ability to recover if #1 were to throw long. Each defensive player guarding his man without the ball plays between the ball and his man as in 20 defense. X1 plays #1 very tight. Good pressure here is important so that #1 doesn't have the opportunity to find the open man. We want the ball handler putting the ball on the floor.

X1 then has the job of making #1 move downcourt at a forty-five degree angle. We are less concerned with the direction #1 takes than we are with preventing him from beating our defensive man handily. In Diagram 13-1, #1 dribbles lefthanded in the direction of #2, who begins to clear out. X2 follows #2 part of the way, but then realizes he has a good chance of surprising #1. X2, therefore, runs-and-jumps (runs and surprises) on the outside shoulder of the dribbler.

THE ROTATION

As X2 returns to jump the dribbler, #2 is left unguarded and must be picked up quickly. As we indicated earlier, there are no ironclad rules to determine who will pick up the open man during the rotation. For that matter it is not required, nor even preferable most of the time, that every player join in the rotation. Proximity and judgment will usually determine these factors. The direction of the rotation, however, is determined by the direction taken by the dribbler. If, as in Diagram 13-1, he moves downcourt to his left, players rotating on the perimeter will do so in a counterclockwise direction. The initial defender of the dribbler, however, (X1 in Diagram 13-1), sprints back looking for the open man in a clockwise direction. The reverse patterns are in effect if the dribbler comes downcourt to his right as we will illustrate later.

In Diagram 13-1, X5, anticipating and then observing X2's run-and-jump move, decides to leave his man to pick up #2. X4 could choose to pick up #5. However, in this case, he remains guarding #4, and X3 stays on #3. X1 never breaks his stride. Playing with his back to his teammates, he doesn't know at the outset when his help is coming. Therefore, he plays #1 tight until in his periphery, he spots X2 leaving and surprising his man. X1 then heads downcourt around the perimeter in a clockwise direction to pick up the open man. In this case, it happens to be #5. However, it could have been #2, if X5 chose to stay on #5. It also could have been #4, if X4 moved to #5 on X5's move to #2, and so on.

We usually end up in what really amounts to a three-man switch. Very seldom would there be as many as four different men changing their defensive assignments. The most typical situation is the one diagramed with X1 picking #5, X2 picking up #1 and X5 taking #2. The other most prevalent move is a simple switch between X1 and X2.

POSSIBLE RESULTS OF RUN-AND-JUMP

For the play to end with ultimate success at this point, #1, as a result of being surprised by X2, might lose the ball on a steal by X2, charge X2, travel with the ball, or pass the ball to #2 with X5 intercepting. In Diagram 13-1, we have not accomplished any of the ideal possibilities suggested. However, we have succeeded in making #1 pick up his dribble. At this point X2 is harassing the ball handler. X5 is trying to prevent the pass to #2, who is #1's closest outlet. X1, X3, and X4 are similarly working to prevent the pass to the other offensive players. If the play were to end successfully at *this* point, #1 might attempt a pass which would be intercepted, or take too much time to find the outlet, which could prevent the ball from getting past the mid-court line within ten seconds.

INDIVIDUAL RESPONSIBILITIES

Before we move on to see what happens if none of the above possibilities occur, let's go back and review the responsibilities of each player in 30 defense using Diagram 13-1 as the example.

1. *Player guarding initial ball handler (X1)*
   (a) Plays man tight - applies pressure in an effort to prevent ball handler from finding open man. Tries to get ball handler to put ball on floor.
   (b) Avoids letting the ball handler slice quickly to the middle of the court. The job of the man guarding the ball handler is to encourage him to place the ball on the court with a dribble at a forty-five (or more) degree angle while keeping pressure on the ball. Playing the run-and-jump does not mean a player may let up when guarding the man with the basketball.
   (c) Stays with his man until he sees in his periphery the run-and-jump man attacking dribbler - then enters rotation looking for open man.
2. *Players guarding men one perimeter pass away (X2 and X3)*
   (a) First responsibility is to prevent pass from ball handler to their man.
   (b) When ball handler starts dribbling *away* from them, they start giving ground in the direction (and to the extent) of the dribble. They are still playing man-to-man, however, and must always be able to get back to prevent a pass.
   (c) When ball handler starts dribbling *toward* them, they start thinking about the proper surprise point to initiate the run-and-jump. The correct point to surprise the dribbler would vary. It would be dependent upon the distance from the dribbler and the speed with which he dribbles. For example, if #1 were dribbling very fast, X2 could surprise him from ten to fifteen feet away. If the dribbler was coming slowly, X2 should not leave until he was approximately six feet away.
3. *Players guarding men two or more perimeter passes away (X4 and X5)*
   (a) Same as 2a above.
   (b) Same as 2b above.
   (c) When ball handler starts dribbling *toward* them, they begin to prepare for rotation. For example X5, in Diagram 13-1, must decide whether to come up and play the possible pass to #2 on X2's run-and-jump or stay where he is and let X1 pick up #2. The decision depends on whether or not he feels he can get the ball, as well as the jump on #2. If #2 decides to break, X5 *should* go for him.
   (d) If X5 is 6'10" and not very active, he probably should not make a decision to enter the rotation unless #2 was going all the way to the basket. X5 probably would not want to play #2 whom, we may assume, is a 6'0" guard.

Diagram 13-2 is a continuation of Diagram 13-1 and illustrates that the 30 defense does not necessarily conclude after one run-and-jump play. The run-and-jump option remains in effect throughout the entire possession.

#1, after being surprised by X2, attempts to get the pass to #2. X5 tries to intercept the pass but is unsuccessful. X5 then stays tough on #2, who dribbles the ball toward the sideline in the direction of #5, who is now covered by X1. Admittedly, we have quite a mismatch here with X1 on #5. However, we have always felt that the temporary mismatch is overrated. A mismatch like this could be brutal under the board, but more often than not, it doesn't get that far. I am convinced the mismatch is overrated from an offensive standpoint and often fails when the offense stops everything to exploit it.

In Diagram 13-2, X1 chooses to run-and-jump the new ball handler, #2. The rotation begins again. This time, X4 picks up #5, who is the offensive player initially left uncovered as a result of the run-and-jump. X3 picks up #4 and X5 comes around the perimeter to take #3.

RUN-AND-JUMP IN THE HALF COURT

Suppose now that #2 gets the pass off to #5, or for that matter to any of the other offensive players. Does the run-and-jump option terminate now that we're in the half-court? Definitely not! In fact, we believe the defense can be even more effective in the half-court.

The only difference between the run-and-jump in the half-court as compared to full-court relates to the element of surprise. The closer the opponents get to their basket, the closer the man running and jumping should be to the dribbler before he starts his move. At the same time, however, the distances between the players in the half-court are much shorter. Consequently, there are more opportunities to surprise an opponent three or four steps away. Close to the basket, the offensive player tends to speed up his dribble thinking of a driving lay-up which enhances the run-and-jump move.

Let's continue the action of the previous diagrams into the half-court. We'll attempt to illustrate how the run-and-jump can be an effective means of stopping the dribbler who thinks he has a good one-on-one move on his opponent. You will also notice some more *matching back up* on the part of the defense as the opponent gets closer to the basket. We'll pick up the action in *Diagram 13-3* on the assumption that the ball has been passed around a few times and some movement has occurred on the court. Each of the players, however, is still guarding the same man he had at the conclusion of the last rotation since no dribble has occurred.

#4 has the ball about fifteen feet from the basket as the other offensive players attempt to clear out for him. #4 thinks he can beat X3 and begins his drive to the basket. X4, however, suddenly crosses the lane to run-and-jump #4. This should be a very effective surprise since, admittedly, it does take courage for X4 to leave his man that close to the basket. As #4 starts his dribble, X5 begins to rotate back in front of #5 and X2 comes back in front of #3. X1, of course, tries both to play #4 and the baseline. We allow X1 to double-team #4 with X4 temporarily.

LINE-OF-BALL PRINCIPLE IN 30 DEFENSE

In *Diagram 13-4,* #1 begins his right-handed dribble down the opposite side of the court. In this case, #2 decides to remain back to serve as a possible outlet for #1. X2, however, continues his move forward in the direction of #1's dribble. If #1 wishes to pass back to #2, we let the pass go as per our *line of ball* principle covered in 20 defense. Should #1 pass to #2, X2 would come back to press the new ball handler while the next closest defensive player (depending on the direction #2 takes) would look for the opportunity to surprise #2.

In Diagram 13-4, X3 runs-and-jumps #1. X4 picks up #3, who takes off looking for the pass from #1. Since #1, dribbling right-handed, moved upcourt to his right, the rotation in Diagram 13-3 is in a clockwise direction around the perimeter. X1 comes back in a counterclockwise direction looking for the open man.

Diagram 13-3

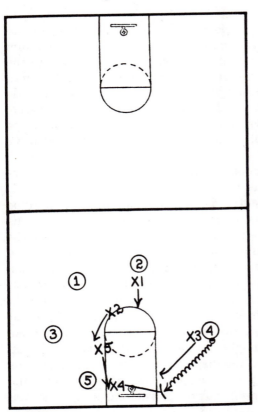

Diagram 13-4

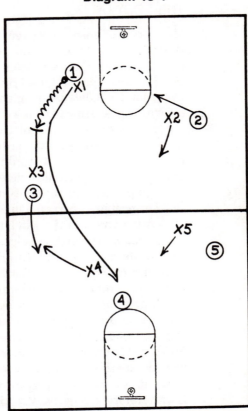

In Diagrams 13-1 through 13-4, we have illustrated the run-and-jump defense against an offense that moved the ball around the perimeter exclusively. The perimeter in these diagrams is that oval or circular shape that would appear if a line were drawn from one offensive player to the other.

One might question at this point what we would do if the ball handler managed to break into the middle despite our efforts to move him downcourt at a forty-five degree angle. Would the run-and-jump still be in effect? Yes! However, the surprise factor would become more critical.

For example, in Diagram 13-4, if #1 broke down the middle past X1 and X2 instead of going right, as he does in the diagram, X4 could, but probably should not, run-and-jump him. However, he should wait until #1 is closer to him if he does, unless he intends to tackle him. If X4 was to run-and-jump #1 without the element of surprise, the move would almost certainly result in a quick basket for the offense off the fast break.

Therefore, if the ball handler does break free into the middle, we immediately sprint back to stop the break and then build back out into 32 Defense.

THE POST UP

Most press offenses, however, employ a *post up* in an effort to get the ball into the middle. At the same time, of course, most defenses will put forth maximum effort to keep the ball around the perimeter and prevent the pass to the middle. If the post up used by the offense is similar to the one illustrated in **Diagram 13-5** defensing it should not pose critical problems. X4 must do everything possible to beat #4 to the middle of the perimeter. His only job is to stick with #4 and prevent the pass. X4 will, of course, give around if #4 becomes located beyond the line of ball. It is important to note that if X2 run-and-jumps #1, X4 would *not* enter into the rotation. The rotation is entered into by perimeter defenders only. This would be true when the run-and-jump occurs in the half-court as well.

The post up illustrated in **Diagram 13-6** is more difficult to cover. This type of move represents the kind of press offense that has been used against us more frequently in recent years. #1 starts down the sideline to his right covered by X1. #3, in this particular play, chooses not to make his move immediately. However, after X3 runs-and-jumps the dribbler, #3 leaves the perimeter and button-hooks into the middle. Who covers #3 posting up into the dangerous middle? Once again, there are no hard and fast rules. X4 could come up and try to prevent the pass to #3. Doing so, however, could present some problems. #4 is now one pass away on the new perimeter which links him directly to the ball handler. X2 might observe the #1 to #3 pass setting up and feel as though he could beat it. The distance involved would make this difficult however. In Diagram 13-6, X1 sees #3 post up on X3's run-and-jump. He, therefore, circles back to pick up #3. No matter what happens, X1 should make the circle move also. If X4 rotates up to #3, X1 would keep going to defend #4.

THE REVERSE DRIBBLE

Diagram 13-7 illustrates the 30 defense against the ball handler who reverses his dribble when the run-and-jump is used against him. As #1 dribbles hard left, X2 runs and surprises. X1 continues downcourt to pick up the open man.

#1, however, instead of picking up his dribble, turns and reverses direction with X2 chasing him this time. X3 then might run-and-jump the dribbler, which would key X2 downcourt looking for the open man.

The reverse dribble can be used to neutralize the intended effect of the run-and-jump. However, with the exception of a possible mismatch, there is still nothing lost by using the defense against this type of move. The defense has still initiated the action and there is always the possibility to get some things accomplished. At the same time, the dribbler who reverses on the run-and-jump (as well as the player who waves the rest of the offense quickly downcourt) is, in a sense, being set up for the 40 defense in which we *stay* double-teamed.

Diagram 13-5

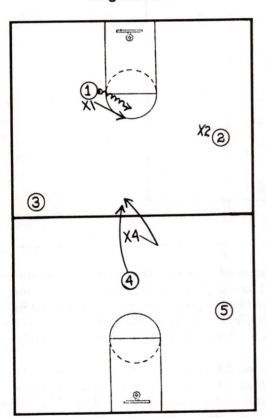

Diagram 13-6

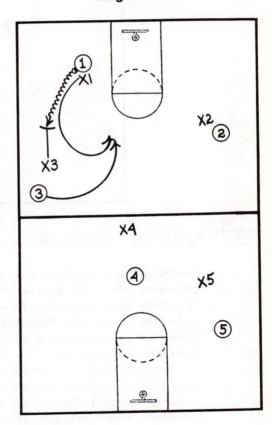

Diagram 13-7

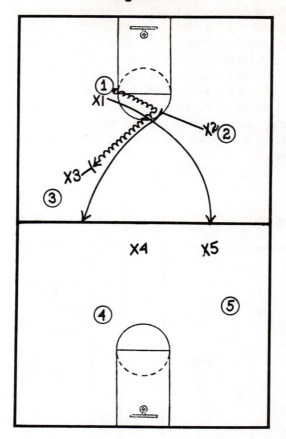

teaching the run-and-jump

Teaching the run-and-jump is predicated almost entirely on our pressure man-to-man drills (20 defense). We introduce the run-and-jump to our players by putting four-against-four full-court on the perimeter and walking through it the first time around. Subsequently, however, all our work on 30 is handled through the whole-method approach after 20 defense has been completely absorbed by the players.

We think the best way to develop confidence in the run-and-jump initially is to teach it briefly to the varsity team, then have them spring it against a junior varsity or freshman team that has had no exposure to it. Much like the previously mentioned experiment conducted at our camp, the results are usually excellent.

We do feel it is important for the coach to call defensive signals when the run-and-jump is scrimmaged during half-court work. The offense in these situations is not permitted to observe the coach's call. The reason for this once again relates to the importance of surprise. We've often asked our players if the run-and-jump is difficult to play against. Invariably they tell us it is not, if they know it's coming.

Surprisingly, the dribbler is still the main objective of our run-and-jump defense. Good things usually happen for the defense if the dribbler is truly surprised. Surprise forces the dribbler to do something he did not anticipate having to do. If he is not a great player, he may not make the best decision.

As coach, you can decide whether to make the run-and-jump a separate, signaled defense or simply tell the team in basic man-to-man pressure that they may jump a dribbler when they think he can be surprised. It really makes little difference. However, I still like the idea of controlling when we play 30 defense by making it a separate call. The additional advantage is that knowing ahead of time perhaps puts us in a better position to rotate.

Our Olympic team of 1976 was told to jump the dribbler anytime a player felt he could surprise the dribbler. The only reason we did not make it a separate defense was the time factor. Our whole season for the Olympics was combined into approximately seven weeks.

If you do decide to make the run-and-jump a separate defense, I would make one coaching point. Make sure the players hide the fact they are in the 30 defense by appearing to be in their typical man-to-man pressure. When we first made it a separate defense, we found that the players were waiting for someone to run-and-jump the dribbler. Therefore they were not playing good individual defense.

The run-and-jump has been a fun defense for us and continues to be an important part of the University of North Carolina's defensive scheme.

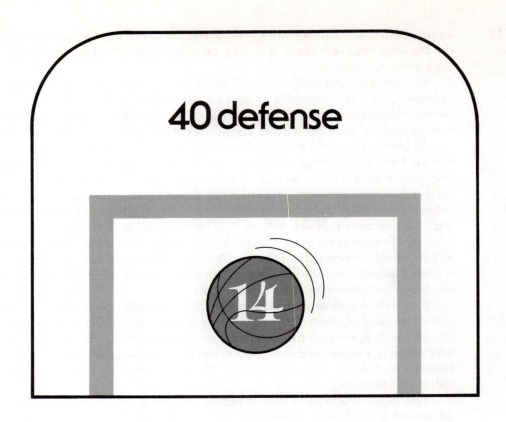

40 defense

If I had to summarize our *40 defense* in a single sentence, I probably would say it was a zone press, disguised initially in a man-to-man alignment. That well could be the briefest definition in this book, but it really does tell a good part of the 40 story.

There are several reasons the man-to-man disguise of our zone press in 40 is important to us. To begin with, we are adding another defense with which the opponent must contend. A multiple defensive system such as ours works best when we avoid letting the offense know what to expect. By showing #1 the same man-to-man alignment in 40 that he sees in our 20 and 30 defenses, we hope to keep him guessing longer. In fact, if things go as they should, the opponent should continue to be in doubt, even after the ball is dribbled and an apparent run and jump defense appears to be setting up.

Actually, 40, which we refer to as our Scramble defense, could be described as an extension of the run-and-jump. It was designed to support and strengthen it. As we indicated in the previous chapter, many ball handlers try to offset the run-and-jump move by reversing their dribble on it. In 40 defense, however, the initial defender of the dribbler does not continue upcourt to look for the open man. Instead, he stays for the double-team as the defense makes the transition from man-to-man defense to a two-two-one zone press.

We feel that one of the most effective defensive plays in basketball is the double-team of the dribbler *once his dribble is used.* This is what we look to accomplish with our 40 defense. The overwhelming majority of teams have a separate man-to-man press offense and a separate zone press offense. By showing man-to-man defense initially, we hope to get the ball handler to put the ball on the floor. As soon as the dribble occurs we go for the double-team. Under these circumstances we think we have a pretty fair chance of intercepting the pass. Once the press is broken, however, we are back into man-to-man defense just as we would defend against the fast break. The 40 defense therefore starts in man-to-man, changes to a zone press, and ultimately reverts back to man-to-man.

During some years, we continued from the zone press back to a zone. However, after several years of experimenting, we felt it was preferable to go back man-to-man once the press was broken since this is the same defense we use to defend the break. We feel it is easier for our players to go back man-to-man than to find the right spots in the zone under these circumstances. The exception to this is our 42 defense, which we will describe later in the chapter.

Like the run-and-jump, the 40 defense works best when it is used sparingly. Overexposure tends to weaken it. However, although its major purpose is one of support, we will go to it a little more often in certain situations.

For example, the 40 can be used to advantage when the opponent has three big men in the lineup at the same time. The zone press usually forces several players to handle the ball. This likely would include some of the big men whose ball-handling skills may be lacking.

Similar to the run-and jump, the 40 is an aggressive attack that can take the opponent out of its game. Therefore, we will use it more frequently against highly organized teams which want to control tempo.

The defense would also be effective against a team that likes to have one ball handler bring the ball up against the press.

Like all gambling-type defenses, however, the 40 lends itself to risk. Sometimes the transitions from man-to-man zone and then back to man-to-man again do not go smoothly. The change back to man-to-man defense after the press is broken is a particularly hazardous time. There may be difficulty picking up the right man. Our goal at that point is to avoid getting hurt with a lay-up. Usually we can avoid it. However, we are vulnerable to that same open fifteen- to twenty-foot jump shot we spoke about in the previous chapter on the run-and-jump.

There is another possible area of concern with 40. Since we line up man-to-man initially, we can not predesignate zone assignments. A player could find himself anywhere on the floor at the time the switch is made from man-to-man zone. For example, if the opponent uses its big man to throw the ball in bounds, our X5 probably would find himself part of the initial double-team. Aside from the fact that this requires every player to learn each position, I don't think this could hurt a team terribly unless X5 was extremely slow. If this were the case, a team might prefer to go with a straight zone press (50 defense) and make X5 a permanent goaltender.

A comparison of the initial diagram in this chapter to that of the previous chapter on the run-and-jump illustrates that the 30 and 40 defenses are initiated identically. **Diagram 14-1** picks up the action after the in-bounds pass has been made to #1. Each player picks up his man and the defense stays man-to-man until the dribble takes place. Just as in 30 defense, if no dribble occurs, the defense remains straight man-to-man which is our 20 defense.

#1 puts the ball on the floor which keys the defensive transition. However, even during this early stage of the transition from man-to-man to zone the difference between 30 and 40 should be inconspicuous. X2 leaves his man for the same run-and-jump move he makes in 30 defense. X3, X4, and X5 react similarly to their moves in 30 with the following exception: In 30 defense, they are given the option to rotate to different players or stay with their original man. In 40 defense, the dribble serves as the key that the double-team is on. Therefore, they must leave their men and move towards zone positions. X1 remains with #1 for the double-team. This marks the only dramatic change between 30 and 40 which takes place when the dribble occurs.

Diagram 14-1

Diagram 14-2

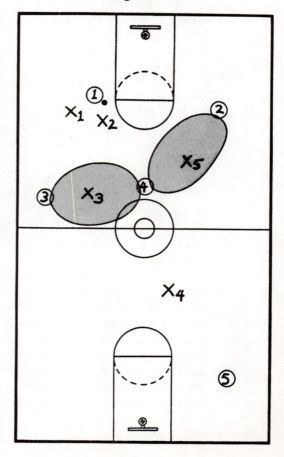

Diagram 14-2 illustrates the completed transition from man-to-man to zone. The defense is now in a two-two-one zone press. X1 and X2 form the double-team. X3 and X5 serve as interceptors and X4 is the goaltender.

How do the players determine which positions to assume in the two-two-one zone press? Of course, the double-teamers always consist of the ball handler's defender plus the defensive man who makes the run-and-jump move. It is important to note that if #1 had dribbled in X3's direction, X3 would have made the run-and-jump move, thereby becoming a double-teamer.

The rule for determining the positioning of the interceptors and goal tender is not quite as precise. Those filling the interceptor positions will be the two players who find themselves closest to those positions as the double-team occurs. However, a player should remember that if the ball handler dribbles *away* from him, and he is one pass away from the ball, he will be the interceptor concerned about the middle of the court. The remaining player, other than the interceptor, takes the goaltender's spot.

As a general rule, most press offenses provide the ball handler with three near outlets. In Diagram 14-2, the interceptor spots, therefore, become the holes between #3, #4, and #2. The overlapping interceptor territories are shaded accordingly in the diagram.

When the double-team occurs, X3 finds himself in perfect position to assume the interceptor position between #3 and #4. On X2's run-and-jump move (Diagram 14-1), X5 must rotate toward #2 in the same way he might in 30 defense. X5, therefore, fills the other interceptor role. X4, spotting X5's move, stays back to assume the goaltender's position.

Of course, sometimes a mixup will occur at this point. This forming of two-two-one zone is probably the most difficult part of our 43 and 44 defense. We can get hurt during this transition from time to time, but fortunately it does not seem to happen too often. Keep in mind that the defense is used sparingly and camouflaged initially. The intent, therefore, is to catch the offense off-balance and get the ball handler to pick up his dribble. When these factors work well for us, the double-team can be a very imposing obstacle for most ball handlers. Because of this, we can sometimes find ourselves temporarily out of position without getting badly hurt.

We also might scout a team's press offense and subsequently be better prepared to fill the two-two-one spots.

INDIVIDUAL RESPONSIBILITIES

As we indicated earlier, the rules for each of the three positions in the two-two-one zone press must be learned by every player. These rules are relatively easy to learn. *Diagram 14-3* is used to illustrate the rules pertaining to the perimeter pass. *Diagram 14-4* covers the same for the pass into the middle which we refer to as the *gut* pass.

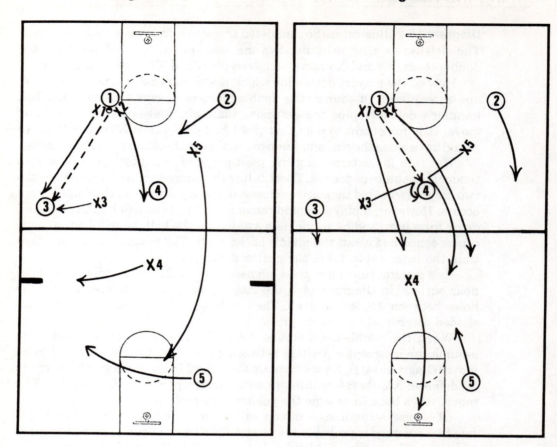

Diagram 14-3   **Diagram 14-4**

_____RULES FOR DOUBLE-TEAMERS

(A) Perimeter Pass—Same Direction   When a perimeter pass is thrown in the double-teamer's direction, he turns and chases the ball. Example: Diagram 14-3 − #1 passes to #3. X1 chases the ball in the direction of #3 hoping to form part of the new double-team on #3. If the pass had gone from #1 to #2, X2 would have sprinted to join #5 in double-teaming #2.

(B) Perimeter Pass—Opposite Direction   When a perimeter pass is made in the opposite direction of the double-teamer, he moves back quickly toward the middle to become an interceptor. Example: Diagram 14-3 − #1 passes to #3. X2 comes back as an interceptor toward the middle of the court. This move toward the middle is very important and follows our _line of ball_ principle. If #1 throws to #3, it is very unlikely that #3 will throw back to #1. The #1 to #3 pass makes the middle a logical area for the offense to attack. For this reason,

X2 must sprint back as fast as he can to cover that area. Again, had the initial pass been made from #1 to #2, X1 would have sprinted to the middle to become an interceptor.

(C) Gut Pass—Pass to the Middle If the gut pass connects (such as the #1 to #4 pass in Diagram 14-4), the rule for the double-teamers is very simple. They quickly turn and sprint back on defense. The gut pass is dangerous. Its completion instantly keys the defense out of the two-two-one zone and into the fast-break defense, which is our 22 defense.

RULES FOR THE INTERCEPTORS

(A) Perimeter Pass - Same Direction When a perimeter pass is thrown in the interceptor's direction, he charges it on the outside and challenges to form part of a new double-team. Example: Diagram 14-3—X3 comes up on the outside of #3. He tries to slow down any quick dribble on the part of #3 while waiting for X1 to join him for the new double-team. Had #1 thrown to #2, X5 would have charged #2 on the outside shoulder, maintaining control so that if #2 dribbled he could slow him down. When a perimeter pass is made in the opposite direction of the interceptor, he then becomes the goaltender. Had #1 passed to #2, X3 would sprint back and become the goaltender.

(B) Gut Pass If the interceptors are unable to stop the pass into the middle, the nearest man to the completed pass challenges the receiver. The other interceptor quickly sprints back. Example: Diagram 14-4—#1 completes the pass to #4 and everyone comes upcourt quickly except X3. X3 tries to slow down and bother #4 in an effort to give everyone else a little extra time to get back. The press has now been broken and our only interest at this point is getting back quickly to form a strong man-to-man defense in the opponent's frontcourt.

RULES FOR THE GOALTENDER

Perimeter Pass When a perimeter pass is made, the goaltender moves in the direction of that pass to become an interceptor. Example: Diagram 14-3—X4 moves to his left in the direction of the #1 to #3 pass to become an interceptor. Had #1 thrown to #2, X4 would have become the interceptor to his right.

Gut Pass When the gut pass is completed, the goaltender races to the basket to serve as goaltender. In Diagram 14-4, X4 is the goaltender.

CHANGING BACK TO MAN-TO-MAN DEFENSE

Earlier in the chapter, we indicated that the 40 defense starts out man-to-man, changes to zone, and ultimately returns to man-to-man defense. It is at this point that the defensive numbering system outlined in our philosophy of defense chapter breaks down slightly. We should try to clarify this briefly before proceeding. The 24 and 23 defenses go back to 22. 34 and 33 similarly go back to 32. One might expect then that the full-court versions of 40 defense go back to 42 as well. Instead, we take 43 and 44 back to 22, which is our man-to-man defense.

Theoretically, we could stay in the same two-two-one press alignment throughout the entire play as we do in 42. However, by switching back to man-to-man, we choose to be a little more conservative in the opponent's frontcourt after gambling in the backcourt. There are additional possibilities a coach may wish to consider. For example, it would also be quite easy to come out of the two-two-one press alignment into a one-two-two zone if this were considered advantageous for personnel reasons.

Getting back to the transition we make from the two-two-one press into man defense, the question arises as to exactly when this change should take place. Of course, as we stated earlier, if the gut pass succeeds, we are automatically back into 22 defense. Otherwise, the hash marks in the opponent's frontcourt (Diagram 14-3) serve as guide. We can form the double-team prior to the ball penetrating that point anytime we can do so. Once the ball penetrates the hash marks in the opponent's front-court we are sprinting back, talking, and trying to pick up our man.

44 DEFENSE

Our 43 defense, described in the previous pages, is used as part of the white series following our field-goals. It also can be called after a made foul shot or in an appropriate out-of-bounds situation. 44 defense is listed as part of our green series in our philosophy of defense chapter. However, the green series (designed to prevent the throw-in) is rarely used. Most teams, alerted to the press, now work to get the ball into play very quickly after an opponent's fieldgoal. The defense, however, does have more time to organize its attack following a successful foul shot. Therefore, we generally call the 44 defense during our huddle at the foul line.

In **Diagram 14-5,** 44 has been called. X1 is attempting to keep #2's throw-in away from #1. X2 stations himself behind #1. If #2 tries to throw the pass to #1 over X1's head, X2 is there to stop him. X1 joins X2 for the double-team as soon as the ball is dribbled or if he catches it in full stride.

In Diagram 14-5, #1 gets free for the pass from #2. X2 acts like he is going back to #2. However, he returns quickly to double-team #1 as soon as the ball is dribbled. The dribble is always the key activating our hunt for that two-two-one zone press. From that point forward, 44 continues upcourt identically to 43.

If the pass were made to #1 and he held the ball while players cleared out, the defense would become identical to 43. The only difference between 44 and 43 would be an attempt to prevent the in-bounds pass and perhaps the opportunity for a quick double-team.

The 44, 43, and 24 defenses look exactly alike when the opponent takes the ball out of bounds, since we are in man-to-man with the man guarding the player in-bounding the ball back as a safety. The differences between the three defenses take place on the dribble.

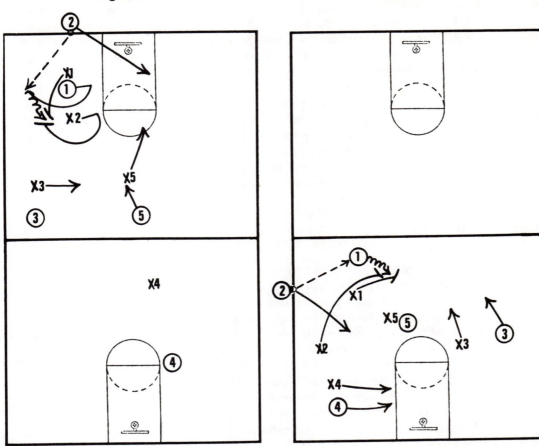

Diagram 14-5

Diagram 14-6

42 DEFENSE SUICIDE PRESS

Although, as indicated earlier, we do not bring 44 and 43 back into 42, we nonetheless do have a 42 defense. The 42 defense can be called as part of the blue series or at the foul-line huddle. It can also be used in a sideline out-of-bounds situation as illustrated in **Diagram 14-6.** Regardless of when it is used the switch from man-to-man to zone in 42 does not take place until the dribble first occurs in the opponent's *frontcourt.*

In Diagram 14-6, #2 has the ball out of bounds on the sideline. The defense is lined up man-to-man. X2, however, is slightly off #2 to encourage the throw-in away from the basket. #2 throws the ball in to #1. The moment #1 dribbles the ball in the half-court the switch is made to the two-two-one zone press. Since #1 dribbles to his left, it becomes X2's responsibility to come up from behind and form the double-team with X1. We maintain that two-two-one zone press all around the half-court until a shot is taken or the action is otherwise stopped.

The 40 is a gambling-type of defense at any point on the floor. Still, the full-court versions (43 and 44) usually provide the defense with the opportunity to protect and race back when the going gets rough. When we run it in the half-court we *are* back. The *suicide press*, as we've nicknamed 42, is a *do or die* defense which can result in an easy shot for the opponent. However, despite the name we give it, and its risks, 42 is not used exclusively in desperation-type situations.

42 is a bold, attacking-type defense which lends itself to surprise, especially since we come from behind the dribbler to form the double-team. We go to it whenever we want to speed up the tempo and feel we can use a good change of pace. For example, we sometimes will call it when the opponent has gradually ebbed away at our lead and is gaining some momentum. The sudden switch from a passive-type defense, used to protect the lead, to one that is strongly aggressive often starts to change the momentum.

teaching the 40 defense

We introduce our defenses to our players in the same manner we have presented them to the reader in this section of the book. Therefore, 40 defense is not introduced until the run-and-jump has been fully covered.

After quickly running through the principles of the 40 defense in the whole-method approach, we turn to part-method for habit building purposes.

We begin the four-on-four drill, illustrated in **Diagram 14-7,** by giving #1 the ball in the double-team situation with the dribble used. #1 has three outlets in #3, #4, and #2. These offensive positions can be played by managers if necessary since our primary goal here is to teach the interceptors how to play the pass. For example, X5 is free to try to outguess #1. However, we usually suggest that he try to encourage the #1 to #2 pass instead of the #1 to #4 pass. If completed, the #1 to #4 pass would break the press. The lateral pass from #1 to #2, however, would give us another opportunity to apply the double-team deep in the opponent's backcourt.

Later in the same drill, we have #1 (or a manager in #1's position) make several completed passes to each of the three outlets. This is done to give each player practice at moving into the required position on each pass. This simple drill serves the purpose of making certain that every man on the squad becomes familiar with the rules governing each position in the two-two-one alignment.

Since the 40 defense is used for support purposes primarily, we do not work to perfect its execution with an excessive amount of drilling. Consequently, most of the exposure our players get to 40 comes about through the whole-method approach during our scrimmages.

One such scrimmage situation, which gives us excellent practice at 40, is our *press offense-defense game*. This full-court game is described in detail at the conclusion of our chapter on the full-court press offense.

Diagram 14-7

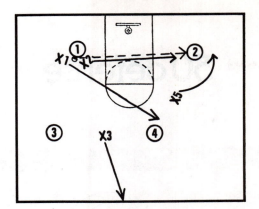

50 defense

Our 50 defense is simply an undisguised, old-fashioned, pure zone defense. There is nothing really unique or exceptional about it. However, we do feel that it fits in quite well to our overall scheme of things. Change for the sake of change is important to us. So let's review briefly to see how 50 compliments the defenses we have covered thus far.

In 20 defense, we attack with straight man-to-man pressure all the way. In 30, we start out in straight man-to-man but change to a rotating-type man-to-man attack. In 40, we again show our man-to-man alignment initially. However, we switch to a zone press when the ball is dribbled and come back into man-to-man when the press is broken.

Therefore, by initially showing a pure zone, we feel that we are giving the offense still another look with our 50 defense.

We used to come back into a zone defense from each of our presses out of the 40 and 50 defenses. However, we later decided to go back to man-to-man after 54 and 53, or 44 and 43. In those defenses, once our double-team was beaten, the situation was similar to defending a fast break after a missed shot. We also would be able to pick up more quickly and execute more effectively since we practice defending against the fast break after a missed shot.

During the period when we returned to a zone, we thought it might be a good idea to build toward the day of a 30-second time clock. The combination of a full-court zone press back to a zone could be very effective when the offense is up against the pressure of the clock. Although we have never believed strongly in the extensive use of zones, we think it does take time to break a good one.

The zone press used in our 54 and 53 defenses is the same as the one used in 40. Both incorporate the same two-two-one alignment. Of course, in 50 defense there is no initial camouflage of the zone press, as there is in 40.

Aside from the additional look it gives us, there is one other advantage gained by showing our zone at the start in 50. By doing so, we are able to designate specific zone assignments to our personnel. We will elaborate on these designations throughout the chapter. In 40 defense, we pick up man-to-man before going into zone press. Therefore we can't designate which part of the zone press each player will cover.

In 54 and 53, just as in 44 and 43, the gut pass breaks the press and we come back quickly. We believe it is important for our full-court presses of 50 and 40 to both lead into man-to-man, once broken down.

Most of the general comments and cautions discussed in the previous chapter on the 40 defense apply to 54 and 53 as well. Most zone presses are intended to speed up tempo, disconcert the opponent, and force them out of their usual style of play. The risk taken for these advantages is greater vulnerability to some easy baskets. Once again, especially in this concluding defensive chapter, we want to emphasize that each of our secondary defenses is used for its change of pace value in support of our predominant 20 defense. Having used them strategically as such, we think they have served us quite well.

Our 52 and 51 defenses are the two straight half-court zones in our defensive repertoire. 52 is the one-three-one trapping zone which is designed to clog the passing lanes and slow down perimeter passing. It is more aggressive than our 51 defense, and gives us a good change of pace. It is also a relatively easy zone to teach.

The zone we will describe for 51 in this chapter is the one-two-two. We have used however, the two-three and the two-one-two zones just as often. The point zone, also used as a 51 defense, has been our favorite for some years and is basically a match-up zone.

51 is our most *passive* defense. The alignment we use will vary from year to year depending upon our personnel as well as the type zones we expect to have played against us most often. If, for example, we anticipate seeing a good deal of two-three zone during a particular season, we may choose that alignment ourselves for 51. Doing so gives us valuable offensive practice at the same time we're working our defense.

The term *passive* calls for some clarification. Actually, no defense should ever be passive in the literal sense. For us, the description is used for comparative purposes. When we go directly into 51 defense, we often do so because we must place a high priority on avoiding further foul trouble. Therefore, we stop taking the initiative defensively for the moment. We play back, let the offense shoot from the outside and hope that we can still box out and get the rebound. However, even within the scope of this philosophy we do make exceptions. When we're up against an exceptionally strong outside shooter, we tell our players to *point him tough*. By this, we mean ". . . know where he is in the zone at all times. When he gets the ball, get out on him and make him give it up . . ." As a general rule, however, we will give the offense the prerogative of shooting uncontested from any point outside of twenty-one feet.

These are our usual thoughts, and our goals in relation to 51 defense, especially when used in conjunction with our red series. The circumstances under which we go to the red series are detailed in our philosophy of defense chapter.

54 defense

54 defense can be signaled in out-of-bounds situations under the opponent's basket when there is a dead ball. It also can be called during our foul-line huddle, which is when we usually use it.

Somewhat unlike the other "fours" (24, 34, 44), 54 cannot be described as a prevent-type defense in the strictest sense. At times, we may put some pressure on the offense to get the ball into play. However, we do not mind if the ball is passed into the corner spots shaded in **Diagram 15-1**. We do try to prevent the ball from being in-bounded to the middle, however.

Since we can designate zone positions to our players in 50 defense, let's look at our initial one-two-one-one line-up in Diagram 15-1 and discuss the reasons for our designations.

X5 is picked to guard the offensive player responsible for making the in-bounds pass. There are several reasons for this choice. First, since 54 will often be used after our successful foul throws, X5 will usually be close to the endline, unless he happens to be the foul shooter. Secondly, we like to have a tall player on the double-team and since we are encouraging the pass to the corners, the man guarding the player making the throw-in will usually be part of the initial double-team. Having our tallest player on the initial throw-in also prevents an easy long pass from out of bounds.

Shot-blocking ability is important to us in the goaltender's spot (X4 in Diagram 15-1). If our best shot blocker happened to be X5, we would place him in the goaltender's position and put X4 defending the in-bounder. If neither were shot blockers, we would put X4 back.

Size is also a factor in determining the player to fill the spot assigned to X3 in Diagram 15-1. Since most teams in-bound the ball to the right, we prefer to have X3's height advantage over X2 in that likely double-team spot.

Speed and quickness are helpful assets in the interceptor positions, which are usually filled by X1 and X2.

In Diagram 15-1, #1 makes the in-bounds pass to #2. Once this pass is completed, our initial one-two-one-one alignment changes to the same two-two-one press described in our 40 defense chapter. Therefore, there is nothing new for our players to learn. X5 and X3 move to double-team #2. X1 and X2 fill the interceptor positions and X4 is back as goaltender.

If #1 takes the ball out on the other side of the basket and makes the

Diagram 15-1　　　　　　　　　　　**Diagram 15-2**

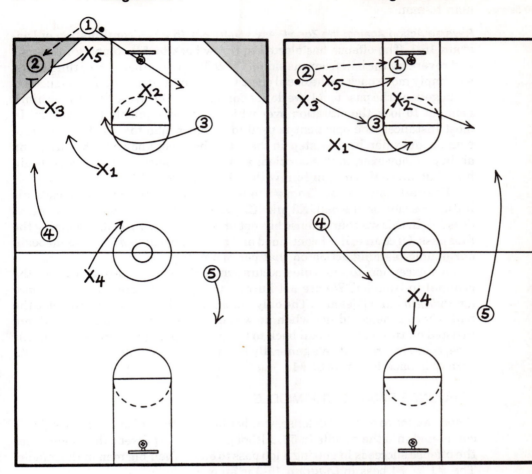

in-bounds pass to #3, X5 and X2 double-team #3. X3 and X1 would move to the interceptor spots and X4 still would be back as goaltender.

The rules governing the two-two-one zone press are identical to those of our 40 defense and are detailed in that chapter. Very briefly in review, those rules, applicable to 50 defense, are as follows:

Offense Completes Gut Pass　A successful pass into the middle breaks the press. The defense sprints back quickly as they would after any missed shot, picking up man-to-man. The most underrated part of a full-court zone press is the strength of sprinting back on defense while the offense believes they have an advantage.

Offense Completes Perimeter Pass　When a perimeter pass is completed, the defense attempts to re-establish the two-two-one zone press by double-teaming the receiver. Once the ball penetrates the hash marks in the opponent's frontcourt, the press is considered broken and we attempt to pick up man-to-man.

Reverse Action Against the Zone Press   **Diagram 15-2** is a continuation of Diagram 15-1. The offense has elected to throw back to #1, stepping in-bounds and reversing the ball from one side of the court to the other. When this occurs, we simply move back to the usual one-two-one-one alignment. If #2 is successful in getting the pass to #1, we do not double-team #1. We actually give him a moment to look the situation over while #5 moves quickly toward him. In most instances, the opponent is used to a bigger man taking the ball out of bounds and when he does step on the court, he is not known for his dribbling ability. If, however, in this position, #1 were a dribbler, X5 could not contain him, but we could contain him with help from X2 or X3.

Basically, on the pass from #2 to #1, we have X5 trying to go back to his initial position on the ball. X3 and X2 go back to their original alignment, as does X1. In this way our defense has not broken down with double-teaming the first pass. Of course, if #1 continued and threw the ball to #5, we would begin our double-teaming action on that perimeter pass.

An exception to our rules occurs when the ball is passed back to the original in-bounder. We are not hurt by this pass, but are prepared to once again *begin* our 54 defense. The only difference is that #1 can now dribble the ball whereas he could not when he was out of bounds. Of course, if a team insisted on throwing the ball back to the man stepping in bounds, X2, in this case, could intercept it. We generally have him come to intercept it only if #2 turns his back to throw to #1.

IN-BOUNDS PASS TO THE MIDDLE

Before we move on to 53 defense, we should cover the in-bounds pass which is completed into the middle in 54. Although we try to prevent this, sometimes the offense succeeds in getting a lob pass to one of their big men in the middle. The #1 to #4 pass in **Diagram 15-3** is an example.

In an effort to counteract this play and stay in the press, each defensive player must move straight back, as illustrated in the diagram. X5 must make a quick recovery. He turns and picks up the receiver, #4. Now we are again in the same one-two-one-one alignment and proceed in much the same way we did when #1 was making the in-bounds pass. The one difference, of course, is that #4 is in bounds and has his dribble alive. This should present no problem, however. If #4 dribbles to his right, X3 and X5 would double-team him. If he dribbles left, X5 and X2 would double-team him.

Occasionally, the offense will attempt to offset a tight press by throwing long on the in-bounds pass as in **Diagram 15-4**. This is likely to happen if X3 and X2 press the near outlets too closely. When this occurs, X1 usually is able to cut off the receiver and impede his progress until X3 can come up for the double-team. X4 then moves cautiously to take one of the interceptor spots. X5 sprints back to the *middle* to take the other interceptor position. X2 hustles deep into the goaltender's position.

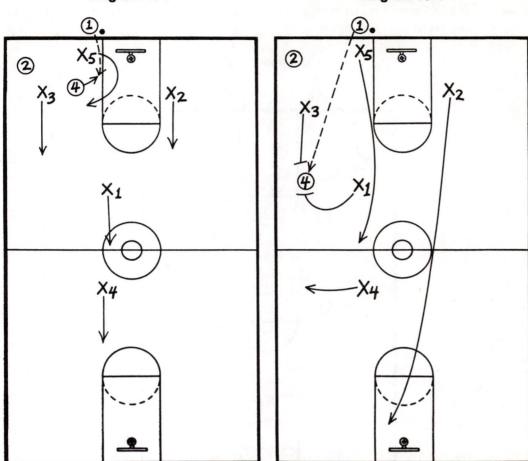

Diagram 15-3   **Diagram 15-4**

53 defense

In 53, we line up clearly in a two-two-one zone press alignment as illustrated in **Diagram 15-5**. The 53 Defense can be used after a made foul shot, or called on a sideline out-of-bounds play at three-quarters court, or on a dead-ball situation after a time-out. On the pass from #1 to #2, X1 merely tries to contain #2 until he begins to dribble hard. At that point, X2 comes up to join X1 for the double-team. X3 and X4 search out the interceptor spots, while X5 is back as the goaltender. If #2 dribbles slowly, X2 would continue to give ground until he chose to surprise #2 by sprinting back quickly for the double-team. Once the double-team is formed, 53, which also goes back to man-to-man (22), proceeds identically to 54. If #2 decided to dribble down the sideline, our entire defensive formation would continue to drop back hoping to make something happen around the mid-court line with a double-team of X1 and X3. X5 would move over as an interceptor, X4 would be goaltender, and X2 would be an interceptor.

Diagram 15-5

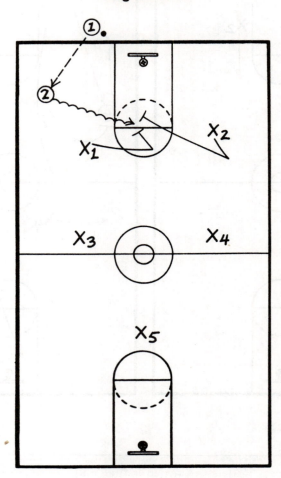

52 defense

When used as part of our blue series, the 52 defense consists of a half-court zone press which evolves into a one-three-one zone trap *after one pass*.

52 defense also can be called part of our red series. When we use it as such, as well as in out-of-bounds situations close to or underneath the opponent's basket, we line up directly in the one-three-one zone.

In **Diagram 15-6**, the 50 defense has been signaled with the offense in possession in their backcourt. We are not in the red series. Therefore, we line up initially in the one-two-one-one zone press formation.

Diagram 15-6   **Diagram 15-7**

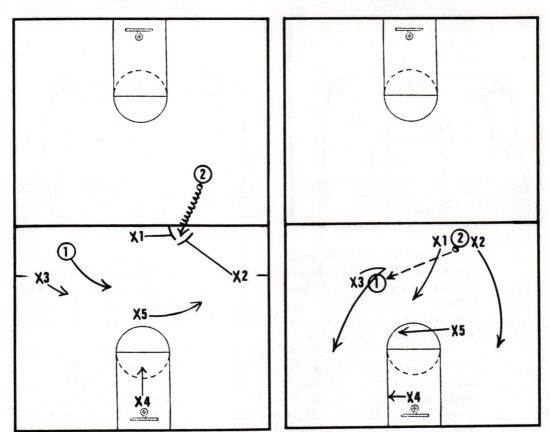

X1 is stationed in the point position close to the ten-second line. X3 and X2 are high on the wings near the hash marks. X5 is just above the free-throw circle and X4 is in the goaltender's position near the basket. Our objective here is to play for *one* double-team between the ten-second line and the hash marks. If we don't get the interception from the one double-team, we are back in the normal 52 defense, which is the one-three-one as we use it in the red series.

In diagram 15-6, X1 and X2 move to double-team #2 the moment he dribbles past the ten-second line. X5 and X3 search out the interceptor spots and X4 is back protecting the basket or can cheat up once the double-team takes place.

Diagram 15-7 shows the move to our one-three-one alignment as #2 manages to get the pass off to #1. The moment this pass is made, our players are immediately keyed into our one-three-one trapping zone. We wish to steal the pass from the *one* double-team, but if unsuccessful we now are committed to the one-three-one passing lane zone, as illustrated in **Diagrams 15-8A** and **15-8B**.

Diagram 15-8A	Diagram 15-8B
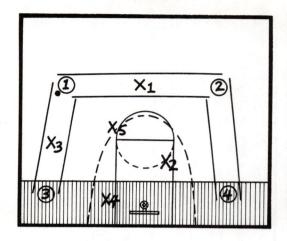	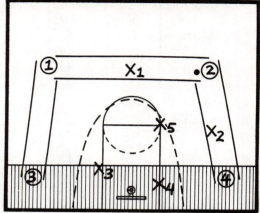

We first observed this one-three-one trap zone several years ago in a game against the University of Kentucky. Coach Adolph Rupp's fine team used the defense very effectively to prohibit our quick perimeter swing of the ball. Although we were fortunate to win the game, we decided to adopt the defense because it was so effective. We also correctly anticipated that it would be a relatively easy zone to teach.

Actually the term *trap* zone is probably a misnomer. What we're really trying to do with this particular alignment is block the passing lanes, as we have emphasized by outlining these lanes in Diagrams 15-8A and 15-8B. We would like to force the offense to resort to *lob* or *bounce* passes which are slower, if they intend to keep the ball moving along the perimeter. The double-team is encouraged and therefore we should be ready for it defensively.

PERSONNEL PLACEMENT IN THE ONE-THREE-ONE TRAP ZONE

There are no firm rules for personnel placement in the one-three-one zone. We ourselves will vary our personnel in the positions shown in the diagrams. However, if teaching simplification is of prime importance, it will probably be easiest to keep X4 and X5 on the posts and assign X1, X2, and X3 to the point and wing positions just as we do in 51 defense.

Since the point man in the zone is responsible for bothering the important guard-to-guard pass, it helps if he happens to be tall for a guard. However, we have not hesitated using the defense even with a 5′ 10″ point man.

The diagrams show X2 and X3 on the wings. I don't think it makes much of a difference which wing either player is assigned to occupy with one possible exception. If the opponent is scouted to consistently come downcourt on the side occupied by X2, it might be preferable to keep X2 there. X3's extra height could be helpful in terms of rebounding strength on the other side. Otherwise, both wings have essentially the same responsibility. Note X2's position in Diagram 15-8A when #1 has the ball. When the ball is passed to #2 (Diagram

15-8B), X2 must come back quickly into the passing lane between #2 and #4.

We do like to have our best rebounder, usually X5, in the middle of the one-three-one zone. X5 has the job of facing the ball handler and staying between the ball and the basket in the path outlined by the dotted lines in Diagrams 15-8A and 15-8B.

X4 has the job of staying low in the lane until the ball is passed to within six feet of the baseline area (shaded in the diagrams). Whenever the ball penetrates this shaded area, X4 comes out to cover. When the ball is outside the shaded area, X4 stays low, moving within the *inside* boundaries of the lane to face the ball.

Now let's move the ball around the half-court in the next few diagrams to see how the zone shifts.

BALL IN THE CORNER

Diagram 15-9 #3 has the ball in the corner of a pass from #1. Since the ball has penetrated within six feet of the baseline, X4, following the rule, comes out to pick up #3. X3 turns and joins X4 for the double-team on #3. X4, who is not likely to be the fastest man on the court, has a relatively long way to come to pick up #3. You might wonder how he manages it. This is one of the keys to the defense. Remember, we said that our goal was to block the passing lanes. If X3 has done his job well, #1's pass to #3 would have to be a slower pass than #1 would normally make. It might be a bounce pass, or perhaps a lob pass over X3. This would give X4 sufficient time to move from the lane to the corner with his hands up. Meanwhile, X5 is observing his rule to stay between the ball and the basket within his *cone*-shaped path around the lane. With the ball in the corner, X5 finds himself in the low-post area vacated by X4. In that spot, he should be in front of any offensive low post. X5 also has a great distance to cover on the #1 to #3 pass. He must move quickly and hope for a lob or bounce pass.

Diagram 15-9

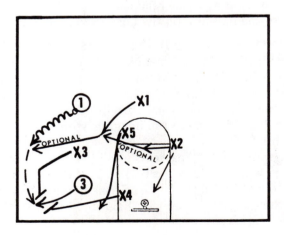

On the #1 to #3 pass into the corner, X1 comes over to block off any offensive high post. The defensive movement could end at this point. If it does, it would probably result in #3 throwing back to #1, if he can get the pass off through the double-team. However, we could carry the play one step further. X1 has the prerogative of leaving the high post and sprinting to the side to block the #3 to #1 pass. If #3 turns to face the sideline out of the double-team, X1 should definitely make this move. X2 watches X1 when the ball goes to the corner initially. If X1 makes the move to block #1 (as the optional movement arrow indicates), X2 must come over to cover a possible pass into the high post.

If all works well, the result of the play is a double-team with each near outlet covered. The play can be particularly effective if #3 is not too tall and has difficulty seeing over the double-team. However it is extremely important that this optional move on the part of X1 be used sparingly. If the offense comes to expect it, they will prepare to counter it with the cross-court pass since we have no defenders on the weak side.

The entire play might not materialize if #3 shoots before the double-team occurs. If he does, we hope the shot will be rushed and that our rebounding coverage will be adequate.

It is important to note that to assure good rebounding coverage throughout 52 defense, X1 must assume the responsibility for rebounding on the weak side. X1 will have to move quickly to the side away from which an outside shot is taken to improve rebounding out of this defense.

Diagram 15-10   #1 gets the pass from #3. X3 and X4, the double-teamers in the corner, must sprint off with X4 returning to the lane and X3 moving up to the passing lane. X1 jumps into the passing lane between #1 and #2. X5 returns up the imaginary dotted line to stay between the ball and the basket.

Penetration Dribble   By concentrating on clogging the perimeter passing lanes the defense is, in effect, inviting the offense to penetrate dribble as #1 does in *Diagram 15-11*. X5 and X1 try to stop #1's penetration by faking at him (hopefully getting him to pick up his dribble) and then backing off. X3 is designated to stop the dribble and stay with him.

To continue showing the reactions of our defensive players in 52 defense we will take the ball around the horn to the other side of the court.

Diagrams 15-12 and 15-13   In Diagram 15-12, #1 chooses to lob pass over X1 to #2. X1 turns to face #2, but remains in the passing lane. X2 sprints out to the passing lane between #2 and #4. X3 moves quickly to the lane while X4 moves to the other side of the lane, as diagramed. Remember, X4 should not leave the lane until the ball comes to within six feet of the baseline. X5 crosses the lane to find that spot on the imaginary line between the ball (#2 in this case) and the basket.

In Diagram 15-13, #2 passes the ball to #4 in the corner. X4 sprints out to double-team with X2. X1 moves back in front of a possible high post. X5 moves down the lane between the ball and basket while X3 adjusts very little. We now have the same situation as in Diagram 15-9 except that the ball is located in the other corner.

Diagram 15-10   **Diagram 15-11**

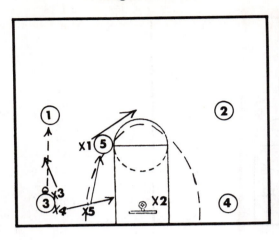

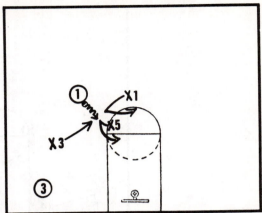

Diagram 15-12   **Diagram 15-13**

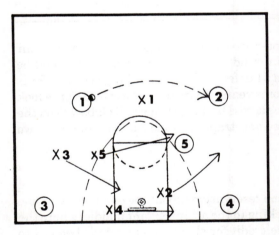

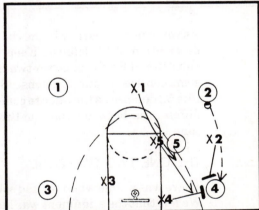

MOVING DIRECTLY INTO THE ONE-THREE-ONE

We introduced the one-three-one zone in this chapter as it evolves from our half-court zone press. In **Diagram 15-14** we show how the defense is set up when the offense has the ball underneath its own basket.

X4 is placed on the offensive player making the in-bounds pass. If the ball is in-bounded outside of six feet, X4 moves into the lane. However, as in Diagram 15-14, if the ball is passed into the corner, X4 and X3 move to double-team the receiver. Once the ball is put into play, the defense proceeds as previously described.

Diagram 15-14

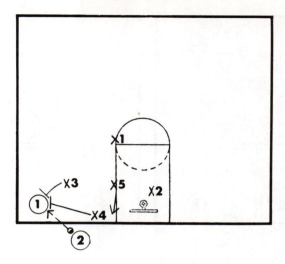

51 defense

As we indicated earlier in the chapter, we will use the one-two-two zone for our description of 51 defense. Keep in mind that any number of zones could be substituted for the one-two-two in 51 defense. One of the things we look for is some contrast to our 52 defense. Some years, we try to have our 51 defense look like 52 defense as the offense comes across half-court. We will elaborate on the differences between the one-three-one trapping zone and the one-two-two zone.

THE ONE-TWO-TWO ZONE

There was a time when we had some reservations about the one-two-two zone. We felt that the alignment was lacking in the all-important middle, where the offense likes to have the ball. The credit for changing our minds belongs to Coach Jack McCloskey, formerly of Wake Forest University, who brought the defense to our conference from the University of Pennsylvania. Coach McCloskey's Wake Forest teams used the one-two-two zone extremely well. They hustled their people in and out of the middle very effectively. We considered their adaptation of the one-two-two to be the most difficult of the straight zones to attack.

Diagrams 15-15 and *15-16* illustrate individual positioning areas of responsibility in the alignment.

The player assignments in the one-two-two zone are similar to our 52 defense designations. However, much of the similarity between the two zones ends at this point. The heavy work load in the one-two-two zone is handled by X4 and X5. They must move farther and faster to get the job done in 51 than is

Diagram 15-15

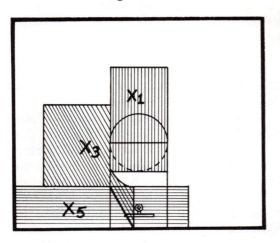

Diagram 15-16

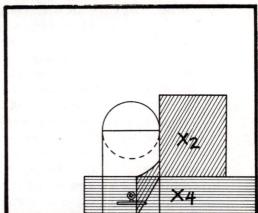

required of them in 52. The reason for this difference will become evident as the ball is moved around the perimeter in *Diagrams 15-17* and *15-18*.

Diagram 15-17 shows the position of the one-two-two zone when the ball is at the top of the free-throw circle. Whenever the ball is anywhere in the high middle area designated by the dotted lines in the diagram, we want X1 to be all over the ball-handler. The moment the ball leaves that area, either through a pass or a dribble, X1 backs off into the middle of the zone, which then changes to more of a two-one-two alignment.

As the ball shifts to the side in Diagram 15-17, X4 moves along with it in the direction of the basket. X3 moves out to stop the dribbler and X2 comes back into the lane. Note that X5 comes out of the lane as soon as the ball begins to move. In 52 defense, the low post stays low until the ball is on its way to the

Diagram 15-17

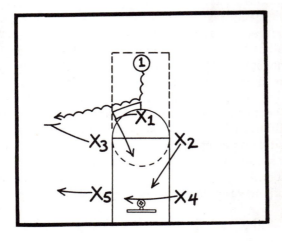

Diagram 15-18

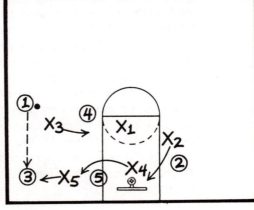

corner. However, since we will not be bothering the perimeter pass in 51 defense, #1, in Diagram 15-18, is free to pass the ball swiftly to #3 in the corner. Therefore X5, who is responsible for #3 in the corner, can't afford to sit

In Diagram 15-18 the pass is made to #3. As the ball moves to the corner, X3, who double-teamed the receiver in 52, now has the job of backing off in order to prevent a pass into the high-post area. X5, already on the move toward the corner, comes out all the way with his hands up, protecting baseline. X4 comes to front the low post if an opponent is there.

Note that the moves by X4 and X5 as the ball swings around the horn represent the biggest challenge to the one-two-two zone. To illustrate this point, let's go back to Diagrams 15-15 and 15-16 for a moment. Note the length of X4 and X5's territories. There is a lot of distance to cover here. Imagine the ball located in the lower right corner of Diagram 15-15. X5 then would be fronting the low post within three feet of the lane while X4 would be heading toward the receiver in the corner. Now, if the ball is quickly passed out of the corner and around the horn, both X4 and X5 must travel the entire length of their territory within three passes, in order to protect on the other side. This is why we indicated earlier that the X5 and X4 positions were most important to this defense. Both defenders must move approximately eight to ten feet on each pass in order to give the zone proper protection in the low post and corners.

Although they are both straight zone defenses, 51 and 52 give the offense different looks. This is in keeping with our overall defensive philosophy. 52, with its emphasis on blocking the passing lanes and double-teaming in the corner, is much more aggressive than 51. However, as we indicated earlier in the chapter, we prefer to be less aggressive when we go to 51. Therefore, the one-two-two suits our needs under these circumstances. We also feel that 51 is a little better rebounding defense than 52 since all five defenders are relatively close to the basket. A quick comparison of Diagrams 15-9 and 15-18 should bear this point out.

teaching 50 defense

By the time our players are introduced to 50 defense, there is relatively little left for them to learn which can not be covered through the whole-method approach. This is particularly true of our 54 and 53 defenses, since the rules for the two-two-one zone press are identical to those of 40 defense. This is one of the advantages we gain with the straight zone presses of 50 defense. For example, if you were to compare the initial diagrams of our 53 and 43 defenses, you would notice two entirely different looks. Yet, we manage to gain the extra look in 50 without increasing our teaching time.

Our *press offense-defense game*, described at the conclusion of chapter eight, is a strong testing ground for all of our presses. During these games, the defense is constantly exposed to offensive counter moves, such as #3's post up in Diagram 15-1.

Very little part-method drilling is required to teach 52 defense. Most of the teaching time devoted to the one-three-one trapping zone is spent discussing individual responsibilities with the players.

Initially, we may put some tape on the floor to highlight X5's perimeter territory, as shown in Diagram 15-8. We then move the ball around the half-court and instruct X5 to stay between the ball and the basket on this tape track we have laid out for him. The tape usually can be removed very quickly. X5 has a relatively simple job in 52 defense.

X4's responsibility is easy for him to learn as well. We tell him to stay in the lane (on the ball side) until the ball is on its way to the corner (six feet out from the baseline). When the ball is headed to the corner, he is to sprint baseline to pick up the receiver.

X2 and X3, on the wings, are taught their responsibilities in relation to their proximity to the ball. If the ball is on their side, they stay in the passing lanes and are ready to come back for the double-team on a pass into the corner. If the ball is on the opposite side, they move in toward the lane. They are told to keep their eyes on X1 and be prepared to come over to the high post if X1 leaves it while the ball is in the opposite corner. We also teach the wings as well as the point the importance of moving whenever they are in the passing lanes. By taking a step in one direction and then back in the other, the space taken up by the defender is increased considerably and makes the perimeter pass more difficult to execute.

X1 has the most difficult responsibility in the one-three-one trapping zone. His duties are described to him as follows:

1. Stay in the passing lane when the ball is high. Bother the guard-to-guard pass. The pass will be made, but your job is to slow it down by making them throw it over your head.

2. When the ball goes to the corner, sprint to the high-post position and prevent the pass into that area.

   2a. *Optional:* If you wish, you may come out and play the outlet pass from the corner. Do not use this move too often, and do not use it if the offensive corner man is big.

3. You must help out with rebounding on the weak side where we lack board strength. Look for those long rebounds that often come off the corner shots.

Our 51 defense is taught much the same way. We show each player his territory in the one-two-two zone and briefly outline his responsibilities. The only part-method drilling we do in 51 is designed to show X4 and X5 how to move on each pass. This is done simply by passing the ball around half-court and having the post men move far enough on each pass to cover their full territories. X4 and X5 are taught to keep their feet wide, their knees bent, and to move quickly as soon as the ball is on its way to the receiver.

All of our additional work with the 50 defense is done through the whole-method approach. Our scrimmages provide the coaching staff with the opportunity to spot problems which become more readily apparent in game-type situations.

situations,

practice planning

4

situations

A good *situations* team can add at least two victories to its record each year. By situations, we mean the little things in a game which can bring about winning or losing, such as foul-shot and jump-ball alignments and last-minute strategies. We will cover these and other situations from both the offensive and defensive viewpoint in this chapter.

defensive foul shot

Since gaining or losing even a single possession could make the difference in the outcome of a game, a team should be prepared to make the most of every foul-shot situation. Our defensive foul-shot alignment is designed to give us the best possible result, regardless of whether or not the opponent makes the shot. The free throw, generally, is successful seven out of ten times. Considering this, and the fact that the made foul shot lends itself to a good press opportunity, one of our major considerations is to be ready to attack the opponent's press. We, therefore, introduced our defensive foul-shot line-up in our chapter devoted to the press offense. However, we also want to make certain we gain possession when the shot is missed those three out of ten times.

In *Diagram 16-1*, the opponent's #3 is at the foul line. X5 must make his first step toward the shooter. If #4 is bigger than X5, X5 should box out #4. If #4 is smaller, X5 may simply go for the ball after contacting #4 with the first step.

X4's job is somewhat different, since X3 is behind him. X4 makes contact with #5 and holds. As soon as the basket is made, X4 sprints downcourt. If the shot is missed, X4 tries to get the rebound and make the outlet pass.

We place X3 on the baseline for three reasons. First, it puts him in a better position to take the ball out of bounds quickly, if the foul shot is successful. This is vitally important to us if we are going to be pressed. Secondly, X3 will be in rebounding position, which gives X4 a better chance to get a step on the defense downcourt. Finally, X3's position at the baseline allows him to block out an offensive man if the opponent chooses to have an offensive man just outside the lane. When the foul shot is attempted, X3 moves in just as the ball touches the rim. He should allow no one between himself and X4, thereby, forming a double-team block, just as in football. If #3 is a ninety-percent foul shooter, X4 could take off immediately, hoping to get an easy basket at the other end.

X1 must move in front of the foul shooter. This prevents a possible tip back to the shooter and gives X1 a chance for a long rebound. It also helps X1's timing in his move for the outlet pass, regardless of whether or not the shot is made.

In *Diagram 16-2*, we face a different offensive foul-shot line-up. When our opponent places a man close to the baseline, such as #2, it is very important for X3 to be on the *baseline* side of that player. The rules do not specify which team is allowed inside position in the area three feet beyond the lane. Therefore, X3, who will be taking the ball out of bounds, can and must rush to take the baseline side of #2. Should #2 get the baseline, he may move in freely for the offensive rebound before X3 can step in front of him.

#2 also could choose to move to the other side. If he does, X3 would move to that side behind X5. X4 then would not be able to release as quickly.

offensive foul shot

The offensive foul shot is another situation for which we must prepare. Since we expect to make at least seven of ten shots, our preparation is aimed principally at setting up our press after the foul shot is made. For those three anticipated misses, however, we want a good chance to recover the rebound and still protect against the opponent getting a quick score on us.

In 1967, we were shooting poorly from the foul line early in the year. It became apparent that we needed an offense for the missed foul shot. It got so bad, in fact, that a friend of mine who is a Monsignor, suggested that one of the players, who was making the sign of the cross before shooting the foul, stop doing so. The Monsignor said, "He's making the Church look bad."

It was at this point that we moved to arrange the situation which would give us a good chance to get the ball back on the missed shot. Obviously, we didn't tell our players the reason for the change. We continued to show confidence in their ability to make the foul shot.

To give us our best chance of regaining possession, we placed our two biggest men to the side of the opponent's smallest inside man. The rules state that the defensive men must take their positions on the inside first. Therefore, we waited until the defensive players established their positions and then moved our taller players (#4 and #5 in **Diagram 16-3**) to the side of the opponent's smaller man (X4).

I remember a game we played in the 1968 Holiday Festival against St. John's. My friend, Lou Carnesecca, the coach of St. John's, protested vigorously when the referee made his defensive foul-shot men keep their positions. Lou had told his players to line up according to size and then change positions, if necessary, according to the spots taken by our offensive players. It was very humorous to see the four post men revolving back and forth across the lane until the referee finally told the St. John's players they had to choose their positions first and remain there. (I'm sure Lou knew the rules, but just wanted a chance to talk to the referees.)

The idea of our two biggest men covering the opponent's smallest man came from my football background. I remembered the *stunting* we tried to do in an effort to block a kick. Our #4 and #5 men likewise stunt on X4. In Diagram 16-3, #5 would give the signal to #4. If #5 intends to move out to the foul shooter, #4 would slip baseline for the offensive rebound. If #5 signals that he will move to the baseline behind X4, #4 comes in on the foul-line side. #3 bumps X5, and attempts to tip back to #1 on a missed foul shot. #4 or #5 also may tip back to #1. It is easier to *tip back* than it is to control a rebound since the tip back requires only one hand. A player can reach higher with one arm than he can with two.

#2, the shooter, knows the defense we will be using before he shoots. He then concentrates on making the shot which keys the defense. #1 is the safety on defense.

Should #5 be shooting the foul shot, #1 would be safety and #2 would position himself against the opponent's big man. #3 and #4 would stunt on X4.

During one season, we lined up for the offensive foul shot as in **Diagram 16-4**. The diagram illustrates a game that has begun between players jockeying for position behind the inside men. Our big men, #4 and #5, stay on the lane. #1 and #3 stay back on each side until the shooter is handed the ball. At this point, either #1 or #3 move into position behind X4 or X5. This was devised knowing that the defense can not move in the visual field of the shooter to disconcert him. If, for example, X2 moved with #1 after #2 has the ball and #2 subsequently misses the foul shot, the rule states that #2 is entitled to another foul try. Only one of the two offensive players involved (either #1 or #3 in Diagram 16-4) moves into position behind the defensive inside man. The other is back on defense. Usually the taller of the two players will come low, although this is not the case in Diagram 16-4. However, if X2 moved with #1 *before* #2 was handed the ball, #3 would go in and #1 would be back on defense. #4 and #5 should make their first step into the lane with the foot nearest the baseline. If the foul shot misses, we want #4 and #5 to look for the tip out to #1, since it will be difficult to go up and catch the ball over X4 and X5.

Diagram 16-1

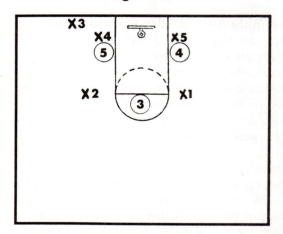

Diagram 16-2

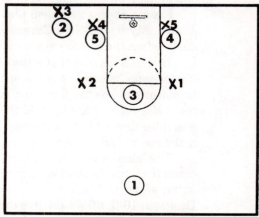

Diagram 16-3

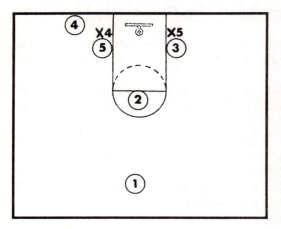

Diagram 16-4

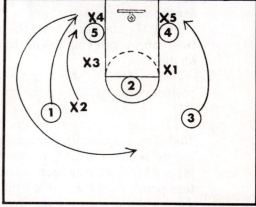

As we have stated many times throughout this book, we always want our team prepared for the unusual. This includes the foul-shot situation. When we played Boston College (coached by the great Bob Cousy) in the 1967 NCAA Eastern Regional finals, they used the set shown in *Diagram 16-5*.

Diagram 16-5

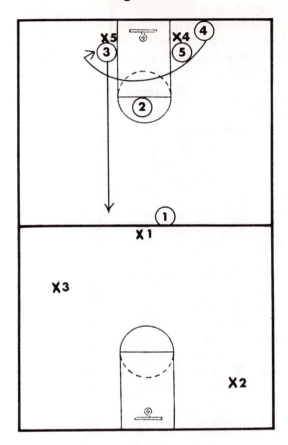

Their plan made them a threat to score if we missed the foul shot. It also gave our shooter something to think about, since he would have to get back on defense very quickly after shooting. We did change our alignment under these circumstances by moving #4 over to X5 on the lane and sending #3 back on defense with #1. You can see that if #2 missed the foul shot, we had an excellent chance to score on any long rebound. #4 and #5 would also be ready to tip back to #2, the shooter.

We practice the offensive foul-shot situations when we are working on our full-court press defense.

jump-ball situations

We will usually average seven to eight jump balls each game. In addition to those which begin each half and the ones resulting from the usual number of loose balls, our defense tends to create jump-ball situations. Therefore, we want to do as much as we can in the way of preparation, to get as many of the resulting possessions as possible.

Our theory on jump balls is that we must gain possession each time our player controls the tip and fifty percent of the time the opponent's player controls it. We have a jump-ball summary chart for each game to determine how we approach our goal. The chart is shown in **Diagram 16-6**.

Diagram 16-6

Jump-Ball Summary Chart

U.N.C. vs. Opponent   Date _____
Place _____

Jump Ball Summary			Good Plays
Between	Control		Interceptions.
NC50 vs OPP55	NC50	NC12	
NC22 vs OPP31	OPP31	NC50	Recoveries:
NC50 vs OPP55	NC50	NC22	
NC30 vs OPP41	OPP41	OPP14	
NC22 vs OPP41	NC22	NC12	Forced Jump:

Draw Charges:

TOTAL

Controlled by UNC   4   Opp.   1

We have achieved more often our goal of stealing fifty percent of our opponent's tip than controlling 100% of our own. We do manage to get about eighty percent of the latter.

The importance of the jump-ball situation in the late stages of a close game can not be overemphasized. We have won some close games by controlling a tip, or stealing an opponent's control of the tip late in the game. In these situations, we will generally use one of the time-outs we've carefully saved for the last few minutes.

I remember, only too well, one game we lost because of a jump-ball situation. We were playing sixth-ranked South Carolina in the Finals of the 1971 ACC tournament. We had won the ACC regular season Championship, but now had to win the tournament to go to the NCAA.

We had managed to control the tempo of the game against their huge 6'11", 6'10", and 6'8" front line. With six seconds to go in the game, we were leading by a 51−50 score, but South Carolina had the ball. It was at that moment that we managed to get a jump ball. Our only big man at 6'10" was jumping against South Carolina's 6'3" Kevin Joyce.

We immediately called time-out to be sure that we would gain possession, or at least get the ball away from their basket. A minute earlier, we had taken a time-out in a jump-ball situation at mid-court. When the jump ball was tossed, we managed to tap it forward to our fine jumper, Bill Chamberlain. We thought that South Carolina would expect us to try this again and therefore gamble in an effort to get the possession. Anticipating their reaction, we planned another play using Bill as a decoy. *Diagram 16-7* illustrates the way the two teams lined up for the jump ball at South Carolina's free-throw line. South Carolina is represented by the X's.

Diagram 16-7

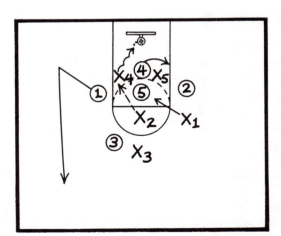

Diagram 16-8

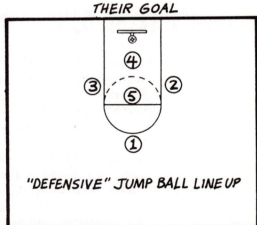

THEIR GOAL

"DEFENSIVE" JUMP BALL LINE UP

Our plan was for #1 to move off the free-throw circle just before the players got set. By doing this, #1 would be free to move as the referee began the toss. #5, the jumper, was to hit the ball downcourt on the side toward which #1 would be releasing. Chamberlain, our #3 man, was to block out any South Carolina player going after the tapped ball.

We expected South Carolina in this *no-control* situation to gamble by having all four of its players moving in the circle early. Surprisingly, they all stood completely still except for John Roche (X1), the All-American guard, who violated the rule by moving in front of our #2 man.

Our #4 man moved to the wrong side of X5. However, as it turned out, he would not have prevented the outcome. Amazingly, South Carolina's Joyce managed to control the tap. He got the ball to 6′10″ Tom Owens (X4) who scored the winning basket in an unbelievable finish.

We could easily have tapped forward to Chamberlain again, but in this case, I was guilty of trying to outthink South Carolina, which had only one man back on defense. We never anticipated that the 6′3″ Joyce would time his jump so well and outjump our 6′10″ man. Our #1 man was wide open. We just couldn't get the ball to him.

As much as it hurts to recall this situation, we're relating it at this point to dramatize the importance of jump-ball situations. We sooner would cite examples of games we won by taking a time-out and subsequently gaining the possession to win the game. Describing this difficult loss, however, will perhaps have a more poignant effect.

We usually line-up for each jump ball as illustrated in Diagrams 16-8 and 16-9.

Diagram 16-8 illustrates the line-up used when the jump ball is tossed at our opponent's end of the court. In this defensive jumpball line-up, we want to be sure our players are near the men they will be guarding if the opponent gains control. Should the jumpball be up against someone other than his own man, the switch must be made before jumping. Each player must have a man and the jumper will be guarding the opponent's jumper until he can switch back to his own man.

Three players are positioned in the defensive half of the circle. The tallest player not jumping (#4 in Diagram 16-8) takes the middle. The next two in height are positioned at either side depending on where their respective men line up. The smallest player takes the middle of the opposite end of the circle.

In *Diagram 16-9*, we are jumping at our end of the court. In this offensive jump-ball situation, we are not as concerned about lining up with the men we are guarding. Should our opponent control the tap, the situation would be similar to defending a fast break. Our offensive jump-ball line-up places our biggest man not jumping in front of our basket. The smallest man is back, while the two in between share the wing position. We use this offensive line-up when the jump ball occurs at center court as well.

The obvious goal in jump-ball situations is to gain possession. A secondary consideration would be scoring off the jump-ball play. This secondary goal, however, should not be pursued at the expense of paying less attention to the primary objective of possession.

When a jump-ball is called, our men move quickly into position. They should quickly determine if this is a no-control, sure-control, or normal jump-ball situation.

A no-control jump ball is one in which the opponent's jumper has at least six inches of height advantage over our jumper. A sure-control situation is one in which our jumper has a similar height advantage over the opponent. The normal situation, which is far more common, is one in which there is some doubt as to which jumper will control the tap.

Our objective is to have our players know where the tap may be headed without disclosing this indication to the opponent. Our jumper calls a verbal signal which freezes one or two possible receivers and simultaneously frees the other two or three men to guess with our opponent's jumper. The verbal signal also tells our team whether the tap will be on the circle, or over our man's head into an imaginary outer circle. Our numbering system is keyed to the positions our men play. The number of digits used signals the distance involved. The exact type of signal used is really not too important. Its only objective should be to key the players to the likely location of the tap.

The no-control is an automatic call for the jumper at either end of the court. In *Diagram 16-10*, we want #2 as the only logical receiver, since he is back on defense and therefore tied down anyway. This frees #3, #4, and #5 to guess the direction of X5's tap and gamble accordingly. We even encourage these three players to move in the lane early. If the violation isn't called, we may steal the ball. If it is called, there is little lost. Our defense will be better organized if our opponents are given the ball out of bounds than it would be if they were to gain possession on the jump ball.

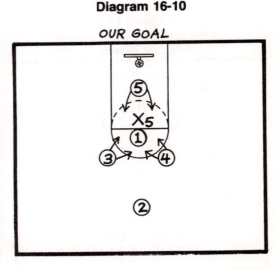

Diagram 16-9

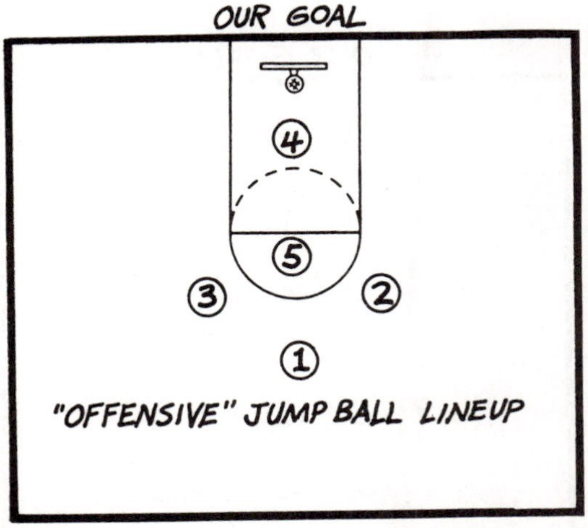

OUR GOAL

"OFFENSIVE" JUMP BALL LINEUP

Diagram 16-10

OUR GOAL

In *Diagram 16-11*, we illustrate a sure-control situation. The dots indicate four possible calls #5 could make to be sure we do gain control. If the forward tap to #2 is called, it signals #3 and #1 that they must be ready to take off and fill the lanes on the fast break. #2 should catch the ball and swing the pass to #1 or #3 near mid-court. Two other good calls would be the long tap over #3 or over #1. If the tap goes long to #3, #4 would block out an opponent in that area, as would #3 before he moved to get the ball. The other good call would be a tap directly to #3 *if* there is only one smaller defensive man defending him.

We wouldn't want the tap going to #4. If something went wrong on the tap, the ball could wind up too close to the opponent's basket.

The same calls illustrated in Diagram 16-11 would be used in an offensive sure-control jump-ball situation.

In *Diagram 16-12*, the long taps over #3 or over #2 would be excellent for possession. #1 and #3 could screen together making this tap over #3 a sure-control. The forward tap to #4 would be used for a quick score. If this tap to #4 is called, #3 and #2 may break to the baseline.

The normal jump-ball situation calls for us to tie down two possible receivers and free two men to gamble. In *Diagram 16-13*, #3 should call any two of the three back men as potential receivers. This frees #1 to play a possible back tap by X3. The other free man will probably guess with X3 on a side tap. However, if that additional free man is #5, he may move into a path of an opponent near him.

In a normal jump-ball situation, we always want our jumper looking to tap to the biggest man in the circle if there is only one opponent near him. Dick Harp, the brilliant coach at Kansas University following Dr. Allen, used Wilt Chamberlain as the receiver for any jump ball in which Wilt was not jumping. The jumper would simply tap it very high to Wilt, and he recovered it as he would a rebound.

Diagram 16-11

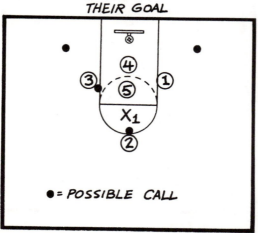

Diagram 16-12

Diagram 16-13

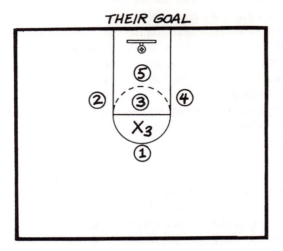

At North Carolina, we have tried some different line-ups on jump balls which we hoped would take the other team by surprise. At times, we have opened the game with everyone stationed along the ten-second line. Once, at the start of the half, we lined up with our players in a straight line from one foul line to the other foul line. Odd line-ups like these, although they occasionally work, are put in for one game, and then cast aside. Most of our practice time devoted to jump-ball situations is concentrated on the fundamental line-ups and strategies discussed earlier. To become a good jump-ball team does take practice. However, it is practice worthwhile.

out-of-bounds situations

When our opponent takes the ball out of bounds, we vary our defense as we pointed out in our philosophy of defense chapter. This out-of-bounds situation does provide a good opportunity to change defenses. When we take the ball out of bounds at the endline, we run our press organization with few exceptions, as described in Chapter 8.

At this point, we will discuss our offensive thinking when the ball is on the baseline, the frontcourt sideline and the backcourt sideline.

When the throw-in is to be made anywhere along the baseline (other than the area six feet from the sideline), we believe the ball is in an advantageous position. Therefore, we look not only for possession, but for a quick two points. Although we do want to know the defense we're facing, we use the same formation against a zone as we do man-to-man when we in-bound the ball. In either case, the out-of-bounds play moves us to our T Game if we don't shoot off the play. We could call another offense if we chose, once the ball is successfully in-bounded.

In **Diagrams 16-14** and **16-15**, we are executing the play against a man-to-man defense. As soon as the referee hands the ball to #3, #5 wheels to set a rear screen for #4. #4 comes off the screen in either direction. Since our first option is to hit #5 rolling to the basket after the screen, we prefer #4 to move as he does in Diagram 16-14. If #4's defender overplays him in that area, #4 should go to the basket and #5 should spin out to the corner as in Diagram 16-15. Occasionally, #5 may start to screen and simply go back to the basket for a pass from #3.

In both diagrams, #1 starts in close and then sprints out to backcourt as a safety valve for #3. #2 is isolated in the extreme corner, hoping to keep X2 from helping out underneath. #3 must do a good job of searching out any opening. There is freedom here for the offense to do as they wish *if* the defense dictates it.

Our move into the T Game comes about in the following manner: #3, after passing to either #4 or #5 in the corner, moves on to the court as a low post. The post going to the basket (either #4 or #5) comes back out as a high post. #2 comes out to the guard position and we are set for the T Game as described in Chapter 4.

Diagrams 16-16 and **16-17** show the same initial alignment with different moves against a zone. #3 may pass to any of his four teammates and come on to the floor as a low post. The object on any in-bounds pass is to move into a quick one-three-one offense against the zone and then to our T Game for continuity. If our opponents go from a zone to a man-to-man defense at this point, we will attack them during the change.

Diagram 16-14

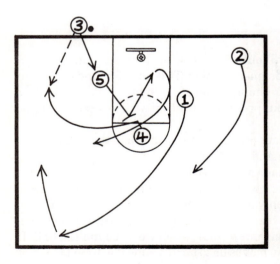

Diagram 16-15

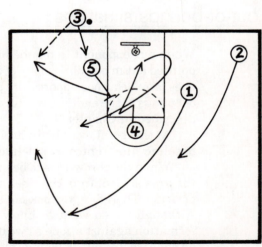

Diagram 16-16

Diagram 16-17

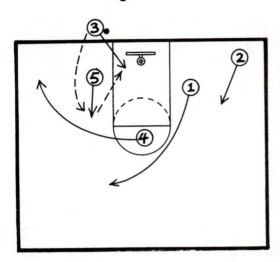

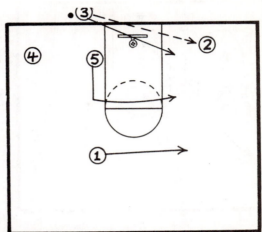

Diagram 16-16 illustrates one play which has given us many baskets against a zone. #5 backpedals to the left of the foul line as #4 moves to the sidelines. #2 holds his corner position until the in-bounds pass is completed. He then moves to a wing. #1 moves back as the point man. #3 chooses a lob pass to #5, who returns it underneath to #3. #5's second look would have been to #2 who could have been able to hit #3 underneath on #2's side. After one swing of the ball, we fall into our T Game with either #3 or #4 becoming the corner man while the other assumes the low post. #5 is the initial high post in our T Game.

Diagram 16-17 shows #3 passing directly to #2 in the extreme corner, and following his pass to the low post. #5 and #1 come across forming our one-three-one, although #2 is situated more toward the baseline than at a wing position.

#2 (who shoots from the corner during practice) may put the ball up. If he does, we would have good rebound coverage from #3, #4, and #5. If #2 doesn't shoot, he looks to either #3 or #5. Regardless of where the throw-in occurs, #5 will be located in a good place to have the ball against a zone.

The sideline out-of-bounds play either in the frontcourt or the backcourt calls for the same line-up. Here, the main objective is sure possession.

During some years, we used special plays from the sideline out-of-bounds situations in our frontcourt against man-to-man. The rule change, which brought about the common foul not being shot until the bonus, created more sideline out-of-bounds situations. This influenced us to look for some set, special out-of-bounds plays from the sideline. If these plays don't work, they take us into our Passing Game. For example, if we wish to run a Basic Cut play from the sidelines, we do so as illustrated in **Diagrams 16-18** and **16-19**.

Diagram 16-18
Diagram 16-19

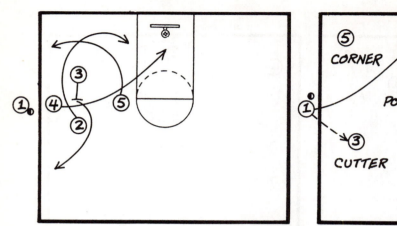

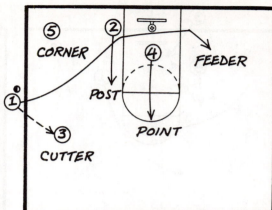

Each time we are awarded the ball in the backcourt, we line up on the sideline, as illustrated in **Diagram 16-20**. We guard against a surprise press in this manner. The quarterback may release the line-up, however, if the press is not in effect.

All four in-bounds men are in line with #3 and perpendicular to the sideline. In Diagram 16-20, #4 takes one step and bolts to the basket as he looks for a pass from #3. #2 moves away from the basket to receive the pass. If #2 is covered, he moves off a rear screen set by #1. If #3 throws to either #1 or #5, #2 sets a rear screen for #3 and then cuts. After screening, #1 should be free for an outlet pass from #3. #5 is the emergency outlet if needed, but he is mainly concerned with becoming a good post up for #1, as we move to press organization. #3 moves off #2 to the far side of the court for balance and press organization.

Diagram 16-20

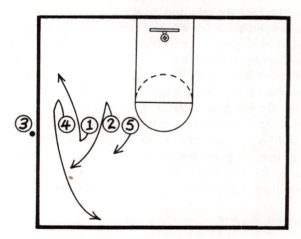

Diagram 16-21 The only difference in the frontcourt line-up shown in the addition of a possible scoring play for #3 after the throw-in. #2 sets the rear screen for #3. After receiving the pass, #1 attempts to hit #5, posting up in the top half of the foul circle. #5 may look to pass underneath to #3 for a lay-up. If that pass is not open, #5 throws to #4 in the far corner and follows his pass to the high post. #3 takes the low post and we are in our T Game.

We also have used a free-lance line-up as a change. The free-lance line-up allows the players to do what they please to get open.

A free-lance line-up is also used for change in the frontcourt. After the successful throw-in from our free-lance line-up, we move into our Passing Game.

Diagram 16-21

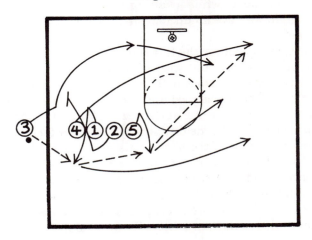

unusual situations

Once again, we want to restate a point mentioned earlier in this book. It is our job, as coaches, to prepare our team for any situation. This includes even the unusual situation such as the *basket-hanger*. Although we have not encountered the basket-hanger to date, we have seen some teams use it against others as a short interval surprise. Therefore, we still take a few minutes of practice time to cover its possible use against us. We want our team to know what to do if the opponent were to leave one of its men at its basket and play a four-man zone against our five offensive players.

Obviously, we would not leave one of our men back with their basket-hanger. However, we would exercise more careful shot selection against their four defenders, and when a shot was taken, our #1 man would sprint back on defense.

One might question the need to spend any time at all covering a play which rarely comes up in a game. The answer is that these unlikely situations may be used more often against teams reputed to be unprepared for them.

Aside from risking the loss of points due to surprise, the team which is unprepared for the unusual may require additional time-outs to cover them when they do occur unexpectedly in a game. We feel strongly that time-outs should be used very carefully so several remain available for the closing minutes of a close game. We will now cover those important last-minute situations.

last-minute situations

HOLDING THE BALL FOR THE LAST SHOT

Under certain conditions we will try to control the ball for the last shot of the half and, of course, the last shot of the game. In both situations, we move into our Four Corners delay while awaiting the right moment for that last shot. However, should we have an uncontested lay-up while waiting, we would go for the basket.

The decision to wait for the last shot of the first half is dependent on the strength of our opponent, the score of the game, and the momentum at the time. Obviously, these factors will vary from game to game. Therefore, we have no set rule. There is a good psychological lift gained by controlling the ball for a time and then scoring at the buzzer. We certainly don't want to take the last shot too soon. The ideal timing would allow for little else other than our own possible tip-in, if the shot is missed.

When I served as an assistant to Frank McGuire at North Carolina, he had the bench stand with seven seconds left on the clock. This signaled the players that the shot was to be taken in four or five seconds. Coach McGuire wanted the last shot to come from the outside. He feared the offensive charging foul that could result from a drive. We have adopted this concept of having the bench stand as a signal. However, we do so at ten seconds. The extra three seconds allows us to move into our one-four alignment from the Four Corners.

As for the shot itself, we do like some type of penetration to put pressure on the defense. Undoubtedly, the defensive players will be told not to foul. This, we feel, makes them even more vulnerable to the penetrating drive.

The decision about holding the ball for the last shot of the game depends on the same factors mentioned earlier relative to the half. We will wait to take the last shot when behind by a point, if we are playing a heavily favored opponent. If the score is tied, we usually hold for the last shot, regardless of the competition.

One such close game that comes to mind occurred during the Finals of the 1969 NCAA Eastern Regionals against Davidson. With the score tied and 1:30 left on the clock, Davidson decided to wait for the last shot. Since we do not like to go down to the wire in a tie situation without possession, we moved into our aggressive 32 defense (half-court run-and-jump). At 1:12, Gerald Tuttle, one of our guards, made a great surprise move on the dribbler which drew a charge and gave us the ball.

We played our Four Corner delay until fifteen seconds remained on the clock. We then called a time-out. The players were told to stay in Four Corners until the bench stood. At that point, we wanted the ball going to Charles Scott.

We told Charles to penetrate, look for the shot, but pass to the open man if Davidson doubled-teamed him. Everything went well. Charles penetrated into the top half of the foul circle. Then, two Davidson players came at him. Charles went straight up for a jump shot and the ball swished through at the buzzer.

I asked Charles later if he saw an open man at the point he was doubled-teamed. Charles, who was an extraordinary pressure player, replied, "I never saw a Davidson man near me!"

We used to set up the last play with a specific player designated to take the last shot. We later decided against the idea. We found that even when the defense put strong coverage on our designated player, he still felt he had to take the shot according to plan. We now think the best strategy is to get the ball to the man our opponents *think* will have it. Then we want that player to hit the open man or take the open shot.

LENGTH OF COURT FOR SCORE

We have had good success with two special plays designed to take us the length of the court for a score. We also have a play which should get us to half-court for a time-out.

We begin all three of these plays similarly with a line-up in our backcourt at the top of the free-throw line from which the players sprint out to designated areas. We practice the plays from the defensive foul-shot situation as well, without the line-up, since the ball remains dead after a made foul shot.

One play, called *100*, takes us to mid-court, where a time-out is called. If the captain will remind the timekeeper not to start the clock until the ball is touched in bounds, this play should take no more than one second off the clock.

The *200* play continues from the 100 play *without* a time-out. The 200 would be used if we had no time-outs left and had to go the length of the court to score within a few seconds. We will cover such a situation toward the conclusion of the chapter.

The *500* play is a desperate situation which requires us to go the length of the court to score in one second. We would use 500 if, for example, our opponent went up by a point with a foul shot, leaving one second left on the clock. Another time for its use would occur if we were down by three on an opponent's field-goal with a few seconds left. We then would ask for a time-out and hope to have it acknowledged in time to leave us two seconds. We then would try 500 hoping to get a field-goal in a second. If we made it, we again would ask for a time-out with one second showing on the clock. At that point, if we were able to keep the opponent from in-bounding the ball, we would have possession under our basket, a second left on the clock, and a chance to win the game with a quick field-goal.

Each of these last-minute situations illustrates the value of using time-outs conservatively and wisely throughout the game. We feel we should keep a minimum of two time-outs for the last two minutes of a close game. The team also should be thoroughly prepared for these last-minute situations so that each time-out serves as a review rather than a learning experience. Toward the conclusion of this chapter, we will cite an example of one particular game, which will illustrate the value of accumulating time-outs for last-minute situations. First, however, let us diagram the 500 play.

Most coaches can put in something which would take them to mid-court in one second, and from there to a shot at their basket in another second or two. Many of the questions we get at clinics regarding these situations relate to the need to go full-court for one last shot in a second.

We will diagram the 500 play from the defensive foul-shot situation. Let us assume the score is tied and the opponent has another foul shot coming. We call 500, knowing if the foul shot is made we still will have a chance with a second left on the clock (and a good timekeeper). If the shot misses, we should go into overtime.

Diagram 16-22   We put in a substitute #5 man for our #1 player since we don't need ball-handling skill now. We also may put in a substitute for #2 to throw

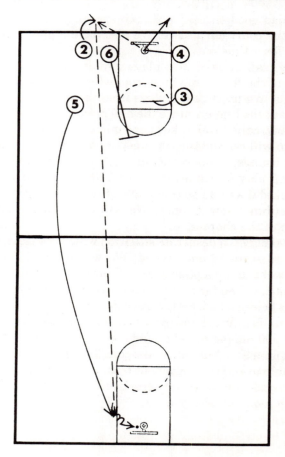

Diagram 16-22

the long baseball pass. Substitute #5, shown as #6 in Diagram 16-22, takes the inside position in the foul lane. If the foul shot is made, #4 grabs it out of the basket and passes it out of bounds to #2. #5 starts downcourt as the foul shot is taken. #3 and #6 try to get in somebody's way after the foul shot is made. We are hopeful of getting #5 one-on-one against the opponent's small man. #2 aims the ball in front of our basket. Ideally, #5 catches the pass and scores, although we are quick to admit it is not a percentage maneuver.

500 has failed more times than it has worked for us. However, for the times it has worked, it was worth practicing.

100 and 200 have been successful more than they have failed. The 100, which takes us to half-court for a time-out, has only failed once in several years. Our exact alignment on the 100 and 200 changes each year. However, we use the same principle annually. We have a big man set a screen and then move somewhere along the ten-second line to receive a spot pass from the end-line.

LAST-MINUTE SITUATIONS ON DEFENSE

Our strategy on last-minute situations, from a defensive point of view, is determined by examining all the pertinent factors before making a decision. Once again, these factors are the strength of the opponent, the score, and the momentum.

If our opponent apparently is holding the ball for the last shot when the score is tied, we usually will gamble to steal the ball unless it means giving up the lay up. We use our 32 run-and-jump defense for last shot situations until only fifteen seconds remain. At fifteen seconds, however, we stop gambling, play good defense, and hope for overtime. We also will be ready to call time-out if we get a rebound or if the opponent scores.

If our opponents appear to be going for the last shot even though they are one point behind, our decision on defense is based on the caliber of the opposition. If the team is one we should beat, we will usually pretend the score is tied and attack from a defensive viewpoint. We dislike the idea of having one shot determine the game's outcome if we are playing against a weaker opponent.

The situation would be different if we were playing a team much stronger than ourselves. If the stronger opponent, behind by a point, elected to go for one shot, we probably would go into a zone and allow them that last shot from the outside.

We do have what we call a *prevent* defense. This is used when our opponent must go the length of the court to score. If possible, we substitute to have three big men and two of our quickest men in the line-up. One big man will cover the in-bounder tightly. The other two big men are playing a zone on each end of the defensive foul line.

Our two quick men are stationed in a two-man zone parallel to the ten-second line and several feet on the frontcourt side. By using this formation, we will be allowing any short pass into their backcourt. However, we will be trying to block or intercept the long pass anywhere near the basket.

After going through the rules prior to the 1962–63 season, I noticed that it was permissible for the offensive team to call time-out after scoring if the defensive team had not begun to throw the ball into play. We began to work on calling time-outs in this situation and had become proficient at using it during practice. We usually had the player closest to the basket grab the ball as it dropped through the net to make sure we could get the time-out. The official probably would not allow this more than once, but we wanted to be sure to make use of the rules.

The first time we had the opportunity to use this kind of time-out occurred during our game with Wake Forest in January, 1963. With eight seconds to play, Wake Forest scored, which put them ahead by three points. We took time-out and set up a play to score inside. Our captain, Larry Brown, was instructed to tell the official that we would be calling time-out if we scored. We did score the basket inside and asked for a time-out with four seconds to play, trailing by one point.

When the time-out was awarded to us, Bones McKinney, the Wake Forest coach was irate. He went out on the floor to argue with the official, but the time-out held. Unfortunately, we did not prevent Wake Forest from getting the ball into play. We fouled then as soon as the ball was in-bounded and Wake Forest made the two foul shots to win the game.

The point we're making is to be sure that, as coach, you know the rules thoroughly so that you can use them in the right situations. I believe Jack Nicklaus made this comment about golf: "If you know the rules, you sometimes can get a very good lie (placement of the ball) and it will work to your advantage." The same applies to basketball. We have won a few games on the basis of knowing the rules and using them to our advantage.

Throughout this chapter we have emphasized the importance of using time-outs wisely so that as many as possible remain available for the closing moments of a close contest.

One game, which may help to illustrate this concept, as well as several last-minute situations discussed earlier in the chapter, took place in 1974.

We were playing Duke University in our final ACC regular season game. Duke had played extremely well and with seventeen seconds left in the game, the score was 88–80 in their favor. Many of the fans were filing to the exits as Bobby Jones, fouled while shooting, went to the free-throw line for us.

During the time-out called by Duke prior to Bobby's shots, we told the team that we would go into our 54 zone press (described in Chapter 15) on Duke's throw-in if Bobby was successful at the line.

Bobby sank both foul shots and our 54 defense worked well for us. Walter Davis, our outstanding swing man who was just a freshman at the time, stole the in-bounds pass and got the ball to guard John Kuester, who sank the lay-up.

The eight point deficit had suddenly been cut in half with thirteen seconds left to play in the game. We quickly called time-out, and reviewed each player's assignment for the 54 defense that we planned to use again.

Once again, we prevented the successful throw-in as Walter Davis deflected the toss, this time, out of bounds off a Duke player. Eleven seconds remained.

It was now our ball underneath our own basket. We ran our regular out-of-bounds play, missed the shot, but scored on a Bobby Jones tap-in to bring us within two points.

Six seconds were left. Again, we called time-out.

During each of these time-outs, we reminded the players that if Duke did get the ball in-bounds, we were to foul immediately to stop the clock. This time, Duke succeeded with its in-bounds pass and we quickly fouled them as planned. There were four seconds to go.

Duke's foul shooter missed his first attempt at the one-and-one. We called our last time-out the instant we gained possession. Three seconds remained on the clock.

Now here is a key point. Since all our time-outs were now used, we could not go to our 100 play. The 100 could have brought us to mid-court in a second. This would have left us two seconds to score from mid-court after setting up a special play during a time-out. Instead, we had no choice but to go the full length of the court and score within three seconds. This, obviously, would be more difficult to accomplish and as such, it should dramatize the value of each time-out. Even though we had used ours judiciously during the game, our chances of tying the score would have been greatly enhanced at that moment, if we still had one more time-out left to us.

In this instance, however, our good fortune was with us a while longer as the 200 play we had worked on in practice came through for us. We made a perfect pass to Walter Davis well beyond the ten-second line. Walter dribbled once inside the hash mark and put up the ball. It swished the nets for our eighth consecutive point in seventeen seconds to tie the score at the buzzer.

We won this remarkable game in overtime by a 96–92 margin.

All teams, ourselves included, would like nothing better than to win all tight games in this exciting manner. However, as we illustrated with examples of the close ones that got away from us, it doesn't always happen this way. Nonetheless, we believe the team well-prepared for these situations, will win a few extra games each season. We, therefore, consider them important enough to work on daily.

All last-minute situations are covered during the final fifteen minutes of practice. This is the time we also devote to our delay and catch-up games. By playing five minute overtime scrimmage virtually every day of practice, almost every conceivable situation will occur at some point in time.

The players learn our philosophy and techniques through frequent repetition and discussion. We may not always accomplish the ideal in these situations. However, we are prepared for them.

This, of course, is a coach's job; to organize, prepare the team, hope for execution and a little bit of luck!

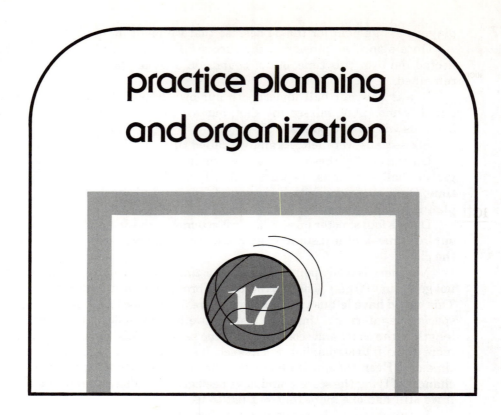

practice planning and organization

The organization, the preparation, the execution, plus a coach's entire philosophy is implemented in the all-important practice session. We realize there have been some basketball teams which have played better than they have practiced. In almost every case, however, a team will play as it practices over the long haul. Since we strongly believe this, it would be hard for us to overstate the value we place on our practice sessions.

Practice time for a basketball team has a two-fold purpose. Individual skills should be improved while the players must learn to blend their talents in an effort to meet the overall needs of the team. Each player's motivation should be to walk off the practice floor a better player than he was when he arrived for the session. The coach has the responsibility of helping each player meet this goal. In addition, the coach must plan each session so that sufficient time is spent utilizing individual talents within the team concept.

Our practices are treated much like a disciplined classroom. There is one difference, however. In most classrooms, the instructor does not have the problem of keeping away several hundred people who wish to observe class each day. We have solved this problem to some extent. On Wednesdays and Fridays, our practice sessions are open to our students, faculty and alumni. Mondays, Tuesdays, and Thursdays are closed practice days.

On closed practice days, we spend more time introducing new concepts, since our players are better able to concentrate on instruction. We scrimmage more and work on things already known to the players on open days. We do insist that practice spectators sit in the second balcony away from the practice floor. This enables the coaches to criticize a player when necessary, without creating embarrassment to the young man. Incidentally, we believe in enthusiastic praise as well as constructive criticism during practice.

Confidence can and should be built during practice sessions through deserved praise. We believe we can become a confident team. We also look to praise achievements that can build individual confidence as well. Confidence, we believe, is the sum of hard work and execution. However, praise will bring this confidence factor along more quickly than if praise were withheld.

practice session rules

We do have some rules which govern our practice sessions. Some of these rules are maintained out of tradition. Each, however, is designed to bring about discipline, pride, and high team morale. A few rules involve the coaching staff as well. We are fortunate to have three coaches available for most practices. Although an assistant coach may occasionally miss practice with other duties, it should be an extreme situation which would prevent the head coach from being at a practice.

The only reasons a player may miss practice would be due to an injury, a home emergency, or study purposes. Missed practice sessions rarely occur, however, since a player usually organizes his time well during the season. Our players also appear to enjoy practice, which is probably the major reason we do not have this problem. Being late to practice would also constitute a violation of our rules; it has occurred only twice in recent years for the reasons mentioned above.

No one is allowed to disturb a player or coach during practice unless it is an extreme emergency. I have never taken a phone call during practice in all my years of coaching. I also have refused to talk to anyone during our practice time. Our managers head off anyone who may want to talk with me. This would include alumni, the chancellor, or the athletic director. There are twenty-two other hours in the day when I can be reached. The same holds true for our players.

At no time during our practice sessions will a player sit or kneel. The one exception would be to allow the winners of a particular drill to sit down during the water break. A coach never sits down during a practice session either.

When the coach is speaking, all eyes must be on the coach. When a player is speaking, all eyes, including those of the coach, must be on him.

No player may offer an excuse to any criticism during practice. Although a player is encouraged to ask questions pertaining to our execution, it can not be associated with his criticism. We do, however, encourage the players to discuss any concerns they may have after the practice session or in my office the next day. There is simply too much to accomplish during the practice session to take time out for this on the court.

When a coaches' whistle blows, action is stopped immediately. If it is time to change ends on the floor for a drill, the whistle signals a fast sprint to the other end of the court.

There is no swearing by anyone at anytime on the practice floor. Swearing will not be tolerated regardless of whether it is used to indicate disgust or directed toward another individual. The same rule applies for any outward display of temper. We sometimes have some poor calls when our managers and graduate assistants referee. Nonetheless, a player is never permitted to question a call, nor comment on it. The carryover into a game situation should be obvious here, in terms of avoiding the possibility of drawing a technical foul.

Finally, tremendous effort is demanded from all our players at practice. There is never a time to slow down or rest. Each player must make a great effort to appear enthusiastic. By acting this way the player will often *become* enthusiastic even if this was not his inclination when he first took the court.

discipline and the peer pressure concept

The above-mentioned rules are rarely violated. We think the reason for this is that our players consider them fair, and in the best interest of the team as well as its individual members. However, if a rule *is* broken, we punish as a team. We believe in group punishment for an individual infraction. The same applies when an individual fails to accomplish the *emphasis of the day*, which will be discussed later in the chapter.

My close friend, golfing companion, and a most competent psychiatrist, Dr. J. Earl Somers, of Chapel Hill, N.C., gave us this *peer pressure* idea back in 1966. Earl related it to some interesting case histories he had studied from the World War II era. It seems that during the war many soldiers were greatly tempted to leave their trenches when the firing began. However, most resisted the urge to leave, despite their fear and the great danger involved. It later was determined that their motivation for remaining under fire was their desire not to let their buddies, or even their lieutenant, down. Although most of the men felt they were fighting a just war, it was their loyalty to their peers and leader, not to a set of ideals, which motivated them to fight.

With this insight given to us by Dr. Somers, we began to aim all motivation toward a player *not letting his buddies down*. We have found this peer pressure method far more effective in building team morale than motivation created by fear, reward, or any other means. Here too, the carryover is obvious since basketball is so much of a team sport. When one player lets down in a game, it not only reflects on the individual player, it hurts his teammates as well. The same applies to practice. When a player breaks a rule or fails to do what is expected of him, it will ultimately hurt the entire team. Consequently, the entire team is punished for the individual's infraction. The punishment usually consists of several sprints run by all team members because an individual did something wrong. When the individual realizes that he is making everyone run sprints for his infraction of a rule, he is less likely to repeat an infraction in the future.

In recent years, we have begun to wonder whether we have created a monster in this *buddy system*. Our players are so anxious to please their teammates they actually may try too hard in given situations. This can be a problem with a conscientious young man who is very sensitive. In these situations, I will talk to the player and assure him that the team accepts him and everyone makes mistakes. Hopefully, this relieves the pressure. Still, I would rather have players that were really concerned about pleasing their teammates than a team in which the individuals could care less and go on their own.

The coaching staff gives a great deal of attention to being fair in its criticism as well as in administering punishment when it is necessary. Young men want to be disciplined, because this shows care and interest. But the discipline has to be fair. We make a very strong effort to treat each member of the team equally, realizing of course, that there are individual differences among our team members. Some players respond better than others to criticism. Others require more praise. Each is a person, however, and I believe all persons are loved by our Creator. Therefore, we should extend the dignity of personhood to every human being since he is loved and accepted as such.

The late, internationally known theologian, Paul Tillich said, "God accepts us as we are, therefore, we must accept others as they are." Dr. Thomas Harris sums up a similiar philosophy with the title of his excellent book *I'm OK, You're OK* (New York: Avon, 1971).

Our coaches attempt to practice this same philosophy of acceptance in our relationship with each player. Therefore, we criticize the act rather than the person. Coaches must push players to a point beyond which the players would like to stop. We accept them individually, as they are, regardless of whether or not they respond to the discipline. However, if they are to be on the team, they have a responsibility to work hard for the overall good of the team.

planning practice

At North Carolina, our preparation for the first practice session begins in the early summer. Since we usually know about the personnel with whom we will be working, we can begin to formulate our offense, defense, and special situations early in the year.

We start by reviewing the past season to determine what has and has not been effective for us. The knowledge of our personnel, combined with our previous year's experience, helps us decide what we will add and delete from the system during the coming season. Our work on fundamentals is more constant, although in our re-evaluation of the previous season, we may uncover some fundamental which needs more attention.

Once we determine our objectives for the year, the next step is to decide how to teach them. We want our entire system for the season introduced to our players before the first game. NCAA universities may begin practice on October 15th. This gives us approximately six weeks of practice time before our first game.

In some states, high schools may not begin to practice that early. In addition, many youngsters play both football and basketball in high school. Those who go out for both sports may not be available for basketball practice until a week or so prior to the first game. If we were faced with this problem, we would not attempt to incorporate all our offenses or defenses before the first game. We would add something each week and have a big review during the Christmas holidays.

Our six week pre-season practice is vitally important. In a sense, it is the most significant period of the year for us since we are forming habits which will prevail all season. The work load is a tough one for our players during this period. After they graduate, they often refer to it as *boot camp*. Invariably, however, our players look back to the pre-season practice period with a sense of pride, since they completed it successfully. They also realize how instrumental this pre-season practice is to whatever degree of success the team achieves during the season. Our pre-season practices do not last more than two hours (excluding running). However, the players stay very active throughout each season.

To organize these practices, we compose a *Master Practice Plan*, illustrated in **Chart 17-1**. We make certain to include everything in this plan that we wish to introduce to our players, as well as the order in which we want the material introduced.

Our Master Practice Plan then is broken down into a *Weekly Plan* (**Chart 17-2**) and ultimately into daily practice plans which are posted on the bulletin board prior to practice each day.

We include two thirty-minute meetings per week during the pre-season period, using the classroom method of lecture and questions. We even test our players on these lectures during the Thanksgiving holidays. Our Monday meeting is devoted to a discussion on our weekly objectives. At our Wednesday meeting, we usually show a training film. This will consist of clips from past games, illustrating a particular phase of the game we are working on that particular week.

FORMAT FOR DAILY PRACTICE DURING PRE-SEASON PERIOD

We do have a fairly standard format for our practices held during the six week pre-season period. This format is illustrated in **Charts 17-3** through **17-9**. These are actual daily practice plans picked from each of the six weeks which preceeded our 1972–1973 season.

Stations   Prior to the formal start of practice, each player must complete the *stations* listed on the daily practice plan before doing any free shooting. Each station takes no more than a few minutes to complete. However, they can help a player improve considerably over the course of a season.

The universal gym set (used for the purpose of strengthening the legs and upper part of the body) as well as the shooting-form station are worked daily. The other stations are varied from day to day.

The shooting-form idea was an outgrowth of a personal struggle with my golf swing. My practice swing was usually sound. However, my form deteriorated rapidly once that little white ball was staring up at me. One golfing magazine I read suggested that a golf swing could be grooved over the winter by swinging the club without involving the ball.

During the summer that followed, I asked John Lotz, one of my former assistants and former head coach at the University of Florida, to have our young summer campers shoot the ball to each other initially rather than at the basket. John, who was an outstanding shooter during his playing days, subsequently found that the youngsters were better able to concentrate on his suggestions regarding their form when they were not disconcerted by the end result of the shot.

Bill Guthridge, my present chief assistant, is another great teacher of the game. Bill has carried this concept one step further by having our campers sit on the floor and shoot the ball against a wall while he works on their form. This approach eliminates possible mistakes resulting from faulty weight distribution. It enables the shooter to concentrate exclusively on the upper body and the proper release of the ball.

The shooting-form station preceeding formal practice gives our players the opportunity to check on their form daily by having them take many shots against a wall or in the air before shooting at a basket. We want them to use the shooting-form station to check for backspin of the ball. We also want them to exaggerate the follow-through by fully extending the elbow and unlocking the wrist downward from the *fully* extended arm. Whether our players are shooting in practice or in a game, we hope to see the fully extended elbow and unlocked wrist *until the ball is in the basket*.

The time devoted to all stations takes up about seven minutes. The players must plan their time accordingly, since stations must be completed before the official start of practice. On meeting days, the squad must complete stations before the meeting. After the meeting, one of our seniors will lead the team in the calisthenics and stretching for warm-up purposes.

To begin practice on non-meeting days, a loud whistle brings the players to mid-court. They sprint to the center circle on the whistle just as we want them to sprint to the bench on a time-out call during a game. During this discussion at mid-court, the coach reiterates the practice objectives and the emphasis of the day. He also tries to build some new enthusiasm for the practice ahead.

Emphasis Of The Day   This is listed at the top of each daily practice plan and usually is tied into our weekly objectives. The emphasis of the day is a particular aspect of the game we want our players to concentrate on during the entire practice session. We vary the emphasis from session to session. However, important basics such as "going to the offensive board" are repeated often.

It is important to make the emphasis of the day something which can be executed easily if a player is mentally alert and putting forth effort. It is equally important to spot the player who does not carry out the emphasis. Otherwise, it loses its purpose.

When a player fails to carry out the emphasis of the day, a loud whistle stops practice. The entire team groups at the endline, and sprints are run by every member of the squad for the player who *let the team down*. We usually run no more than one or two sprints for a player's failure to carry out the emphasis. We are not interested in the running for its own value at this point. Our main concern is the purpose it serves to remind the players of the daily emphasis.

Initial Drills   We begin our daily practice with a running and passing drill for the entire squad. We usually alternate between the fast-break drill, the pass-and-cut lay-up drill, the Four Corners passing drill, and the pitch-ahead lay-up drill.

We then work a defensive drill for the entire team.

Dummy Offense   The next five minutes are usually spent on *dummy offense*. I have never been particularly fond of dummy offense either as a player or a coach, but we do feel it is necessary to effectively teach a set offense. We have even run our free-lance Passing Game in dummy offense and found that it helped us learn to move the ball more quickly.

We work the dummy offense at both ends of the court by dividing the squad into the blue and white teams listed on the practice plan. The coaching assignments for this, as well as all split squad activities, are made at our noon-time meeting when the staff reviews the day's practice plan.

Explode To Basket Drill   This drill usually follows dummy offense. This drill is the closest we ever come to playing one-on-one. It was originally used as a means of teaching individual offensive moves without defense. At the time, we were primarily concerned with teaching a player to make a crossover move and drive hard to his weak hand. We felt that if a player went through the daily motions of driving to his left, presuming that was his weak side, he would soon become adept at the move. If the player's natural preference was to go to his left, we made him drive right, or to the basket.

In subsequent years, we added a screen to the drill to help the player learn to drive off the screen and teach the screener to roll to the basket. Finally, we felt the same drill presented a good opportunity to teach defense at the point of the ball. Since the drill is brief and the distances short, the defense player need not worry about the embarrassment of being badly beaten. Therefore, in addition to the offensive benefits mentioned earlier, the drill now helps us teach good defensive position on the ball and *boxing* out the shooter for rebounding position.

To facilitate the explode to basket drill, we divide an average twelve man squad into four groups of three players each. We divide the squad according to size so that the players in each group are relatively equal in size. Both the left and right sides of the baskets are used at each end of the court. One man serves as a passer in a guard or center position. He fakes a crosscourt pass, then hits his man coming to the ball. The receiver then drives on his defender. The three men rotate the passer, driver, and defender positions after each play. In essence, they are playing one-on-one basketball.

Defense Oriented Four-on-Four Work   The next period involving four-on-four work is vitally important toward the building of our defense. To establish our four-man groups, each player is assigned to a particular group on the first day of practice. Ideally, each group will consist of two frontcourt men and two backcourt men.

Our breakdown during this period involves one four-man group working defense against another group, while the third group works on shooting form at the opposite end of the court. The rotation varies daily so that the groups do not play against the same four men continuously.

The four-on-four work during this period is defense-oriented. We begin on fundamental defense and build up through all our 20 defense principles within three weeks. The offense participates in these drills primarily to help the defense. Nonetheless, the offensive players do get some work accomplished on passing, dribbling, screening, cutting, and offensive rebounding.

We try to give each of the four-man groups a minimum of seven minutes on defense. Therefore, this period lasts approximately 21 minutes. It may run a little longer during the first three weeks of practice.

From this point on in practice, our daily plan will vary depending upon the offense and defense receiving our attention that day. Since the players have just completed some solid four-on-four defensive work, we usually move to an offensive part-method drill. The particular drill used may be any one of the part-method drills described in the offense section of this book. We generally work the drill at both ends of the floor dividing the squad into the blue and white teams described earlier.

A defense part-method drill usually follows at this point. We first review the defensive principle taught during the previous practice session before going on to a new principle.

It is during this time allotted to part-method drilling that we sometimes divide the team into frontcourt men at one end and backcourt at the other. When this is done, each group works a particular part-method drill applicable to its needs.

Competitive Drill Prior To Water Break   When our part-method drilling is completed, we move into a competitive drill or game prior to the water break. The games we usually alternate during this period are the secondary-break drill, described in Chapter Seven (Diagram 7-7), and the press offense-defense game which is covered in detail at the conclusion of Chapter Eight. We also will play a three-on-two continuity game in this period, which is used more for fun than to simulate an actual game situation.

The Water Break   Our water break is held approximately one hour after practice begins. I had never heard of a water break in practice until 1963. At that time our physiologist, Dr. Carl Blyth, presented us with facts which convinced us that a water break is not only helpful, but imperative as a preventative of a possible serious health problem. In these matters, we work very closely with our outstanding trainers John Lacey and Marc Davis, and the Sports Medicine Department under the leadership of Dr. Joseph DeWalt at the University's Medical Center on campus.

Early in the year, our players will lose between five to twelve pounds per workout. We monitor this closely. Any player losing more than ten pounds per workout is encouraged to help himself at *any* time to the water we keep available for this purpose on the scorer's table.

Five-on-Five Whole-Method Work   Whenever we wish to introduce any new concept to our players, we do so after the water break. This is the period devoted to our five-on-five whole-method teaching. Everything done in practice after the water break is facilitated through five-on-five work. This whole-method time is spent either in half-court work or in a full-court scrimmage. Most our early pre-season work is done in the half-court, emphasizing defense for the first twenty minutes and offense for the remaining twenty minutes.

Any time we work half-court, regardless of whether the emphasis is on offense or defense, we always want to employ the *transition*, discussed in our chapter on the 20 defense. Therefore, when the offense misses a shot the defense always breaks.

During the past few years, we have even strengthened this emphasis. We now have the defense quickly jump out of bounds after the practice opponent's field-goal and rush the ball into play. For example, suppose we are working half-court offense and the offense scores. The defense jumps out of bounds and puts the ball into play quickly. The team originally on offense must now defend the fast break before it can continue on offense. The defensive signal is called quickly and the break is defended. The coach then blows the whistle and the original offensive five go back to offense again. They put the ball into play at the other end of the court this time and head upcourt to their original basket. By simulating a fast break after field-goals in practice, we remind our players that they must always be ready to make that vitally important, quick transition from offense to defense and from defense to offense. Also, we are giving the team practice at quickly calling, and reading, the defensive signals which follow every North Carolina field-goal.

Full-Court Scrimmaging   We probably should do more pre-season full-court scrimmaging than we presently do. However, we also believe that an offense or defense should be well prepared before putting it to the test in a game-like situation. Therefore, we do not get to our initial full-court scrimmage work until approximately two weeks after the start of practice. This will consist of two ten-minute controlled sessions.

By the fourth week, we are usually scrimmaging this full forty-five minute whole-method period three times a week. The players not participating in the scrimmage will shoot foul shots at the portable baskets, work on individual weaknesses, or stand on the sideline waiting to be substituted into the game.

Last Five Minutes Our last segment of the formal practice session is devoted to situations which often arise in the last five minutes of a game. During this period we work on our delay offense and catch-up on defense. By the third week of practice we use this time period almost daily for a five-minute overtime scrimmage. When the overtime game is concluded, organized practice is completed and organized running begins.

Conditioning and Sprints I have always believed in the value of sprints ever since my own playing days at the University of Kansas, when they were used by Dr. Allen at the conclusion of every practice.

There are many differing opinions on sprints. Some coaches believe it is important to conclude practice with something the players find highly enjoyable. Others feel the value of sprints lie only in their benefit as a means of getting the players in top condition. Although our organized running program does help our conditioning very early in the pre-season period, we look to sprints more for the psychological value they provide the team. We feel, and our players seem to agree, that there is much to be gained from being pushed to work harder. This kind of effort builds *mental toughness* and, usually, the harder a team works to achieve its goals, the stronger will be its determination to accomplish them.

We give our seniors a re-evaluation questionnaire to complete at the end of each season. To the best of my recollection, no one in the history of our program has voted to discontinue the sprints we run at the conclusion of practice.

Incidentally, there is a way each player can eliminate the need to run one or more sprints during a particular practice session. Every time a player draws an offensive foul either in practice or during a game, it eliminates a sprint for him at the time of his choosing.

The distances which make up a sprint are determined by the coach. A *super* sprint will consist of a run to one-quarter court and back, plus a run to half-court and back, plus a run to three-quarter court and back, plus a full-court run and back. A *junior* sprint consists of endline to endline run and back. We particularly like this latter distance because we can relate it to our players in terms of the need to run quickly into offense and quickly back into defense.

Each type of sprint must be run within a designated number of seconds. However, every player is given his own designated time in which to run a particular distance. This is in keeping with our practice of expecting maximum effort based solely on the individual capabilities of each player. We refer to this as the *Scott* rule after our great player of the late 1960's, Charles Scott, whose tremendous speed was one of his many natural talents.

At the time Charles came up to varsity, we expected all our players to run the super sprint in thirty seconds or less. Charles would hardly work up a sweat in the half minute allotted to the run. Twenty five seconds was a more realistic time for him, whereas a player like 6'10" Rusty Clark did the very best he could when he ran the distance in twenty-nine seconds. It was at that point that we changed the rule and established expected finish times based on individual capability. The Scott rule has worked well for us.

While on the subject of individual capability, it is important to point out that the coach must become thoroughly familiar with the endurance capacity of each player. We want our players to work very hard because we feel it is good for them. However, the health of our young men comes first and must never be jeopardized. This is why we can not be specific in terms of suggesting a designated number of sprints and their duration after a typical practice. This will vary depending upon a variety of conditions which affect each practice session and each individual player. The coach always must use good sense and discretion in these matters. I might also add that our trainer always is instantly accessible during each practice session.

PRACTICE FORMAT AFTER START OF SEASON

The preceeding format covers our typical practice session during the six week pre-season period. After the season begins, the format does change, although the variations are slight in the month of December.

As of January, we eliminate some of our drills and cut the session down to ninety minutes. We also discontinue most of our part-method teaching and rely more heavily on the whole-method approach. However, we do, continue using the explode to basket drill along with the four-on-four work described earlier.

On a pre-game day, we do not discuss the team we are about to play with our players. Instead, we work our team at aspects of play we know will require good execution based upon the coaching staff's knowledge of the opponent.

For example, if we know the upcoming opponent uses full-court pressure defense, we will work our players at press offense in preparation for the game, without discussing our reasons for doing so. We take this positive approach because we want our players to concentrate more on improving themselves as opposed to worrying about the opponent.

On the day before a game, we usually put in about one hour of hard work trying to build confidence by praising good play and conclude the practice with a one-and-one foul-shot competition between the blue and white teams. The idea is to see which team can finish first. Presuming there are six players on the blue team and six on the white team, each must put in twelve consecutive foul shots before that team can retire to the dressing room.

We believe in giving the players one or two days a week off during the season. We usually choose the day after a game as one of those days off. During the pre-season period, the players are off every Sunday plus two of the six Saturdays in that period.

These well-earned days off not withstanding, we want our players to look forward to practice, and to enjoy the experience. Most of all, we want them to consider it a privilege to be allowed to practice and we believe they feel this way. At the same time, we on the coaching staff feel that we have been blessed with an outstanding group of young men through the years who have made our jobs on the practice floor equally gratifying.

Chart 17-1   UNC Master Practice Plan (1975–76)

October 15 — Mile Run, Objective Data, Picture Day, Dinner Meeting

Period I   October 16–18 (6 Hours)

  I. Fundamentals
    A. Selecting Squad
    B. Conditioning
    C. Prepare new drills for clinic
    D. Shooting Form - Foul-Shot Ritual
    E. Individual Defense
      1. Stance
        a. on ball
        b. without ball
      2. Position
        a. on ball
        b. without ball
      3. Feet Movement
    F. Individual Offense
      1. Passing - All Types
      2. Dribbling
      3. Offensive moves with ball
    G. Rebounding
      1. Offensive
      2. Defensive
  II. Team Offense
    A. Fast Break
      1. Primary Break Organization
      2. Secondary Break
        a. into Passing Game
        b. with shot
      3. Part-Method
        a. Two-on-One
        b. Three-on-One
    B. Introduce Passing Game
      1. High-Low Post
        a. from initial set
      2. Double Low Post
        a. from initial set
        b. from secondary break
  III. Team Defense
    A. Introduce 22 Defense
      1. Cover basic principles in pick up at half-court except covering screen either on ball or away
      2. Picking up against fast break

Chart 17-1   UNC Master Practice Plan (1975—76) Continued

Period II   October 20—25 (12 Hours)

    I. Fundamentals - (Review Period I)
       A. Add Screening

   II. Team Offense
       A. Continue Fast Break
          1. Add Three-on-Two
       B. Continue Passing-Game Offense
          1. Part Method
             a. post movement
             b. perimeter movement
          2. Still no screen on ball
          3. Very little dribbling
       C. Introduce Offense #4 (Delay Game)
          1. As keep away
          2. Against zone press
       D. Introduce Press Offense (Dummy only)

   III.Team Defense
       A. Continue 22 Defense as in Period I
          1. Add screen principles
          2. Initiate 22 from sideline out-of-bounds situations
       B. Introduce 23 and 24 Defense

Period III   October 27—31 (10 Hours)

    I. Fundamentals
       A. Continue all Fundamentals from Periods I and II
       B. Begin alternating days of each fundamental
       C. Squad selection completed

   II. Team Offense
       A. Continue Passing Game
          1. Entries to #3 and #5 against man-to-man pressure
          2. Begin screen at point of ball option
          3. Begin perimeter dribble option
          4. Begin full-court scrimmage (Passing game only)
       B. Fast Break Completed
          1. Also at end of press offense
       C. Continue Offense #4
          1. Begin against man-to-man
          2. Build confidence with half-court work
       D. Press Offense
          1. Against man-to-man
          2. Against zone press (Experiment with our 54)

   III. Team Defense
       A. Review all principles in 22, 23, 24
       B. Defense against break completed
       C. Introduce Run-and-Jump whole-method
       D. Begin calling signals after scoring in half-court offense

Period IV   November 3—8 (10 Hours)
                 Blue-White Game (2 Hours)

   I. Fundamentals
      A. Review first three periods
      B. Out-of-bounds situations - Offensive and Defensive
      C. Foul-shot situations
      D. Jump-ball situations
      E. Pre-game warm-up
   II. Team Offense
      A. Passing Game
         1. Complete against man-to-man
         2. Introduce against zone or combo
      B. Continue and Improve Fast Break
         1. From all defensive work
         2. Competitive break games
      C. Complete #4 Offense
         1. Begin overtime scrimmage each day
      D. Complete Press Offense
         1. From dead-ball situation
         2. Against three-quarters court pressure
         3. Play press offensive-defensive game
   III. Team Defense
      A. Introduce 42 Defense
         1. Entry to 42 as part of series with 22 and 32
         2. Part-Method on double-team and slides
      B. Add 43 defense to 22 and 32 for series
      C. Incorporate 44 Defense into system
      D. Review all team defense to date

Period V   November 10—15 (10 Hours)
                 UNC vs. Russia (2 Hours)

   I. Fundamentals
      A. Review all situation work
      B. Begin special situation work
      C. Review and discuss individual fundamentals
      D. Talk about USA rules—Differences of International rules
   II. Team Offense
      A. Review differences of zone and man-to-man in passing game
      B. Review fast break
      C. Review press offense
      D. Introduce #2 Offense
         1. Dummy for first two days
         2. Against zone only
         3. Entry to #2 game
         4. Explain logical scoring situations

Chart 17-1   UNC Master Practice Plan (1975—76) Continued

III. Team Defense
  A. Continue work on half-court series (22—32—42)
    1. Must get signal
  B. Continue work on full-court series (23—33—43)
    1. Must get signal.
  C. Introduce 51 defense (Point Zone)
    1. Five-on-four defense initially
    2. Explain principles similar to man-to-man
    3. Back from 44 and 43 defense
  D. Introduce 52 Defense
    1. Similarity to 51
    2. As part of zone series (51—52—42)

Period VI   November 17—21 (10 Hours)
    DEFENSE EMPHASIS WEEK

I. Fundamentals
  A. Individual defense review
  B. Defensive foul-shot situation
  C. Defense against all out-of-bounds situations
  D. Defense after losing jump ball
  E. Go for record on defense drill #1

II. Team Offense
  A. Complete #2 Offense
  B. Introduce #1 Offense
    1. Wing option
    2. Post option
    3. Dribble option
    4. Entry to above three
  C. Practice against all our defenses with emphasis on the defense

III. Team Defense
  A. Review principles of 20 Defense
  B. One day for 30 Defense emphasis
  C. One day for 40 Defense emphasis
  D. Scrimmages (ten minutes) with each series (half-court, full-court, and zone); Chart these
  E. Review 51 and 52 Defense
  F. Introduce 54 Defense
  G. Review defense against break (22)
  H. Part method of 43, 44, and 54 Defense back to 51 Defense
  I. Drawing charges worth two
  J. Missing signal costs one draw charge
  K. Pictures posted of past defensive stars at North Carolina

Period VII November 24−29 (14 Hours) - Thanksgiving
       First game - 29th!
       Review of Periods I−VI

  I. Fundamentals
    A. Review all to date
    B. Last-minute situation in detail
      1. at meetings
      2. in practice
    C. Quarterback meetings
    D. Pre-game warm-up
    E. Game traditions

  II. Team Offense
    A. Review #1 Offense (When to Use)
    B. Review #2 Offense (When to use)
    C. Review #3 Offense (When to use)
    D. Review #4 Offense (When to use)
    E. Review #5 Offense (When to use)
    F. Introduce catch-up offense
    G. Review press offense
    H. Review fast break
    I. Cover unusual situations
      1. Triangle-and-two defense
      2. Box-and-one defense

  III. Team Defense
    A. Review 22, 23, 24 Defense (When to use)
    B. Review 32, 33, 34 Defense (When to use)
    C. Review 42, 43, 44 Defense (When to use)
    D. Review 51, 52, 54 Defense (When to use)
    E. Review series defenses
    F. Cover unusual situations
      1. Basket-hanger
      2. Against our offense #4
    G. Introduce 41 Defense (Point and One)

COMPLETES PRE-SEASON PRACTICE

Chart 17-2   Weekly Practice Plan   **(Oct. 16−21, 12 hours)**

Objectives: Fundamentals
                            Conditioning
                            Fast-Break Offense
                            Passing Game
                            22, 23 Defense
                            Introduce Offense #4 and Press Offense

Period:

  I Warm-up   Fast-Break Drill #1
                            Dummy Offense
                            Four Corners passing drill
                            Dribble & Pivot
                            Defense Drill #1
                            Defense Drill #2
                            Explode Drill (Dummy and with towel)
                            Pass and cut to basket

 II Four-on-four   Foul-shot ritual
     Shooting   Spin ball in air
                            Use of backboard   (Just like camp week)
                            Stopping for jump shot
                            Adjustment Drill (Overhead pass for offense: Defensive Drill #3)
                            Transition Drill (Defensive Drill #4)
                            Support Drill (Defensive Drill #5)
                            Dribble-used Drill (Defensive Drill #6)
                            All-Purpose—combine Defensive Drills 3, 4, 5, and 6

III Offensive   Fast-break organization (with Box-out) Dummy
     Part-Method   Press organization drill - Dummy
     Drills   Big men—offensive rebounding game
                            Little men—outlet pass—two-on-one—three-on-one
                                           advancing ball circling
                            Passing Game—part-method—Post work
                            Shooting games from spots
                            Screen-and-roll

IV Defensive Part-   Whistle indicates reverse or slap floor
     Method Drills   Zig-Zag with towel (hands shoulder line) (Defense Drill #7)
                            Prevent and recover (one-on-one, two-on-two) (Defense Drill #8)
                            Combine Drill #8 and Drill #9
                            Boxing out and outlet pass
                            Beating man to ball in lane (Defense Drill #9)
                            Guarding outside shooter (Defense Drill #10)

 V Pre-Water Break   Three-on-two continuity
     Competition   Secondary break game
     (Winner-Losers)   Press offense-defense game
                            Rebounding game

VI Whole-Method   Introduce offense #3
     (Alternate Offense &   Offense #3 movement game
     Defense Daily)   Half-court Offense #3—no dribble—with break
                            Every third pass must go to post or violation
                            Fast break into offense #3

VII	Wind-up (Last fifteen minutes)	Introduce offense #4—Build confidence Backdoor in offense #4 game—part-method Keep-away game Conditioning - running groups Suicide Sprints Crossing in two minutes

Chart 17-3   Practice Plan for Monday, October 16, 1972

TIME	SUBJECT	POINTS TO STRESS
	EMPHASIS OF THE DAY: 　Offense - Catch ball with two hands 　Defense - Two passes away in lane	
	STATIONS - Universal Gym Set - three minutes 　Shooting Form - Spin Ball 　Passing - 2 hand chest pass 　Jump Rope - Weighted Vests	(Johnston)
	Special Exercises - Back (Karl, Washington); 　Groin (O'Donnell)	
4:15	Discussion	
4:19	Fast-Break Drill #1	
4:23	Defense Drill #1	
4:28	Explode Drill (Weak hand)	Pass to driver; fake up underneath
4:31	Group I - Shooting Form - Foul-Shot ritual - 　Spin Ball Group II & III - Four-on-four 　Adjustment Drill #3 -	Position Guarding man with ball; rebounding later
4:37	Rotate Groups	
4:43	Rotate Groups	
4:50	Fast-Break Organization	Secondary Break
5:00	White Team - Zig-Zag Drill #7 Blue Team - Prevent and Recover Drill	Belt-basket #8 - Initial position
5:05	Rotate Ends	
5:15	Defensive Rebounding - Footwork	
5:20	Water Break	
5:25	Introduce rules of Offense #3 　Offense #3 game - Winners Half-court Offense 　Breaking (Near End)	Entry* No dribble, easy pass, movement 　of posts Rebounding Defense Balance; Talk; Blocking Out
5:45	23 Defense with break -	Guarding man with ball; check 　adjustment
6:05	Introduce - offense #4	Show reverse move Middle interchange
6:10	Conditioning - 　Check Bulletin Board for Running groups 　Big Men - Side baskets	

	WHITE			BLUE	
(1)	Hite	(Karl)	(1)	Hoffman	
(2)	Karl	(Elston)	(2)	Harrison	
(3)	O'Donnell		(3)	Bell	
(4)	Johnston		(4)	Washington	
(5)	Jones		(5)	Stahl	

POST PRACTICE REMARKS:

Chart 17-4   Practice Plan for Tuesday, October 17, 1972

TIME	SUBJECT	POINTS TO STRESS
	(Use sweat bands!!)	Exercises for Washington, Karl, O'Donnell Call DeWalt
	EMPHASIS OF THE DAY: Offense - Going to Board Defense - Hand up on Ball	
	STATIONS: Universal Gym Set Shooting Form - Spin Ball Passing - See Coach Guthridge - Toss backs	
4:00	Big Men (Offensive Moves) - Dummy	From #3 game
4:15	Discussion - (Practices)	
4:18	Fast-break Drill #1	
4:22	Dummy Offense - #3 - #4	
4:27	Defense Drill #1 - #2	
4:30	Explode with Defense (No reaching)	Position on Ball; Box out; fake overhead pass
4:35	Group II - Shooting	Form - Backboard
	Group I & III - Defense	
	Adjustment Drill #3	Retreat in direction of ball
	Guard-to-Guard Transition Drill	Hand up
4:43	Rotate Groups	
4:49	Rotate Groups	
4:55	Two-on-one - Both ends - Three-on-two	Keep in air
5:05	Defense Drill #7 - Zig-Zag	Belt-Basket
	Defense Drill #8 - Prevent & recover	Draw charge
5:10	Rotate Groups	Jacknife - footwork
5:15	Boxing out - (both ends)	Footwork - outlet pass
5:20	Water Break	
5:25	Fast break organization	Secondary break; Two beginnings
5:30	Half-court Defense	Defensive Rebounding
	With Fast break	Move on movement of ball Hand up on Ball
5:48	Half-court offense	
	Passing game competition	Screen away
	No dribble	Movement without ball Off. Board Def. against break
6:05	Offense #4 reverse drill—both ends	
	Offense #4—3 possessions each—(competitive)	Corner man initiates reverse
6:15	Conditioning	

WHITE			BLUE	
(1)	Hite	(Karl)	(1)	Hoffman
(2)	Karl	(Elston)	(2)	Harrison
(3)	O'Donnell		(3)	Bell
(4)	Johnston		(4)	Washington
(5)	Jones		(5)	Stahl

POST PRACTICE REMARKS:

Chart 17-5 Practice Plan for Wednesday, October 18, 1972

TIME	SUBJECT	POINTS TO STRESS
	EMPHASIS OF THE DAY:	
	Offensive - Offensive Board - Defense Balance	
	Defensive - Hand-up on man with ball	
	STATIONS - Passing - Coach Guthridge	
	Shooting Form	
	Rebounder - (ten rebounds) - Big Men	
	Ball Handling - Backcourt	
4:00	Meeting	
	20 Series Defensive Film	
	Practice to date	
	(Blazer fitting 2:45–3:30)	
4:30	Calisthenics	Karl - Leader
4:35	Four Corners	
4:40	Dummy Offense Passing Drill	
4:45	Defense Drill #1, #2	
4:50	Explode with defense	Hand up; Taking Fake
4:55	Group III	Shooting (backboard)
	Group I & II	Four-on-four defense
	Adjustment Drill #3	
	Transition Drill #4	Stopping at lane
5:03	Rotate Groups	
5:10	Rotate Groups	
5:18	Big Men - Blocking Out Drill	Let ball hit floor
	Backcourt - two-on-one	
5:25	Big Men - Offensive Rebounding Game	
	Backcourt - Advancing ball - Press offense	
5:32	Water Break	
5:35	Fast-Break Organization	Review secondary
	Introduce Press offense organization	
5:45	Offense #3 game (Winners-Losers)	Offense board
	Every 3rd pass must go to a post	Defense against break
	Defense—Fast break into offense #3	
6:05	23 Defense—without stopping	Hand up; move with movement of ball
	Defense breaking into offense #3	Box out
6:20	Offense #4	Pick up dribble
	One point one minute	
	(Both teams)	
6:25	Keep away game - Number of seconds	
6:30	Conditioning	

WHITE		BLUE	
(1) Karl	(Hite)	(1) Hoffman	
(2) Elston	(Karl)	(2) Harrison	
(3) O'Donnell	(Elston)	(3) Bell	
(4) Johnston		(4) Washington	
(5) Jones		(5) Stahl	

POST PRACTICE REMARKS:

Chart 17-6 Practice Plan for Thursday, October 19, 1972

TIME	SUBJECT	POINTS TO STRESS
	EMPHASIS OF THE DAY	
	Off. - three passes before outside shot	(after throw-in)
	Def. - Blocking out on Board!	
	STATIONS - Passing to throw-backs	
	Shooting Form	
	Jump Rope - Weighted Vests	
4:00	Big Men - offensive low-posts move	
4:15	Discussion	
4:20	Fast-Break Drill #1	
4:25	Defense Drills #1, #2	
4:30	Explode with Defense	Hand up; Taking fake; Moving to get open
4:35	Shooting - Group I - Stopping for Jump Shot	
	Defense - Groups II & III	
	Adjustment - Drill #3)	
	Transition - Drill #4) } Combine	
	Support - Drill #5)	
4:43	Rotate Groups	
4:51	Rotate Groups	
5:00	Zig-Zag Drill - White Team	
	Prevent & Recover - Blue Team	
5:05	Rotate Groups	
5:10	Fast-Break Organization - Press	(Dummy)
5:15	Secondary Break Game	
5:20	Water Break	Blackboard Discussion
		Press offense
5:25	23 Defense (continuous)	Hand up
	with Break	Move on each pass - block out
5:40	Half-court offense #3	Screening away
	Limit dribbling	Six passes
6:00	Offense #4	
	74 − 71 (Two minutes to play)	
6:10	Keep-away	
6:15	Conditioning	

WHITE		BLUE	
(1)	Hite (Karl)	(1)	Hoffman
(2)	Karl (Elston)	(2)	Harrison
(3)	O'Donnell (Johnston)	(3)	Bell
(4)	Johnston (O'Donnell)	(4)	Washington
(5)	Jones	(5)	Stahl

POST PRACTICE REMARKS:

Chart 17-7 Practice Plan for Friday, October 20, 1972

TIME	SUBJECT	POINTS TO STRESS
	EMPHASIS OF THE DAY	
	Offense - Catch ball with two hands	
	Defense - Blocking out	
	STATION - Universal Gym set	
	Shooting spin	
3:00	NCAA Filming Session (TV short)	
3:45	Discussion - (scrimmage tomorrow)	
3:50	Fast-Break Drill #1	
3:55	Four corners passing drill	
4:00	Defense Drills #1, #2	
4:05	Explode Drill with Defense	Taking fake; boxing out; hands up
4:10	Group II - Shooting Form Review	Backboard; foul-shot ritual;
	Group I & III - Four-on-four Defense	stopping for jumper
	Adjustment Drill #3 - (Beat man to Ball)	
	Transition Drill #4	
	Support Drill #5	
	Dribble-Used Drill #6	
4:18	Rotate Groups	
4:26	Rotate Groups	
4:35	Defensive Rebounding	Box out mismatch
	(both ends)	
4:40	Zig-Zag - Drill #7 (B)	forty-five degrees on reverse
	Prevent and recover - Drill #8	with help
4:45	Rotate Groups	
4:50	Dummy Offense #3 from Secondary Break	
4:55	Secondary Break Game	Into Offense #3; Block out
5:00	Water Break	
5:05	23 Defense with break	Box out; hand up; move on each movement
		of ball
5:20	Offense #3 against set defense	Screen away and step back
	Defense against break	Posts & outside men
5:30	#4 offense - 74−71 Two minutes to play	
	(Both teams)	
5:40	Keep-away Game	
5:45	Conditioning	

WHITE		BLUE	
(1) Karl	(Hite)	(1) Hoffman	
(2) Elston	(Karl)	(2) Harrison	
(3) O'Donnell	(Johnston)	(3) Bell	
(4) Johnston	(O'Donnell)	(4) Stahl	(Washington)
(5) Jones		(5) Washington	(Stahl)

POST PRACTICE REMARKS:

Chart 17-8   #21 Practice Plan for Thursday, November 9, 1972

TIME	SUBJECT	POINTS TO STRESS

EMPHASIS OF THE DAY
   Know the defense
   Defense - Move when ball moves

STATIONS - Universal Gym set
      Rebounder - Big Men - Ball handling
        (backcourt)
      Shooting Form

4:00	Big Men - Offense #2 execution	
4:15	Discussion - Chili Tickets	
	1:00 p.m. reception - Tomorrow's plan	
4:20	Fast-Break Drill #1	
	Four corners passing drill Pre-game warm-up	
	Dummy Offense	
4:30	Defense Drill #2	
4:35	Explode with Defense - Hey! Hand up on ball	
4:40	Shooting - Throw Back (zone spots)	
	Defense - Four-on-four with signals	
4:49	Rotate Groups	
4:57	Rotate Groups	
5:05	Fast-Break Organization - Press organization	
5:10	Secondary Break Game - Defending Break	
5:15	Water Break	
5:20	Full-court Series Defense - 53-33-23-43	
	-One team stays on defense	
5:30	Foul-Shot situations - Both ways	Review 54-34-24-44
5:40	Jump-ball situations - Both ways	
5:45	Half-court offense - Review zone off.	
	#1, #2, #3 Man offense	
	Execution	
6:05	Out-of-bounds situations	
	Baseline - sideline	
6:10	Foul Shooting - around horn	
	Winners - Losers	

WHITE		BLUE	
(1) Hite		(1) Karl	(Hoffman)
(2) Elston		(2) Harrison	(Karl)
(3) Johnston (Bell)		(3) O'Donnell	
(4) Stahl		(4) Kupchak	
(5) Jones		(5) Washington	

POST PRACTICE REMARKS:

Chart 17-9   #25 Practice Plan for Wednesday, November 15, 1972

TIME	SUBJECT	POINTS TO STRESS

EMPHASIS OF THE DAY: Boxing Out
                    Off. Board

STATIONS - Universal Gym set
           Shooting Form

4:00	Meeting - Situations - Last Minute
	Zone Offense - quick throw-in getting signal
4:30	Calisthenics - Johnston
4:35	Fast-Break Drill #1
4:38	Defense Drill #1, #2
4:34	Explode with defense
4:38	Dummy offense
4:45	Shooting Form - White
	Defense (Guarding Screener) - Blue
4:55	Rotate Groups
5:05	Boxing out - Both ends
5:10	Scrimmage (ten minutes)
	Blue - Zone Series; White - Full-court series
5:30	Water Break
5:35	Scrimmage (ten minutes)
	Blue - Full-court Series; White - Zone series
5:55	Scrimmage (ten minutes)
	White - Zone Series; Blue - Zone Series
6:15	Keep-away
6:20	Foul Shots - Conditioning

WHITE	BLUE
(1) Karl	(1) Hoffman
(2) Elston	(2) Harrison
(3) Johnston (O'Donnell)	(3) Chambers (Bell)
(4) Stahl	(4) Kupchak
(5) Jones	(5) Washington

POST PRACTICE REMARKS:

appendix:

lettermen under dean smith at north carolina

Name	Class	Degree	Graduate Work	Present Position
Peppy Callahan	'62	AB Educ. (Math)	MAT (Math) '64	Lt. Col. U.S. Air Force, McCord AFB, Seattle, WA
Hugh Donohue	'62	AB (History)		Industrial Relations, International Telephone and Telegraph, New York City, New York
Jim Hudock	'62	BS (Ind. Rel.)	DDS'68	Dentist, Kinston, North Carolina
Harry Jones	'62	AB (Philosophy)	MA (Phil.) '63	College Teacher, New York
Don Walsh	'62	AB (Pol. Sci.)	JD (Law) '65	Head Basketball Coach, Denver Nuggets (NBA) Denver, Colorado
Eddie Burke (Mgr)	'62	BS (Ind. Rel.)		Manager, IBM, Washington, D.C.
*Larry Brown	'63	AB (History)		Head Basketball Coach, UCLA, Westwood, CA
Charles Burns	'63	AB (Sociology)		Sales Rep., Levi Strauss, Lexington, Ky.
Dieter Krause	'63	AB (Recreation)		Col. U.S. Army, Germany
Yogi Poteet	'63	AB (Sociology)	MAT (Educ.) '65	Education Specialist, Department of Army, Petersburg, Virginia
Richard Vinroot	'63	BS (Bus. Adm.)	JD (Law) '66	Attorney at Law, Charlotte, North Carolina
Mike Cooke	'64	AB (English)		Executive, Blue Bell Mfg. Co., Bethesda, Md.
Art Katz	'64	AB (Education)	MAT (Educ.) '66	High School Teacher, Wayne, New Jersey
Bryan McSweeney	'64	AB (Pol. Sci.)	MBA (Prof. Mgmt.) '75	Monex International Ltd., Newport Beach, California
Charles Shaffer	'64	AB (History)	JD (Law) '67	Attorney at Law, Atlanta, Georgia (Pres. Atlanta Bar Association)
Elliott Murnick (Mgr)	'64	BA (Pol. Sci.)		Sports Promotion, Raleigh, North Carolina
Bill Brown	'65	AB (History)		Attorney at Law, Atlanta, Georgia
*Bill Cunningham	'65	AB (History)	JD (Law) '68	Head Basketball Coach, Philadelphia 76ers, (NBA) Philadelphia, Pennsylvania

*Have played pro basketball in United States
**Have played pro basketball in Europe.

Name	Class	Degree	Graduate Work	Present Position
Bill Galantai	'65	AB (History)	MA (Educ.)	Doctoral Program in Administration & Supervision, Baldwin Harbor, New York
Pud Hassell	'65	AB (History)	JD (Law) '68	Attorney at Law, Raleigh, North Carolina
Ray Respess	'65	BS (Ind. Rel.)		Personnel Manager, Caswell Training Center, Kinston, North Carolina
Terry Ronner	'65	BS (Bus. Adm.)		Accountant, Wilmington, North Carolina
Bob Bennett	'66	AB (Pol. Sci.)	JD (Law '69)	Attorney at Law, Los Angeles, California
Bill Harrison	'66	BA (Economics)	MBA (Bus. Adm.) '67	Sr. Vice-President, Chemical Bank, London, England
Ray Hassell	'66	AB (History)		Salesman, Pharmaceutical Company, Dallas, Texas
Mike Iannarella	'66	AB (English)	MA (Eng.) '67; Ph.D.	College Teacher, Massachusetts
Earl Johnson	'66	BA (Pol. Sci.)	DDS'70	Dentist, Raleigh, North Carolina
Jim Moore	'66	AB (Psychology)	Psychology '67	Insurance Executive, Wilmington, North Carolina
Mike Smith	'66	BS (Math.)		Executive, Humble Oil Co., New Orleans, Louisiana
Jim Smithwick	'66	AB (Chemistry)		Pediatrician, Laurinburg, North Carolina
John Yokley	'66	BS (Ind. Rel.)	MD'70	Executive Furniture Mfg., Mt. Airy, North Carolina
Bill Cochrane (Mgr)	'66	AB (Education)		High School Teacher & Coach, Virginia Beach, Va.
Joe Youngblood (Mgr)	'66	BA (Pol. Sci.)		President, Fletcher Auto Agency, Fletcher, N.C.
Tom Gauntlett	'67	AB (Pol. Sci.)	Law (1 year)	Executive, Payne Printing, Dallas, Pennsylvania
*Bob Lewis	'67	AB (Rec. Adm.)		J. F. Kennedy Center for Culture, Washington, D.C.
Mark Mirken	'67	AB (Pol. Sci.)	JD (Law) '70	Vice-Pres., General Mills Corp.
Donnie Moe	'67	BS (Bus. Adm.)	MBA (Bus. Adm.) '73	Area Personnel Representative, Raleigh, N.C.
Ian Morrison	'67	BS (Soc. Welfare)		High School Coach, Kingsport, Tenn.
Fred Emmerson (Mgr)	'67	BA (English)	Law '72	Attorney at Law, Chapel Hill, North Carolina
Ben Thompson (Mgr)	'67	BA (English)	DDS '71; MS '73	Dentist, Winston-Salem, North Carolina
Greg Campbell	'68	BS (Bus. Adm.)		Accountant, Bayonne, New Jersey
Ralph Fletcher	'68	BS (Bus. Adm.)	MBA (Bus. Adm.) '70	Bond Investment, Walnut Creek, California
Jim Frye	'68	AB (Psyc.)	Law (1 year)	High School Coach & Teacher, Orland Park, Illinois
Dickson Gribble III	'68	AB (Chemistry)		Captain, U.S. Army, Ft. Huachuca, Arizona
*Larry Miller	'68	BS (Bus. Adm.)		Real Estate Broker, Virginia Beach, Virginia
Joe Brown	'69	BS (Bus. Adm.)		Mortgage Banking, Raleigh, North Carolina
*Bill Bunting	'69	AB (Education)		Cameron Brown Developers, Raleigh, North Carolina
Franklin (Rusty) Clark	'69	AB (Zoology)	MD '73	Thoracic Surgeon, Fayetteville, N.C.
*Dick Grubar	'69	BS (Bus. Adm.)		Mkt/Mgr-Indus., Weaver Const. Co., Greensboro, N.C.
Gerald Tuttle	'69	AB (Phy. Educ.)		Executive, Classic Leather, Inc., Hickory, N.C.
Bob Coleman (Mgr)	'69	BA (Rec. Adm.)	MS (Rec. Adm.) '74	Superior Sales Corporation, Columbia, South Carolina
Randy Forehand (Mgr)	'69	BA (Zoology)	MD '74	Pediatrician, Richlands, Virginia

294

Name	Year	Degree (field)	Advanced degree	Occupation / Location
Jim Delany	'70	AB (Pol. Sci.)	JD (Law) '73	Comm., Ohio Valley Conf., Nashville, TN
Eddie Fogler	'70	AB (Math)	MAT (Educ.) '73	Ass't Basketball Coach, University of North Carolina, Chapel Hill, North Carolina
*Charles Scott	'70	AB (History)		Post Graduate Student
Ricky Webb	'70	AB (Chemistry)	MBA '82	Dentist, New Bern, N.C.
Gra Whitehead	'70	BS (Bus. Adm.)		Bank Officer, Scotland Neck, N.C.
Leroy Upperman (Mgr)	'70	BA (History)	JD (Law) '73	Attorney at Law, Los Angeles, California
**Dave Chadwick	'71	BA (RTVMP)	D. Div. '80	Pastor, Presbyterian Church, Charlotte, N.C.
*Lee Dedmon	'71	AB (Rec. Adm.)		Teacher and Coach, Gastonia, North Carolina
Don Eggleston	'71	AB (Pol. Sci.)	JD (Law) '74	Attorney at Law, Madison, North Carolina
Dale Gipple	'71	AB (Pol. Sci.)		Sales, Bocock-Stroud, Winston-Salem, N.C.
Richard Tuttle	'71	AB (Recreation)		Recreation Supervisor, Gastonia, North Carolina
*Bill Chamberlain	'72	AB (Recreation Adm.)		Banker, Pittsburgh, Pa.
Billy Chambers	'72	AB (Chemistry)	DDS '75; MS '79	Dentist, Asheville, N.C.
**Craig Corson	'72	AB (Psychology)	MBA (Bus. Adm.) '81	University of North Carolina, Chapel Hill, N.C.
Mike Earey	'72	BS (Bus. Adm.)		Bank Officer, Chapel Hill, North Carolina
**Kim Huband	'72	BA (English)	MS (Rec. Adm.) '76	State Government, Raleigh, North Carolina
*Steve Previs	'72	BA (RTVMP)		President, Bakon Products, Inc., Atlanta, Georgia
*Dennis Wuycik	'72	AB (Economics)		Pres., DMW Enterprises, Chapel Hill, North Carolina
Jon Barrett (Mgr)	'72	BA (Pol. Sci.)	JD (Law) '78	Attorney at Law, Charlotte, North Carolina
John Austin	'73	BS (Ind. Rel.)		Respiratory Therapist, Cone Memorial Hospital, Greensboro, North Carolina
John Cox	'73	BA (Psychology)	MED (Educ.) '75	Coach and Teacher, Roxboro, North Carolina
**Donn Johnston	'73	AB (Pol. Sci.)	JD (Law) '80	Attorney at Law, Greensboro, North Carolina
*George Karl	'73	AB (Pol. Sci.)		Head Coach, Great Falls, Montana, Continental Professional League
*Robert McAdoo	'73	AB (Sociology)		Pro Basketball, Detroit Pistons, (NBA) Detroit, MI
Doug Donald (Mgr)	'73	BS (Ind. Rel.)		Banker, Fayetteville, North Carolina
*Darrell Elston	'74	BA (History)	Accounting '81	Owner, Golf City, Terre Haute, IN, and Graduate Student
Ray Hite	'74	AB (Education)	ME (Educ.)	Assistant Basketball Coach, Western Kentucky University, Bowling Green, Kentucky
*Bobby Jones	'74	BA (Psychology)		Pro Basketball, Philadelphia 76ers (NBA) Philadelphia, Pennsylvania

* Have played pro basketball in United States
** Have played pro basketball in Europe.

Name	Class	Degree	Graduate Work	Present Position
**John O'Donnell	'74	BA (Psy. & Pol. Sci.)	MD Dec. '80	Medical School, University of North Carolina, Chapel Hill, North Carolina
Greg Miles (Mgr)	'74	BA (Pol. Sci.)		Spaulding, Walton & Assoc., Burlington, N.C.
Mickey Bell	'75	BS (Business)		Converse Mid-Atlantic Sales and Promotions Manager, Charlotte, N.C.
Ray Harrison	'75	AB (Rec. Adm.)		Olympic Chemical Company, Greensboro, North Carolina
Brad Hoffman	'75	BS (Business)		Asst. Coach, Athletes in Action Basketball Team (AAU), Laguna Hills, California
**Ed Stahl	'75	BS (Business)		Converse Sales Rep., Raleigh, N.C.
Charles Waddell	'75	BS (Ind. Rel.)		Assistant Athletic Fitness Director at University of North Carolina, Chapel Hill, N.C.
*Donald Washington	'75	AB (Studio Art)		Pro Basketball, Europe
John Rancke (Mgr)	'75	AB (Rec. Adm.)		City Recreation Department, Zebulon, North Carolina
**Bill Chambers	'76	AB (Psychology)	'82	High School Coach and Teacher - Graduate School
David Hanners	'76	AB (Education)		Asst. Coach, UNC Wilmington, Wilmington, N.C.
*Mitch Kupchak	'76	AB (Pol. Sci. & Psy.)	MA (Educ.) '78	Pro Basketball, Washington Bullets (NBA) Washington, D.C.
Tony Shaver	'76	BS (Business)		Coach and Teacher, Episcopal School, Alexandria, Va.
Danny Veazey (Mgr)	'76	AB (History)	MD '81	Medical Student, University of North Carolina Chapel Hill, North Carolina
**Bruce Buckley	'77	BA (Math)	JD (Law) '81	Law School, University of North Carolina, Chapel Hill
Woody Coley	'77	BA (Economics)		Executive, Kenan Transport Company, Richmond, Virginia
*Walter Davis	'77	AB (Recreation)		Pro Basketball, Phoenix Suns (NBA), Phoenix, Arizona
*John Kuester	'77	AB (Education)		Pro Basketball, Great Falls, Mont., Continental League
*Tommy LaGarde	'77	BA (Economics)		Pro Basketball, Dallas Mavericks (NBA) Dallas, Texas
James Smith	'77	BA (Humanities)	MA (Educ.) '79	Assistant Coach, New Orleans Univ., New Orleans, LA
John Cohen (Mgr)	'78	BA (History)		Executive, Jewel Box Comp., New York, N.Y.
*Geff Crompton	'78	AB (Recreation)		Pro Basketball, Great Falls, Mont., Continental League
*Phil Ford	'78	BS (Business)		Pro Basketball, Kansas City Kings (NBA) Kansas City, Missouri
Jeff Mason (Mgr)	'78	AB (Journalism)	JD (Law) '83	Law Student, University of North Carolina, Chapel Hill
**Tom Zaliagiris	'78	AB (Education)		Sales Exec., Classic Leather, Hickory, N.C.
*Dudley Bradley	'79	AB (Sociology & Rec.)		Pro Basketball, Indiana Pacers, (NBA), Indianapolis, IN

Name	Year	Degree	Occupation
Ged Doughton	'79	AB (Political Science)	Banking, Wachovia Bank, Winston-Salem, N.C.
Ricky Duckett (Mgr)	'79	AB (Education) MS (Educ) '80	Asst. Basketball Coach, Harvard Univ., Cambridge, Mass.
**Randy Wiel	'79	AB (Education)	Pro Basketball, Holland
*Dave Colescott	'80	AB (Education)	Pro Basketball, Philadelphia, Continental League
*Mike O'Koren	'80	AB (Recreation)	Pro Basketball, New Jersey Nets (NBA) E. Rutherford, N.J.
**John Virgil	'80	AB (Recreation)	Pro Basketball, Holland
**Jeff Wolf	'80	AB (Political Science)	Pro Basketball, Italy
**Rich Yonakor	'80	AB (Recreation)	Pro Basketball, Italy
Kenny Lee (Mgr)	'80		Student, University of North Carolina

*Have played pro basketball in United States
**Have played pro basketball in Europe.

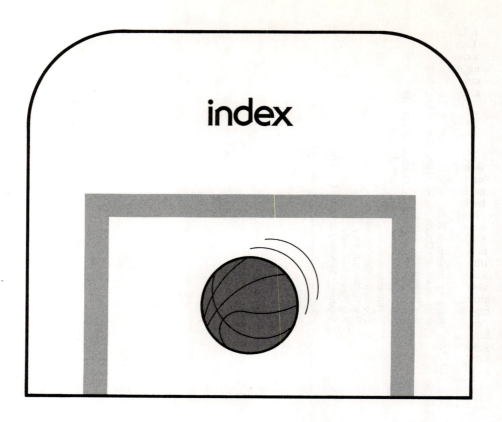

index

U

UCLA:
  advantages of passing game, 29
  Alcindor era, 16
  full-court press offense, 95
  1968 NCAA finals, 76
  team play and winning games, 21
  Wooden, John, 16, 29
Utah, University of, 77

V

van Breda Kolff, Butch, 27
Virginia Squires, 78
Virginia Tech, 77

W

Wake Forest University, 241
Walsh, Donnie, 205
Warren, Mike, 76
Weekly practice plan (*see* Practice, weekly plans)
Winter, Tex, 53

Wooden, John, 16, 29
Wootten, Morgan, 205, 209
Wuycik, Dennis, 21

Z

Zone defense (50 defense), 170, 229−44
  advantages, 229−30
  ball in corner (*diagrams*), 238−40
  full court (*diagrams*), 231−34
  half court (*diagrams*), 235−37
  1−3−1 (*diagrams*), 235−37, 240, 243
  1−2−2 (*diagrams*), 241−43
  passive, 230
  personnel placement, 231, 237−38
  point zone, 170
  responsibilities, 244
  against shot clock, 229−30
  teaching, 243−44 (*see also* Press
    offense-defense game)
  three-quarter court (*diagram*), 234−35
Zone offense, free-lance, 27 (*see also* individual
  offenses)
Zone press, 264 (*see also* Scramble, Zone defense)